RELIGION AND THE STATE UNIVERSITY

Religion
and
the State University

EDITED BY

ERICH A. WALTER

ANN ARBOR: THE UNIVERSITY OF MICHIGAN PRESS

Contents

v

ERICH A. WALTER

Introduction

This book is a co-operative attempt to describe and to define the place of religion in higher education, in the university community, and particularly in the state-supported university. The doctrine of separation of church and state has tended to put most state universities, in their study of religion, in a position of striving for mere objectivity. Some of them seem altogether indifferent. Education in state-supported universities is predominantly secular. Until recently, there has thus been separation not only of church and state but of church and university as well. At best, as Walton Bean puts it, "the position of religion in the American state university is a position of tacit compromise." The problems that arise in developing curricula in religion, and in finding a place for religious worship within the university itself, are the concern of this volume.

The book is intended for students and all those associated with them. It is for students now enrolled or who expect to enroll at state and privately supported universities, and for their parents, teachers, community leaders, denominational church leaders, student personnel workers, and college administrators.

The contributors express a variety of points of view, and many, though not all, represent state universities. No restrictions other than space limitations were placed upon them. Their views are their own. The book does not present any official point of view.

The opening section of the volume establishes the setting of a state university: its pluralistic society and religious life, its

importance as a part of the mind of the state, and the separa-
tion-of-church-and-state principle.

The second section deals with the place of religion in state
university education, the problems of academic freedom, and
the place of religion in the humanities, sciences, and the professions.

The third section is devoted to the university community, the
life of the campus, counseling about religion, religious centers,
common objectives of diverse religious groups, the problems
of students from foreign lands in trying to observe their religious practices and to live their religions, and, finally, to the
value systems or mythology of the present college generation.

The young student arriving on the campus is struck first of
all by the divergent cultural and religious backgrounds of his
new associates. He becomes keenly aware of the pluralistic
aspect of our society, and of religious pluralism specifically.
The first three chapters, accordingly, give three views on the
question what goes into the making of a pluralistic society.
They reflect religious views most commonly held in the United
States—Catholic, Jewish, and Protestant.

"From the very beginning," Will Herberg writes, "America
has been a land of diversity striving for unity . . . the diversities
have been racial, ethnic, cultural, and religious, while the unity
striven for has been the unity of a new 'way of life' reflecting
the 'new order of the ages' established in the New World."

J. Courtney Murray contends "that the pluralist structure of
our contemporary society did not come into existence through a
'peaceful' development. The historical forces that contributed
to the development were not only intellectual but also passionate. They were not only resident in men whose names we
know; they were also to some considerable extent anonymous,
with the strange anonymity that attaches to forces that are
organized. Had the dynamism of development not been thus
complex, it would not have been successful."

Roland Bainton expresses succinctly the university's problem
in offering religion as a study to its students: "If religion has the
answers to such [universal] questions, surely no subject could

be more appropriate in a university dedicated to the quest of knowledge. But now comes a difficulty that is accentuated though not created by religious pluralism. Judaism and Christianity are religions of historic revelation. They announce a way to truth which is not that of the university, because revelation is conceived by all of these religions, at least in their more naïve stages, as something given in times past, a deposit to be accepted and elucidated, not to be questioned, whereas for the university truth is a quest where nothing is to be taken for granted and every hypothesis subjected to critical scrutiny. Truth as a deposit and truth as a quest, can these concepts coexist?"

The chapter "What Is the State University?" by Walton Bean discusses the dual aspect of a state university, as a community of scholars and as a place where young people develop their purposes in life. It operates as a human community rather than a legal entity. In many areas it is guided by tacit compromise and a process of give and take.

The constitutional limitations which a state university faces as an instrumentality of the state; the objectives of these constitutional limitations; the general significance of the First Amendment; the relevance of these limitations to the general question of religion in the curriculum of a state university, and more specifically to religious courses and programs: these form the subject of Paul Kauper.

Kauper is concerned with enlarging the possibilities of teaching and studying religion in state-supported universities: "In view of the place that religion has occupied and continues to occupy in the life and history of man, its influence in the shaping of ideas, its impact on culture and its significance as a unifying and integrating force that provides a high sense of purpose and motivation and opens new vistas of truth, goodness, and beauty, religion must of necessity command some attention at any academic institution both as an intellectual discipline and as a way of life." And he continues: "The university may well take the position that it is derelict to the high purpose for which it was created if it fails to deal in a positive way with religion as a vital force in the life and history of man. Indeed, it is fair to assert that for a university deliberately to exclude from its curriculum all courses with a positive religious content is not simply to fail to teach religion but in itself becomes a telling witness that religion is irrelevant to that process of cultivating the mind and spirit that we call higher education."

What place, then, has religion in the state university? Helen White notes the place of religion as a branch of learning, as one of the great humanities. It involves choice, rejection and selection; it pervades life. She knows the student's relationship to his family, to his teachers, to his counselors, and to his church. She knows the problem of finding a place for religion in a university curriculum and analyzes the problem sympathetically from all points of view including that of the student's parents and of the university administrator. She faces the obstacles; she offers solutions.

Mark Ingraham explores the question of academic freedom, including the professor's and the student's right to express religious views in and out of the classroom. He makes certain distinctions: between freedom of discussion and freedom of action; between the criticism of an opinion or of a person expressing an opinion, and the criticism of the university for allowing certain opinions to be expressed. He points out that academic freedom is distinct from and more comprehensive than the freedom of every citizen, and that it is necessary for the usefulness of the teacher.

Writing about religion and the humanities Theodore Greene posits five general attitudes—of curiosity, of response, of respect, of obligation, and of creativity—and four skills that implement the attitudes: the logical-linguistic, the factual, the normative, and the synoptic skill. "In proportion as we are literate, articulate, and clear-headed in the several complementary languages of human discourse, as we are factually oriented and informed, as we are sensitive and mature in our normative responses, and as we acquire the capacity for synoptic vision," so are we proportionately "equipped for the task of human living." That if they are to perform their proper function, the humanities must play their unique role "to make men more truly human, more humane."

"For the healthy growth of social science we need maturely religious social scientists," Kenneth Boulding states. He believes that the social scientist who fails to achieve this maturity is in proportion incomplete and deficient and cannot fully comprehend the whole experience of mankind. He believes that the problem of the end of human activity is growing more pressing as social science develops, that the potential power in the hands of social scientists is terrible to contemplate because it means control of the minds and actions of men. "What are the right ends of human activity? This question becomes insistent, inescapable." "The future of science, and especially of social science, may depend on our getting better answers than we now have to the question of when ignorance is bliss—or, as a matter of fact, what bliss is anyway! And bliss, curiously enough, is one of the great subjects of religion."

G. E. Hutchinson in a chapter on "Religion and the Natural Sciences," deals with the question to what extent the method we call scientific investigation gives a true and a complete picture of existence. "Scientific investigation," he writes, "though it leads to results that are convergently true, is certainly, and probably permanently, an incomplete mode of knowledge. Since we live in a universe which is not completely known, and probably not completely knowable, we must live our lives using everything at our disposal and not merely the scientifically mapped part of reality. Statements outside the scientific body of knowledge are inevitably made in language which is similarly derived as metaphor from language describing the investigatable world."

George Shuster considers the role of religion in professional education as conducted under public auspices. The student looks upon religion as a moral prophylactic agent rather than a subject for serious study. "But," says Shuster, "dialectic is the method by which religious insights developed from naïve belief to intellectual realization." We avoid theological studies in American universities. They have been crowded out of the curriculum by such studies as the libido psychology of Freud and studies in behaviorism. He pleads for instruction in religion at the same high level of intellectual quality as the student receives in professional studies. This is the challenge that must be provided if the professional student is to rise above religious rusticity.

The American student community is analyzed by Robert Strozier. He shows how inclusive we Americans are in defining "campus," and how incomprehensible our definition is to foreign visitors. In his section on the relation of government, business, and industry to education, and of the various financial aids to students, he underlines the rapidly changing aspects of student life in American universities. He points to the tensions of life at large and to their counterparts in life on the campus.

The specific religious problems that face the average student are the concern of Seward Hiltner. He also outlines the problems encountered in counseling students and suggests what should be done to provide enough trained counselors for the growing student population that is rapping at the doors of American universities.

Glenn A. Olds writes about religious centers. He reviews the various connotations of the term for students and other members of the university community. Growing separation of religious faith and liberal learning gives rise to the religious center on the campuses which is, Olds believes, a symbol of man's persistent need to be made whole. He discusses the patterns and functions of the center, and indicates the trends they have followed.

The trend toward "co-ordination" of the last decade is the subject of Arthur Lelyveld. He cites the University of Minnesota in particular and refers to many other universities, describing the various forms of interreligious programs that are in effect. He describes such interreligious activities as "Religious Emphasis Weeks" and the "World University Service," common to most university communities. He emphasizes that co-operation among the various religions defeats its purpose if it can be secured only at the price of relinquishing their essential differences.

In his Preface to *Saint Joan* Bernard Shaw says: "Though all society is founded on intolerance, all improvement is founded on tolerance." What tolerance means among students of different beliefs and what it requires of each believer is shown by Filmer Northrop in his chapter on students from other lands. Interreligious understanding is most difficult to achieve. Northrop recalls anthropologist Hoebel's study of the legal norms of seven different primitive peoples. So different are these norms that Hoebel had to establish seven different sets of normative and philosophical postulates to describe them. "Interreligious understanding," says Northrop, "requires the same approach. The scientists and philosophers who have studied some of the world cultures—the cultural anthropologists and philosophers of comparative cultures—have found that the behavior and ceremonies of a people of one culture seem meaningless and even silly to an observer from a different culture until the observer learns how to understand, from within the observed culture, what he sees."

After a glance at the changes that have taken place in customs on the college dance floor, Chad Walsh analyzes the changing patterns of "dating." Students, he finds, almost never exchange partners at dances. They "go steady." He considers this custom an expression of a general desire for security. Sex and marriage are taken seriously much sooner than they were formerly. Security is the dominant ideal of the contemporary American student. If he does become interested in religion it is for his peace of mind, to satisfy his desire to be secure.

In conclusion, William Frankena looks at both past and future. He assigns the study of religion a very important place in the state-supported university. He analyzes the philosophy which he finds underlying the separation of church and state and guiding the state university in its treatment of religion, and suggests norms, some means, some ends for future thought and action. Among these he includes some cautionary statements which bear on present practices.

A student entering the University of Michigan in 1858 would in his sophomore year have been shocked by the publication of Charles Darwin's *The Origin of Species*. Asa Gray, the distinguished American botanist, once a member of the faculty of the University of Michigan, reviewed the book for the *Atlantic Monthly*. Science unceremoniously confronted religion. Darwin's theories put men's religious faith to a new test.

The student of 1958 has had the world explode in his face. He and his fellows see the release of atomic energy and stand helpless. Dr. David Bradley's recent book *No Place to Hide* dramatically emphasizes man's plight. Our student may well wonder if there is not a metaphysic to meet today's new scientific challenge. It seems obvious that with his desire to know the world as it should be and not only as it is, he will expect to find the problem thoroughly and authoritatively presented and reviewed at the university.

The editor hopes the reader may come away from this book with a mind favorable toward expanding the study of religion in state universities, toward giving the university student a greater understanding of the values of religion and hence a greater tolerance for them. Students of our day, in their almost hysterical emphasis on the study of science, their preoccupation with the robot, their fascination with "the organization man," and their general impatience toward the man who cannot easily be pigeonholed, seem to be shunted toward attitudes that are absolute; in their excited espousal of a new view, they turn zealot. The editor cannot forego the pleasure of sharing with them a quotation from Jeremy Taylor's sermon, "Against Bitterness of Zeal":

"Any zeal is proper for religion, but the zeal of the sword and the zeal of anger; this is the bitterness of zeal, and it is a certain temptation to every man against his duty; for if the sword turns preacher, and dictates propositions by empire instead of arguments, and engraves them in men's hearts with a poignard, that it shall be death to believe what I innocently and ignorantly am persuaded of, it must needs be unsafe to try the spirits, to try all things, to make inquiry; and yet, without this liberty, no man can justify himself before God or man, nor confidently say that his religion is best; since he cannot without a final danger make himself to give a right sentence, and to follow that which he finds to be best. This may ruin souls by making hypocrites, or careless and compliant against conscience or without it; but it does not save souls, though peradventure it should force them to a good opinion.

"When Abraham sat at his tent door, according to his custom, waiting to entertain strangers, he espied an old man, stooping and leaning on his staff, weary with age and travel, coming towards him, who was a hundred years of age. He received him kindly, washed his feet, provided supper, caused him to sit down; but observing that the old man ate and prayed not, nor begged a blessing on his meat, he asked him why he did not worship the God of heaven. The old man told him that he worshipped the fire only, and acknowledged no other god. At which answer Abraham grew so zealously angry that he thrust the old man out of his tent, and exposed him to all the evils of the night and an unguarded condition. When the old man was gone, God called to Abraham and asked him where the stranger was. He replied, 'I thrust him away because he did not worship thee.' God answered him, 'I have suffered him these hundred years, although he dishonoured me; and couldst not thou endure him one night?'"

The Setting

JOHN COURTNEY MURRAY, S.J.

The Making of a Pluralistic Society — A Catholic View

CHAPTER I

We are not here concerned with all the pluralisms, proper to the political community as such, which have the sanction of the central tradition of politics in the West. The distinction between church and state, and between state and society, entail a pluralistic organization of the community. And this pluralism becomes more complex through the existence within the community of a whole range of institutions that come into being under the operation of the principle of natural association (e.g., the family) or of free association (e.g., all manner of social, economic, cultural, and academic associations).

Our question, however, concerns a society that is pluralist in consequence of multiple conceptions of, and answers to, what are usually called the Ultimate Questions. In this sense societies in the past have been pluralist in manifold fashion. Thus the ancient Christian Empire, with its divisions between Arian or Nestorian and Catholic Christianity; thus too the post-Reformation and post-Revolution "Catholic nation," so called, within which there existed a plurality of attitudes toward the Catholic church, ranging from the most devout fidelity out to the extremes of anticlericalism in the Continental sense. Our current American pluralism, however, has its own quality. Basically, I should say that it is related to the kind of Ultimate Questions that have become the typical concern of modernity as such. All of them are related to the central question, what is man? Thence they proliferate.

What is the rank of man within the order of being, if there is an order of being? Is the nature of man simply continuous with the nature of the cosmic universe, to be understood in terms of its laws, whatever they may be? Or is there a discontinuity between man and the rest of nature, in consequence of the fact that the nature of man is spiritual in a unique sense? What is man's destiny, his *summum bonum*? Is it to be found and fulfilled within terrestrial history, or does it lie beyond time in "another world"? What is the "sense" of history, its direction and meaning and finality? Or is the category of "finality" meaningless? What can a man know? What do you mean when you say, "I know"? What manner of certitude or certainty attaches to human knowledge? Is knowledge a univocal term, or are there diverse modes and degrees of knowledge, discontinuous one from another? Can man's knowledge—and also his love— reach to realities that are transcendent to the world of matter, space, and time? Is there a God? What is God—a Person, a Power, or simply a projection of man's own consciousness? Does God have a care for man? Has God entered the world of human history there to accomplish a "redemption"? Is the theological concept of "salvation" only a reassuring ambiguity? Or has it a content that is at once mysterious and intelligible? What mental equivalents attach to all the words that have been the currency of civilized discourse—freedom, justice, order, law, authority, power, peace, virtue, morality, religion?

All these questions, and others related to them, concern the essentials of human existence. The multiplicity of answers to them, and of ways of refusing them, is in general what we mean by modern pluralism. Integral to the pluralism is the agnostic view that it is useless or illegitimate even to ask questions that are Ultimate.

How did our American pluralist society come to be? To answer the question would be to write the history of what is called "modernity." One would have to begin by deciding whether modernity began with the rise of Gnosticism in the second century or with the fall of Constantinople in the fifteenth century. One would also have to situate American society as in many respects a special type of realization, within the wider context of the modern world. Declining these extensive tasks, I shall be content with one central observation, which I borrow from Professor Eric Voegelin.

It is his contention—and I agree with it—that the pluralist structure of our contemporary society did not come into existence through a "peaceful" development. The historical forces that contributed to the development were not only intellectual but also passionate. They were not only resident in men whose names we know; they were also to some considerable extent anonymous, with the strange anonymity that attaches to forces that are organized. Had the dynamism of development not been thus complex, it would not have been successful.

Moreover, I would further agree with Voegelin's description of the end-result of the development as stated in terms of what he calls the "hard facts concerning the texture of opinion in contemporary democratic societies." "We are not dealing," he says, "with human beings who hold this or that opinion as individuals, but with Christians and secularists; not with Christians, but with Catholics and Protestants; not with plain liberals, but with Christians and secular liberals; not with plain secular liberals, but with old-style liberals of the free-enterprise type and modern liberals of the socialist type; and so forth. This rich diversification of socially entrenched and violently vociferous opinion is what we call our pluralistic society. It has received its structure through wars, and these wars are still going on. The genteel picture of a search for truth in which humankind is engaged with the means of peaceful persuasion, in dignified communication and correction of opinions, is utterly at variance with the facts."

I note this view for a reason. The "genteel picture" is not seldom put forward to describe the university, whose spiritual situation within modern pluralist society is sometimes said to be therefore privileged. However, the picture in its gentility does not fit the facts of this situation. One does not have to probe very deep below the urbanities of university life to find oneself in the midst of the many-sided and confused "religious wars" that in their unbloody form are at once the heritage of modernity from its bloody past and also the essence of modernity itself.

I do not deplore this fact. If the university takes its own function seriously, it ought to find itself in the characteristically modern situation of religious conflict, understanding the adjective to mean conflict on Basic Issues, conflict that is at once intellectual and passionate, a clash both of individual minds and of organized opinions. What I would deplore would be any refusal on the part of the university (and the university sometimes makes this refusal) to recognize its own spiritual and intellectual situation. The university would succumb to a special type of neurotic disorder if it were to cultivate an inflated image of itself as somehow standing in all serenity "above" the religious wars that rage beneath the surface of modern life and as somehow privileged to disregard these conflicts as irrelevant to its "search for truth." To cast up this "genteel picture" of itself would be to indulge in a flight from reality. The only inner disorder that would be worse than this would be a flight to the fantasy that the university is omnicompetent to judge the issues of truth involved in all the pluralisms of contemporary society.

If pluralism in the sense explained is the characteristic fact of contemporary society, it is also the original root of certain problems that are no less characteristic. An increasing preoccupation with the problematic aspects of pluralism is indeed one of the most interesting phenomena of the present time, which distinguishes it from the heyday of classical liberalism, when man's faith in the assumptions, spoken and unspoken, of an extreme individualism was still unshaken. For instance, it used to be assumed, as a cardinal merit of a pluralist society, that the truth would always be assured of conquest if only it were subjected to the unbridled competition in the market place of ideas. But it is now no longer possible to cherish this naïveté. For further instance, it used to be assumed that an ever-expanding variety of conflicting religious and philosophical views was per se an index of richness, a pledge of vitality, a proof of the values of individualism, a guarantee against stagnation, and so on. But history has not left this assumption intact. In a word, it used to be assumed that pluralism represented "progress." But now the question has arisen, whether its proliferation may not be causatively related to certain observable decadences within the area of intellectual life. A few might be mentioned, but without any intention of exploring here the whole subject.

There is, for instance, the advance of solipsism, the view that my insight is mine alone and cannot be shared by another, much less by a community; this view is, of course, the destruction of the classical and Christian concept of reason. There is the dissolution of the ancient idea of the unity of truth, a unity that admits and demands distinctions and differentiations interior to itself, in consequence of which the concept of truth acquires an inner architecture whose structural elements are articulated in accord with a hierarchical principle. There is the consequent dissolution of the idea of truth itself to the point where no assertion may claim more than the status of sheer opinion, to be granted an equality of freedom with any other opinion. In further consequence there has occurred the dispersal into meaninglessness of all that Socrates meant by the "order of the soul." Then too there has occurred that drastic contraction of the dimensions of reason and that severe devaluation of intelligence which usually goes by the name of "scientism," or, if you will, "positivism"—the theory that "truth" is a univocal term, and that the single technique valid in the "search" for truth is the empirical method of science. This theory is the denial of the possibility of philosophy in the meaning that the word has had since Plato.

Other, and not unrelated, decadences come to mind. There is, for instance, the loss of a common universe of discourse which alone makes argument possible; and there is the consequent decay of argument and the corruption of controversy, amid the sterilities of stock polemical attacks and counterattacks, or amid the bottomless morasses of semanticism. But perhaps the ultimate tendency of the pluralisms created by the era of modernity is felt rather in the realm of affectivity than in the realm of reason as such. The fact today is not simply that we hold different views but that we have become different types of men, with different styles of interior life. The gulfs of division, fairly measured, appear almost unbridgeable, not least because man is more than a thinking animal; he is also a creature of sympathies. And the communal experiences today, in the areas of religion and philosophy, are so diverse that they create not sympathies but alienations between groups.

My suggestion then is that the problem of pluralism has begun to appear in a new light. Perhaps the basic reason for this is the fact that we are entering a new era. Whether it will be a better or even a good era is another question that still remains open. In any case, we have reached the end of the era that gave itself the qualification "modern."

This observation is not original. A Catholic theologian, Romano Guardini, has written a book entitled *Das Ende der Neuzeit*. A Protestant philosopher, William Ernest Hocking, has defined today's problem as the "passage beyond modernity." A political scientist, Eric Voegelin, has pointed to the fact that the reduction of man, from image of God down to a mass of biological drives, has "run its whole gamut"; and he has drawn the conclusion that this fact is "for the social scientist the most important index that 'modernity' has run its course." A historian, Geoffrey Barraclough, has done an essay with the title, "The End of European History," meaning in context the end of the history of modern Europe. A Protestant theologian, Paul Tillich, has put forward the thesis that in some identifiable sense an end has been put to what he calls the "Protestant era," which was itself an important aspect of modernity. Arnold Toynbee has gone so far as to popularize the notion that our present era is not only post-modern but also post-Christian.

If these observers, whose points of view are so diverse, may claim credence, it follows that we confront a whole new set of problems. There is, of course, the problem of salvaging those elements of truth and moral value which gave vitality to the whole movement called "modernity." But my question concerns only the manifold pluralisms, in the sense explained, which have been the special creation of modernity. With the dissolution of the age that made them, are these pluralisms somehow and to some extent to be unmade?

It would seem that the process of unmaking them is already importantly afoot. Protestantism, for instance, now feels its own inner discordant pluralisms as no longer an unqualified glory but as something of a scandal. And in the Ecumenical Movement it is in quest of its own unities. Catholicism in turn now feels that certain of its past unities were something of a scandal; there is, for instance, the unity asserted in Belloc's famous thesis that "Europe is the faith and the faith is Europe." In consequence the Church is asserting with sharper emphasis its own proper sacramental unity, altogether universal, altogether spiritual, not enfeoffed to any historical culture but transcendent to every culture at the same time that it is a leaven in all cultures. Again, Europe has realized that its modern pluralisms of many kinds, of which it was once boastfully jealous, are importantly the cause of its own present impotence. The "good European" has now emerged, and his quest is for some manner and measure of unity that will begin for Europe a new history and regain for it a due share of its lost significance in the realm of historical action. The Communist too, whether Soviet or Chinese, cherishes his own dream of a demonic unification of the world. And in the United States, finally, the problem of unity in its relation to the pluralisms of American society has begun to be felt with a new seriousness.

True enough, the problem is not seldom raised in a way that is false. One thinks, for instance, of the New Nativism, as represented by Mr. Paul Blanshard; or of the issue of "conformism," about which there is so much confused talk; or of the current anxieties about internal subversion, regarded as a threat to an American unity ("there are those among us who are not of us"). And so on. But even the falsities attendant upon the manner in which the issue of unity-amid-pluralism is raised bear witness to the reality of the issue itself.

The question has been asked: How much of the pluralism is bogus and unreal? And how much of the unity is likewise bogus —and undesirable? The more general question has also been asked: How much pluralism, and what kinds of pluralism, can a pluralist society stand? And conversely, how much unity, and what kind of unity, does a pluralist society need in order to be a society at all, effectively organized for responsible action in history, and yet a "free" society?

Similarly, certain words have now acquired a respectability that was long denied them—the word "order," for instance, which now is disjunctively coupled with the word "freedom," with the fading of the typically modern illusion that somehow "freedom" is itself the principle of order.

Finally, responsible and informed thinkers can now discourse about the "public philosophy" of America, considering it to be a valid concept which furnishes the premises for dissent, to be identified as dissent even though the public philosophy itself contains no tenets that would justify coercion of the dissenter. In the same fashion serious inquiries are now made into the American consensus—the question being not whether such a thing exists but what it is and whence it came and how it may be kept alive and operative by argument among reasonable men. Moreover, since every social consensus that supports and directs the historical action of a given political community is always to a considerable extent a legacy from an earlier age, questions have been asked about the American heritage and about the manner in which it has developed. Has the America of today been true to its own spiritual origins? Indeed, were the principles that lay at its origins ambiguous to some extent, so as to permit various lines of development, not all of them happy? Is the American man of today an "exile from his own past" (as Geoffrey Bruun said of European man)?

The central point here is that the quest for unity-amid-pluralism has assumed a new urgency in the mind of post-modern man.

In this connection it might be well to advert to the fact that, since St. Augustine's description of the "two cities," it has been realized that societal unity may, broadly speaking, be of two orders—the divine or the demonic. It is of the divine order when it is the product of faith, reason, freedom, justice, law, and love. Within the social unity created by these forces, which are instinct with all the divinity that resides in man, the human personality itself grows to its destined stature of dignity at the same time that the community achieves its unity. Societal unity is of the demonic order when it is the product of force, whether the force be violent or subtle. There are, for instance, all the kinds of force that operate in the industrial society created by modernity (irrational political propaganda, commercial advertising, all the assaults upon reason and taste that are launched by mass amusements, and the like). These forces operate under the device of "freedom," but unto the disintegration of the human personality, and unto the more or less forcible unification of social life on a level lower than that established, forever, by Aristotle's "reasonable man" and his Christian completion. The quest for unity-amid-pluralism must therefore be critical of its own impulses. Its stimulus must not be passion, whether the passion be imperialist (the will to power) or craven (fear and anxiety).

What then might be the attitudes and functions of the university in the face of the problem of pluralism as newly presented at the outset of the post-modern era? The premise of the question is the fact that the Basic Issues have come to matter to men in a new way. Does this fact matter to the university? Many of the commitments of modernity—shared by the university, because it too has been modern—have dissolved in disenchantment. Does their dissolution make any difference to the university? The positivistic universe (if the phrase be not a contradiction in adiecto) has come to seem a wilderness of disorder to the soul of man, which cannot be content to live in chaos since it is always aware, however dimly, that it is natively committed to the discovery of an order in reality or, alternatively, to the imposition of an order on reality at whatever cost both to reality and to itself. Is post-modern man's new commitment to order of any interest to the university?

I know, of course, that the word "commitment," used in regard to a university, raises specters. I am not myself fond of the word; it is more distinctively part of the Protestant vocabulary, which is not mine; and moreover the dictionary adds to its definition: ". . . esp. to prison"! In any case, some nice questions center around the word. Is the university, as a matter of fact, uncommitted? And in what senses or in what directions? Is "non-committalism" an intellectual virtue or is it what Gordon Keith Chalmers called it, a "sin"? Is a commitment to "freedom," understanding "freedom" to be a purely formal category, any more a valid premise of the intellectual life than a commitment to the Kantian *Moralprinzip*, understood as a purely formal category, is a valid premise for the moral life? "Handle so. . . ." Indeed. But *what* am I to do? And analogously in the former case, what is this "truth" for which I am to be "free" to search?

Leaving these interesting questions aside, I might better come to more concrete matters and venture a few assertions of a practical kind. First, I venture to assert that the university is committed to the task of putting an end, as far as it can, to intellectual savagery in all its forms, including a major current form, which is the savagery of the American student (perhaps the professor?) who in all matters religious and theological is an untutored child of the intellectual wilderness. Again, the university is committed to the task of putting an end to prejudice based on ignorance, by helping to banish the ignorance. Unless indeed the university wishes to commit itself to the prejudice that religious knowledge is really ignorance.

The assertion I chiefly wish to venture, however, is that the university is committed to its students and to their freedom to learn. Its students are not abstractions. And whatever may be the university's duty (or right, or privilege, or sin) of non-committalism, the fact is that many of its students are religiously committed. To put it concretely, they believe in God. Or to put it even more concretely, they are Protestants, Catholics, Jews. The university as such has no right to judge the validity of any of these commitments, so called. Similarly, it has no right to ignore the fact of these commitments, much less to require that—for the space, say, of four years—its students should be content to become scientific naturalists within the university, whatever else they, somewhat schizophrenically, may choose to be outside its walls.

The major issue here is the student's freedom to learn—to explore the full intellectual dimensions of the religious faith to which he is committed. He comes to college with the "faith of the charcoal burner," of course. And it is the right of the university to require that his quest of religious knowledge should be pursued in the university style—under properly qualified professors, in courses of high academic content, in accordance with the best methods of theological scholarship, and so on. But this right of the university should itself conspire with the student's own freedom to learn, so as to create the academic empowerment that is presently almost wholly lacking. A college and university student is academically empowered to grow in all the dimensions of knowledge—except the dimension of religious knowledge.

What is the formula for translating the student's freedom to learn about his religious faith into a genuine empowerment? The question would have to be argued; and it might not be possible to devise a uniformly applicable formula.

In any case, the formula of the "religious emphasis week" is hopelessly inadequate; and when it becomes simply a piece of public relations it is also unworthy of a university. Again, the formula of a "department of religion" is no good, unless the "religion" of the department includes the major historic faiths, which is rarely the case. As for a "department of religion *and* philosophy," it chiefly serves to confuse the issue. In its most destructive concrete mode of operation it blurs the clear line of distinction that traditional Christianity has drawn between the order of faith and the order of reason. (Incidentally, it is not for the university to say that this line ought to be blurred, or moved from its traditional position.)

Whatever the concrete formula may be, it must reckon with the factual pluralism of American society, insofar as this pluralism is real and not illusory. There can be no question of any bogus irenicism or of the submergence of religious differences in a vague haze of "fellowship." And here, lest what I said above about the "unmaking" of modern pluralism should be misunderstood, I should add a clarification. It is not, and cannot be, the function of the university to reduce modern pluralism to unity. However, it might be that the university could make some contribution to a quite different task—namely, the reduction of modern pluralism to intelligibility.

This is an intellectual task. It bears upon the clarification of the pluralism itself. The Protestant charcoal burner today knows well enough that he differs from the Catholic charcoal burner, and vice versa. But it is not so certain that either could say why, in any articulate fashion. And if one or the other should undertake to give reasons, they would probably be mistaken, or distorted, or unclear, or even irrelevant. Anyone who has attended a run-of-the-mill college "bull session" will know this.

From this point of view I would specify two general academic objectives that a college or university could legitimately aim at in the field of religious knowledge as its contribution to a clarification of the problem of pluralism.

The first is a genuine understanding of the epistemology of religious truth—or, if you will, of the nature of religious faith. It is precisely here that modern pluralism has its roots. Karl Barth was making this point when he said, in effect, that it is no use discussing whether we believe in common certain articles of the creed, when we are in radical disagreement on what is the meaning of the word with which the creed begins, "Credo." It is in consequence of this radical disagreement that Catholicism and Protestantism appear as, and are, systems of belief that bear to each other only an analogical relationship. That is to say, they are somewhat the same, and totally different. One would expect the mature Catholic and Protestant mind to understand this fact, which takes a bit of understanding.

The second understanding—and academic objectives can be stated only in terms of understanding—would be of the systems of belief, precisely as systems, in their inner organic consistency (whatever it may be), and in their relation to other areas of human knowledge (insofar as these relations are intellectually discernible).

These two objectives are not unworthy of an institution of higher learning. They also coincide with the objectives that the student should be made free to reach. If he did reach them, he would be on emergence from college less a rustic than when he entered. And would not his college gently rejoice? The preservation of rusticities can hardly rank high among the preoccupations of the college dean.

When considered in terms of these two objectives, the practical difficulties appear less formidable than they are sometimes thought to be. There may indeed be some three hundred religious bodies in America. But there are not that many "styles" of religious belief. In fact, there are generically only three—the Protestant, the Catholic, and the Jewish. They are radically different "styles" and no one of them is reducible, or perhaps even comparable, to any of the others. And in each case the style of the epistemology is related to the structure of the theology (or possibly to the absence of a theology).

The academic content of possible courses would be no great problem, except as it involves selection from a wealth of materials. The Catholic theological tradition is a treasury that even lifelong study cannot exhaust. Judaism has its learning, rich and venerable. And today the Protestant has the task of assimilating the already great, and still growing, body of ecumenical theology. No college or university should have to worry about its academic standards if it were to turn its students loose, under expert guidance, into these three great storehouses of thought.

Under expert guidance—that might be the greatest practical problem. Specially trained men would be needed. One could only hope that they would become available as opportunities opened before them. For the rest, I should only insist on one principle. It was stated by John Stuart Mill when he said that every position should be explained and defended by a man who holds it, and who therefore is able to make the case for it most competently. This is, in a special way, a restatement of the principle upon which St. Augustine tirelessly dwelt: *"Nisi credideritis, non intelligetis."* The communication of understanding supposes its possession. I do not myself accept the pedagogical canon that seems to be popular in university circles: every position ought to be explained by one who is sympathetic with it but who personally rejects it. It has never seemed to me that this is a canon of "objectivity" at all. Nor does it insure the communication of a critical understanding of the position in question, given the principle that only an immanent critique, as it is called, can lead to this desirable type of understanding. In any case, my own view is that the only path to genuine understanding of a religious faith lies through the faith itself. The possession of the faith is therefore the proper qualification of the professor who would wish to communicate a critical understanding of it.

These are but a few practical suggestions toward a definition of the role of the university in the face of the problem of pluralism today. In conclusion, it should go without saying that the function of the university is not at all messianic. It is entirely minimal. The Basic Issues, deeply considered, do in the end raise in the mind of man the issue of "salvation." But if post-modern man hopes for salvation, he must set his hope elsewhere than on the university. Henry Adams' gratitude to Harvard for its contribution to his intellectual development is the highest gratitude that the university can merit from man in search of salvation. Harvard, said Adams in effect, did not get in my way. But this is no small cause for gratitude when the issue at stake is salvation.

WILL HERBERG

The Making of a Pluralistic Society — A Jewish View

CHAPTER II

In some sense, all societies, even the most monolithic, have been pluralistic, for there has never been a society without a wide diversity of interests, opinions, and conditions of life. Yet when we speak of a pluralistic society, we mean something more. We mean a society in which these diversities not only exist as a matter of fact but are recognized, accepted, perhaps even institutionalized into the structure and functioning of the social order. In this sense, American society is thoroughly pluralistic, but pluralistic in a very specal way, with its own characteristic freedoms and limitations. The shape of American pluralism helps define the underlying pattern of American life, within which emerge the so-called "intergroup" problems confronting us today, on campus or off, and in terms of which they must be confronted and dealt with.

The pluralism of American society is the product of its history, and therefore reflects its inmost being, for the inmost being of men and their societies is essentially historical. From the very beginning, America has been a land of diversity striving for unity. And from the very beginning too, the diversities have been racial, ethnic, cultural, and religious, whereas the unity striven for has been that of a new "way of life" reflecting the "new order of the ages" established in the New World (*novus ordo seclorum*, the motto on the reverse of the Great

Seal of the United States). This was the vision that fired the imagination of Hector de Crèvecoeur, the author of the celebrated "Letters from an American Farmer," who was so eager to interpret the new American reality to the Old and New World alike. "Here," Crèvecoeur proclaimed proudly in 1782, "individuals of all nations are melted into a new race of men, whose labors and posterity will one day cause great changes in the world." Thus early was the "melting pot" philosophy explicitly formulated, and thus early did the problem of unity amidst diversity, and diversity amidst unity, emerge as the perennial problem of American life.

The conception implied in the image of the "melting pot" (or the "transmuting pot," as George R. Stewart prefers to call it) has always been subject to a misunderstanding that is itself not without significance. When, at least until recently, Americans spoke of the "melting pot" (although the term as such did not come into use until the first decade of this century), they generally had in mind a process by which the foreign "peculiarities" of language and culture that the immigrants brought with them from the old country would be sloughed off in the course of Americanization, and a new homogeneous, undifferentiated type of American would come into being. Against this, the apostles of "cultural pluralism" protested; they stressed the richness of the immigrant cultures, deplored their threatening dissolution, and advocated a multicultural, even multinational society along familiar European lines. Both—the theorists of the "melting pot" and the "cultural pluralists"—gravely misunderstood the emerging pattern of American pluralism.

For American pluralism, through all its changes and mutations, has remained characteristically American, quite unlike the pluralistic patterns prevailing in other parts of the world. The sources of diversity have been different, and the expressions of it even more so. By and large, we may say that since the latter part of the nineteenth century, the sources of American pluralism have been mainly race, ethnicity, and religion, with section or region playing a diminishing, though in some cases still significant role. It is in terms of these that Americans have tended, and still tend, to define their identities amidst the totality of American life. The process of enculturation perpetuates the pattern. "When asked the simple question, 'What are you?'" Gordon W. Allport has noted, referring to certain recent researches, "only 10 per cent of four-year-olds answer in terms of racial, ethnic, or religious membership, whereas 75 per cent of nine-year-olds do so." "Race" in America today means color, white vs. nonwhite, and racial stigmatization has introduced an element of caste-like stratification into American life. For white Americans, ethnicity and religion have been, and still remain, the major sources of pluralistic diversity, though the relation between them has changed drastically in the course of the past generation. It is this change that provides a clue to an understanding of the present-day shape of American pluralism and of the place of religion in American life.

As long as large-scale immigration continued, and America was predominantly a land of immigrants, in the days when "the immigrants were American history," as Handlin puts it, the dominant form of self-identification, and therefore the dominant source of pluralistic diversity, was immigrant ethnicity. Religion was largely felt to be a part of the ethnic heritage, recent or remote. The enthusiasts of the "melting pot" were eager to eliminate this diversity as quickly as possible; the "cultural pluralists" were determined to perpetuate it; but both alike moved within the framework of a pluralism based substantially on ethnicity, ethnic culture, and ethnic religion.

Within the past generation, the picture has been radically transformed. The stoppage of the mass immigration during World War I, followed by the anti-immigration legislation of the 1920's, undermined the foundations of the immigrant ethnic group with amazing rapidity; what it did was to facilitate the emergence of the third and post-third generations, with their characteristic responses and attitudes, as a decisive influence in American life, no longer threatened with submergence by the next new wave of immigration. This far-reaching structural change has, of course, been reflected in the shape and form of American pluralism. Specifically, within the threefold American scheme of race, ethnicity, and religion, a shift has taken place from ethnicity to religion as the dominant form of self-identification, and therefore (as we have noted) also the dominant form of pluralistic diversity. Ethnic identifications and traditions have not disappeared; on the contrary, with the third generation, as Marcus Lee Hansen has cogently shown, they enjoy a lively popularity as symbols of "heritage." But now the relation of ethnicity and religion has been reversed: religion is no longer taken as an aspect of ethnicity; it is ethnicity, or rather what remains of it, that is taken up, redefined, and expressed through religious identifications and institutions. Religion—or at least the tripartite differentiation of Protestant, Catholic, Jew—has (aside from race) become the prevailing source of pluralistic diversity in American life. American pluralism is today (again aside from race) characteristically religious pluralism, and all problems of American unity and diversity have to be interpreted in the light of this great fact.

From this standpoint, the basic fact in the shaping of contemporary American pluralism is the transformation of America in the course of the past generation from a Protestant country into a three-religion country.

Writing just about thirty years ago, André Siegfried described Protestantism as America's "national religion," and he was very largely right, despite the ban on religious establishment in the Constitution. Normally, to be born an American meant to be a Protestant; this was the religious identification that in the American mind quite naturally went along with being an American. Non-Protestants felt the force of this conviction almost as strongly as did the Protestants; Catholics and Jews, despite their vastly increasing numbers, each experienced their non-Protestant religion as a problem, even as an obstacle, to their becoming full-fledged Americans: it was the mark of their foreignness. (This was true despite the much-esteemed colonial heritage of both Jews and Catholics, since it was not the "old American" elements in these two groups that influenced American attitudes but the newer immigrant masses.) In the familiar Troeltschean sense (that is, a form of religious belonging which is felt to be involved in one's belonging to the national community), Protestantism, not any of the multiplying denominations but Protestantism as a whole, constituted America's "established church."

This is no longer so. Today, unlike fifty years ago, Catholics and Jews as well as Protestants feel themselves to be Americans not apart from, or in spite of, their religion, but because of it. If America today possesses a "church" in the Troeltschean sense, it is the tripartite religious system of Protestant-Catholic-Jew.

This transformation of America from a Protestant into a three-religion country has come about not as a result of any marked increase in the ratio of Catholics or Jews in the population— the Protestant-Catholic ratio has remained almost the same for the past thirty years and the proportion of Jews in the general population has probably been declining. It has come about, as I have already suggested, as an accompaniment of the shift in the pattern of self-identification, and therefore also in the source of pluralistic diversity, from ethnicity to religion.

This religious pluralism, built into the very structure of American life, receives explicit institutional expression in the expanding interfaith pattern. The interfaith movement and, even more, the interfaith "idea," articulates the new shape of American life, and therein lies its characteristic appeal to the American mind. Indeed, as the older ethnic identifications tend to fade out with the appearance of a stabilized third generation, there is a growing feeling that unification along interfaith lines is the most appropriate way of expressing the comprehensive unity of the American people. Since the pluralism of American life is so largely a religious pluralism, the symbol of all-American co-operation in every good cause naturally becomes "interfaith."

Thus, the "I am an American Day," originally observed to demonstrate the American unity of the various ethnic-immigrant groups that make up our population, is now celebrated along interfaith lines. "Protestants, Catholics, and Jews, with a Negro chairman, united to celebrate I am an American Day . . ." is how one New York newspaper reported the event last September. Once Protestants, Catholics, and Jews are included, it is felt, then all Americans are included, and the way to include all Americans in any enterprise is to establish it along inter-faith—that is, tri-faith—lines.

This emerging pattern of American pluralism as religious pluralism would seem to be particularly significant for the campus community, for among the younger people on the campus the older forms of pluralistic diversity (ethnicity, re-gionalism) play a relatively small role, whereas the newer categories of religion, with their rich connotation of "heri-tage" and "belonging" along American lines, are acquiring a growing appeal. From this one may not draw any unequivocal conclusions as to the extent or quality of the "religious boom" on the campus or off; one cannot, however, overlook the fact that the problem of pluralism on the campus is (aside from race) a problem of religious pluralism, even more so than it is in the American community at large.

But before we can pursue this line of inquiry much further, we must raise another question. American pluralism, it has often been noted, is not simply plurality; it is also unity: it is, in fact, best designated by the term *pluriunity*—a unity in plurality as well as a plurality in unity. *E pluribus unum*: this phrase, which was originally employed to celebrate the unifica-tion of the thirteen colonies into the new nation, will serve very well as the formula for American pluralism as it has developed through the decades since the Civil War.

What is this unity that has supplied the centripetal force in American life, or (to change the image) the common frame-work within which the pluralistic allegiances find both their freedom and their limits? This unity is the unity of the Amer-ican Way of Life.

It is not easy to put into words just what the American Way of Life is, or how it functions to provide the over-all unity for the pluralistic diversity of American society. Perhaps the most important thing to say about it is that for the American, the American Way of Life is that by virtue of which he is an Amer-ican. Germans tend to interpret their common "Germanness" in terms of "race" (in the peculiar German sense); Frenchmen tend to interpret their common "Frenchness" in terms of "culture"; Americans, with their incredible diversity of race, culture, and national origin, find their unity, their common "Americanness," in their adherence to, and participation in, the American Way of Life. This provides them with their common allegiance and their common faith; it provides them, to use the words of the sociologist Robin M. Williams, Jr., with "the common set of ideas, rituals, and symbols" by which an "overarching sense of unity" is achieved amidst diversity and conflict. If the pluralism of contemporary American society is primarily a religious pluralism, the unity within which this pluralism is expressed and contained is a unity of the American Way of Life.

This means that in effect the "three great faiths" appear to increasing numbers of Americans as three alternative (though not necessarily equal) expressions of their common "Americanness." They are esteemed because they are felt to be at bottom three different versions of the same set of "moral and spiritual values of democracy," that is, of the American Way of Life on its religious side. Interfaith co-operation is understood as the co-operation of those who, whatever their belief, are after all Americans, sharing the same values and commitments. In other words, precisely because the pluralism of American life is so largely a religious pluralism, the overarching unity that contains this pluralism tends itself to be invested with a quasi-sacred character. What a philosopher like Horace M. Kallen states explicitly when he proclaims the "democratic faith" to be "the religion *of* and *for* religions . . . all may freely come together in it," is essentially implicit in the ethos of American life and finds expression in many of its social and cultural patterns.

The peculiar structure of American pluralism—religious diversity given unity through being interpreted as diverse expressions of the same overarching system of values and commitments —confronts Protestant, Catholic, Jew, and secularist alike with a series of complicated and perplexing problems.

The secularist naturally finds embarrassing the almost universal tendency of Americans to identify themselves religiously and to interpret their religious identification as the particular expression of their Americanness; for, under these circumstances, the man who refuses to "belong" religiously tends to be viewed with suspicion as somehow not truly American, very much as Catholics and Jews were looked upon until a generation or two ago. "There is a tendency," Sidney H. Scheuer, a leader of the Ethical Culture movement, recently complained with a great deal of justice, "to regard all people who are not committed to one of the three great faiths as being disloyal to American principles and traditions." This is true also on college campuses, even though on college campuses the proportion of those who refuse to associate themselves with one or another of the "three great faiths" is considerably higher than that among the population as a whole, and there is still a residual tendency, especially among the faculty, to pass off such refusal as evidence of enlightenment and nonconformity. Confronted with these pressures of the environment (soon internalized so that the deviant himself begins to feel something wrong with his attitude), and no longer so sure of the anti-religious gospels and philosophies of yesterday, the secularist has, in recent years, tended to lose his fervor and to discover unexpected virtues of a social and psychological character in religion, provided it is not too "orthodox" or institutionalized for his taste. Thus what might be called a proreligious secularism has arisen in the wake of the great upsurge of religiousness that is sweeping the country today.

On the other side, Protestants, Catholics, and Jews who take their faith seriously are equally embarrassed by the way the religious situation is shaping up, though for rather different reasons. They find much of the religiousness that is engendered when religion comes to serve as a definition of identity and a vehicle of "belonging" in a pluralistic society to be shoddy, superficial, and void of authentic religious content. They are particularly perturbed by the current tendency in American culture to "religionize" democracy, Americanism, or the American Way by turning it into a great, overarching "common faith" to provide a quasi-sacred bond of unity for the multifarious diversity of American life. They see religion becoming progressively secularized in a climate in which secularism itself is becoming proreligious without ceasing to be secularistic.

This secularization of American religion was already well advanced by the end of the last century as far as Protestantism was concerned. "During the second half of the nineteenth century," Sidney E. Mead notes, "there occurred a virtual identification of the outlook of . . . denominational Protestantism with 'Americanism' or 'the American way of life.' . . . The United States, in effect, had two religions, or at least two different forms of the same religion, and . . . the prevailing Protestant ideology represented a syncretistic mingling of the two. The first was the religion of the denominations. . . . The second was the religion of the democratic society and nation" ("American Protestantism Since the Civil War," *Journal of Religion,* January 1956). As long as they remained foreign and therefore marginal, Judaism and Catholicism were little affected by this trend. As they became American, however, they fell under the same influences, and began to exhibit the same characteristic syncretism. What took place, and not in this respect alone, was the "Protestantization" of the non-Protestant religions of America.

It is necessary to understand these concerns of the secularist and the man of faith alike if we are to grasp the profound ambiguity of the present religious situation, reflecting the new type of American pluralism that has emerged in the course of the past generation.

While the new structure of American pluralism is becoming increasingly evident to all observers, it is envisaged rather differently by Protestant, Catholic, and Jew. The tripartite structure of American pluralism is thus reflected in a profound trilogue about the value and significance of the new reality. As Kenneth Underwood has recently pointed out, the three "faith groups" confronting the religious pluralism of mid-twentieth-century America tend to see and emphasize different aspects of it: Catholics "search for signs of a 'reintegration' of Western society" about the natural law, the "public philosophy," and the ageless wisdom of the Church; Protestants find evidence that a "vital diversity of religious groupings has been assured"; and Jews tend to stress the parity of the "three great faiths" in a three-religion country united by common "spiritual values." Perhaps my insistence on the transformation of America into a three-religion country as the key to an understanding of contemporary American pluralism may be traced to this Jewish "angle." I recognize that I am seeing and assessing American reality from a certain standpoint, but I do not think that this standpoint, while of course partial, constitutes much of a distorting bias; rather, I think, it encourages a fresh approach to what is after all essentially a new situation.

From this standpoint, one must recognize that there is great positive value in the contemporary three-religion pluralism. It is, of course, true that pluralism is not simply or unequivocally good, and a unitary society simply and unequivocally bad; no human order is ever simply and unequivocally either one or the other. Nor are the "liberal" arguments for pluralism—that in a pluralistic competition "the truth" will somehow prevail, and that diversity itself is a primary value and pledge of vitality —particularly impressive, especially as they relate to religion. Yet as a Jew, I do feel that the creative dialectic tension between Judaism and Christianity that I see implied in the divine purpose is, in many ways, advanced by our three-religion pluralism, though in other ways stultified; and as an American, I value pluralistic diversity (up to a point) as providing a kind of built-in system of checks and balances upon inordinate power: here I do but follow the logic of the Founding Fathers. It is true that religion is not to be reduced simply to its institutions or to be identified with its institutional power; yet religious institutions do exist, do tend to accumulate power and use it in ways that make limitation and control necessary in the interests of justice. A pluralistic setup, it seems to me, provides such limitation and control in a way that involves the least interference from the outside, and therefore the greatest freedom for religion.

Yet, as I have indicated, I do not regard pluralism or diversity as necessarily and intrinsically good, certainly not an unqualified good. Much of present-day Protestant enthusiasm for "vital and genuine diversity" in religion strikes me as simply an echoing and re-echoing of liberalistic naïvetés, with little relation to authentic Lutheran, Calvinist, or sectarian tradition. Here I find the Jewish position, somewhere between the Catholic emphasis on unity and the liberal-Protestant worship of diversity for the sake of diversity, more plausible, more viable, and more realistically related to the interests of religion and society. At any rate, it seems to offer a fruitful approach to the kind of religious pluralism that is emerging in America today.

The American college campus, particularly the state university, is in many ways a microcosm of the religious pluralism that characterizes present-day America. The tripartite division is taken for granted on the campus, despite a number of groups here and there that refuse to accommodate themselves to it. On the college campus, too, there is the so-called secularist element, a little more self-conscious perhaps, and certainly more numerous, than in the outside world. And in the background looms the "race question," which, though it does not concern us directly at this point, does after all constitute as basic an aspect of American pluralism as the religious pluralism we have been discussing.

I think it is fair to say that virtually all Americans who have given any thought to the matter are thoroughly dissatisfied with the present state of the relations between religion and education, particularly public education. This is true for all levels of the educational system, though it seems to be felt most disturbingly at the level of the elementary school. On the university level, the problems are, of course, very different, though perhaps even more complex, for it is on this level that the concern for objectivity and academic integrity is greatest and the fear of "outside influences" most acute.

It is by no means easy even to formulate the problem, but perhaps it may be put this way: the place that is granted to religion in the university scheme of things, at least on most campuses, does not correspond either to a sound conception of higher education or to the essential requirements of contemporary American religious pluralism.

Public education in this country emerged at a time when "nonsectarianism" meant the exclusion of any particular religious denomination from control or special influence, not the exclusion of religion as such; indeed, the public schools were for decades, and in some parts of the country still continue to be, what one might call generalized Protestant schools. With the increasing number of Catholics and Jews becoming part of American life, especially in the urban centers, this understanding of "nonsectarian" could not long remain viable; the phrase soon came to mean "nonreligious," since there seemed to be no way of meeting the obviously justified complaints of the non-Protestant minorities, who were compelled to send their children to what were essentially Protestant schools, except by altogether eliminating religion from education. This trend played in very well with the ideological secularism that toward the latter part of the nineteenth century began to make substantial inroads among the educated classes in this country. The extrusion of religion from education, especially higher education, was now justified on the ground that religion was of no intellectual significance, little more than an outmoded superstition and at best only the cultivation of private sentiments and ideals. It was in this period that many of the state universities came into being or received their definitive character; it was in this period, too, that many of the older colleges abandoned their church connections and transformed themselves into secular institutions, in this respect indistinguishable from the state universities. It was very much in line with the temper of the times, the temper of modernity.

The official theory ran that the university was neutral in matters of religion, not only as to the various kinds of religion to be found among the American people but as between religion and nonreligion, even antireligion. The university would have nothing to do with religion; let religion be taken care of, insofar as taken care of it must be, by denominational church groups off the campus. But of course this was a delusion; the extrusion of Christianity from the campus (there was as yet no question of Judaism) meant not the pursuit of the academic enterprise without any over-all commitments; it meant the replacement of Christianity by some secularistic pseudo-religion, usually some brand of naturalism or positivism, that soon began to acquire an almost official status. This suited the secularist intellectuals to a T and as long as the modern temper prevailed among the educated classes, the trend went unchallenged. The Catholics established their own institutions; and the Jews of the first or second generation who aspired to a higher education were even more secularist-minded than the rest.

But we are no longer living under the sign of modernity. Within the past generation, a profound cultural change has taken place in the Western world. The mind that has emerged from this change is a post-modern mind. It no longer takes the secularist philosophies of the nineteenth and early twentieth century as self-evident; to many these philosophies have become totally discredited, to almost all they have lost their earlier appeal. The collapse of modernity has not, or has not yet, led to any significant spiritual reconstruction; confusion, anxiety, and search are the marks of our time. But the presuppositions of modernity are gone and with them the presuppositions of religionless education.

It is no longer self-evident, especially among the younger and more sensitive people, that religion is simply emotion without intellectual content. On the contrary, the religious thinkers of today—I have in mind such men as Maritain, Berdyaev, Buber, Tillich, Niebuhr, and of course Kierkegaard, who is to all intents and purposes a contemporary—enjoy a remarkable prestige as vanguard thinkers, not only among "religionists," but particularly among those concerned with so-called "secular" interests—psychiatrists, historians, political scientists, poets, educators, and literary critics. Religion—yes, theology—is recognized as having its intellectual relevance, and no institution of higher learning can be said to live up to its responsibility if it does not take this fact into account.

The philosophies of secularism can no longer claim prescriptive right in the university on the ground that they are not special commitments at all, but simply reason and science. They are special commitments, even quasi-theologies, and this is being widely acknowledged today. What the man of faith now demands, and this demand is beginning to make more sense than it has made for decades, is that his "philosophy," his *Weltanschauung*, his way of seeing and understanding things, his principle of integrating knowledge and experience, be given the same rights and privileges in the academic world as are the secularist philosophies, the same free course of learning and teaching. It is hard to find a ground, apart from the discredited dogmas of secularism, on which this demand can be refused.

If this is the first demand, the second is that the actualities of American pluralism be taken into account in relating religion to higher education. Catholics and Jews certainly have good grounds for complaint on this score. Most of the departments of religion in our colleges and universities (and even more, the administrative machinery of the campus religious work) reflect the older situation when Protestantism was America's "national religion," rather than the present situation in which the three religions of America are on a par, at least as far as public life is concerned. Rarely does a department of religion on a campus include a Catholic, and almost as rarely a Jew, even where large numbers of Catholic and Jewish students are to be found. This is surely indefensible, and the discrimination is not mitigated but rather compounded when the Protestantism that prevails is no more than a debased kind of "liberal religionism." It ought to be possible, and in a number of cases it actually has proved possible, to devise some form of tri-faith co-operation that would achieve the necessary unity and allow for the equally necessary diversity in the work of an effective department of religion. How effective any department of religion can hope to be under the present circumstances is another question.

But while the actualities of American religious pluralism must be taken into account, they must also be transcended. For American religious pluralism, let us remember, has two faces. On the one side, it brings the "three great faiths" together into a common framework; but, on the other side, this framework tends to be their common Americanness, more precisely the "moral and spiritual values" implied in the American Way of Life. These "values" are indeed worthy ones—some, in fact, are admirable—but religions that allow themselves to be defined in terms of the prevailing culture, however admirable, can never hope to be more than culture-religions, devoid of any genuine religious or prophetic power. This is the great danger confronting our historic faiths today, and it is a danger the more insidious because the threat comes from friend, not from foe. Those of us who are concerned about achieving a new relation between religion and higher education ought to be at least equally concerned about safeguarding and, where need be, restoring, the authentic content of faith, for otherwise the religion that is related to education will be little more than a spiritualized version of the current cultural values and convictions.

The "three great faiths" belong together, but they belong together not because they are "religions of democracy." They belong together because they are the religions of the Bible. The real and significant bond between them, in other words, is not that they are all American, but that they are all Biblical: we all, insofar as we are truly Christians or Jews, recognize Abraham as our father and the God of Israel as our God. The differences between the three religions are not trivial; they are very real and often of quite crucial importance, not to be dissolved into a generalized commitment to "religion" or "democracy." Yet they are differences within a common religious framework, usually designated as the Judeo-Christian tradition, and it is this common religious framework that, in my conception, gives ultimate religious meaning to the American tri-faith pluralism and to every effort to relate this tri-faith pluralism to the enterprise of higher education.

ROLAND H. BAINTON

The Making of a Pluralistic
Society — A Protestant View

CHAPTER III

The University of Michigan has long been dedicated to the view that religion belongs on the campus. Many another institution, in recent years, has been moving to the same conviction. All are confronted by the fact that their students are adherents of diverse faiths. In addition to the three main religions in America each with its own subvarieties, there is a fourth, which might be called the religion of Enlightenment, a Christianity attenuated as to doctrine and accentuated as to social idealism. Thomas Jefferson was its high priest and our democracy is its daughter. These three or four varieties have learned after wars of religion to co-exist. They do so because of the triumph of the philosophy of the Enlightenment. Start talking about religious differences with the common man and he will exclaim, "At bottom we are all the same. We believe in God. We believe in goodness; the rest does not matter." This is precisely the point of view, in the Renaissance, of Boccaccio, with his story of the three identical rings representing Christianity, Judaism, and Islam, a story re-employed by that great figure of the Enlightenment Ephraim Lessing as a theme for his play *Nathan the Wise.* It was the philosophy of John Locke, who averred that if he were on the road that leads to Jerusalem it was of no consequence whether he wore buskins, cut his hair short or long, ate or refrained from meat, or had as a guide one clothed in white and crowned with a miter. Such trivial points as these, said he, make implacable enemies of Christians, "who are all agreed in the substantial and truly fundamental part of religion."

This point of view is very prevalent, but it does not so far prevail as to make possible a unified religious program on the part of the three or four groups in the university. The Catholics, the Protestants (especially the Fundamentalists), and the Orthodox Jews will not admit that the points of difference are trivial. The liberal Jews and the liberal Protestants are closer to the philosophy of the Enlightenment, though they too, and notably today, would not relegate doctrine so blithely to the area of the nonessentials.

The degree to which this pluralism obstructs a program of religion in the universities depends somewhat on the reason for which the inclusion of religion is desired. One reason for introducing religion into the curriculum—and a perfectly valid reason—is that religion is a subject of universal interest with regard to which every educated man should have at least a modicum of understanding because religion has been so determinative in the formation of cultures. The number of religions is of no consequence here save to increase the amount and the complexity of the material to be studied. There may still be a question whether or not courses should be taught by adherents of the several faiths. For the most part this would be impossible on budgetary grounds, and even if it were possible to employ a Protestant, a Catholic, and a Jew as professors of religion, similar consideration could not be extended to teachers representing all the religions of the world. The most defensible technique would resemble that used for the languages where a philologian directs a course with the aid of native informants; thus an expert on comparative religion might supplement his offerings with lectures by members of the religions expounded.

But no one of the three main religions in our land is satisfied with only this approach. All would claim that religion is something more than anthropology or sociology or history and that one cannot really understand religion without being religious. The sincere adherent of a faith must desire ultimately, however adroit the approach, to make converts because he believes

that his particular faith has the answer to life's most fundamental questions and problems.

What shall we say of this our universe which increasing
knowledge discloses as ever more appallingly vast, whose extent is measured only in terms of light-years, and whose dura-
tion dwarfs the life of man to less than the span of an insect?
Evidence of staggering intelligence we see in its intricate
structure and delicate balance, evidence of purpose in its
dynamic, creative self-elaboration, and differentiation within
organic wholeness. But is there here any friendliness to man?
In the bleak recesses of stellar space, in the nuclear explosions
of solar radiation, in the erratic and devastating course of
tornadoes, in the eruption of volcanoes, and in the cooling of
planets, is there anything but the inexorable working of an
inscrutable purpose indifferent to mankind? Have we been
accorded by capricious fate a temporary haven on a sun-bask-
ing planet only that, after the mind of man has exploited every
resource for survival, we shall at last succumb when our earth
has become as extinct as the craters of the moon? And what
of all those who have gone before and of those who are yet to
come? What is the destiny of those who have labored in the
morning of man, carving bisons on the walls of their caves,
of those who for millenia followed unchanged the ancestral
ways of the forest primeval? Of those who throughout the
centuries have by searching found out some of the secrets and
added to the treasure house of knowledge? Are they now and
shall we shortly all be resolved into the dust from which we
came without the answers we crave to those riddles? And
what of the grave inequalities that life inflicts, the barbarous
torments that men have suffered at the hands of men? Is there
no vindication? And for those who have so sinned against their
fellows, is there no forgiveness? If we must answer "No,"
straight down the line, what then is the meaning of life and of
mortality? We may indeed say with the resolute poet brooding
over the recession of faith, "Let us be true then, love, to one
another." But how great a place have love and honor in a universe where man alone has evolved and cherishes such ideals?
And to come to our own situation, what is the point of foster-

ing universities and of acquiring more knowledge perchance with the consequence of hastening man's destruction? Or should we perhaps use our science to get it over with and not wait for the great freeze to encompass a burned-out world?

If religion has the answers to such universal questions, surely no subject could be more appropriate in a university dedicated to the quest of knowledge. But now comes a difficulty that is accentuated though not created by religious pluralism. Judaism and Christianity are religions of historic revelation. They announce a way to truth which is not that of the university, because revelation is conceived by all of these religions, at least in their more naïve stages, as something given in times past, a deposit to be accepted and elucidated, not to be questioned, whereas for the university truth is a quest where nothing is to be taken for granted and every hypothesis subjected to critical scrutiny. Truth as a deposit and truth as a quest, can these concepts coexist?

The notion of truth as a quest is derived from our Hellenic heritage. This was the presupposition of Socrates, of Plato, of Aristotle. The idea had a rebirth in the Renaissance when Erasmus applied it to the study of the Scripture. The classic formulation was given by that Renaissance Puritan John Milton, who declared that in theology as in arithmetic the golden rule is, "To be still searching what we know not by what we know, still closing up truth to truth as we find it." He was confident that in so doing truth would emerge. "Let truth and falsehood grapple; whoever knew truth put to the worse in a free and open encounter?" Father Murray asks us whether we can any longer be so naïve as to believe that. Now of course we have seen that the enemies of free encounter can so take advantage of free encounter as to destroy it. But the point was that among a company of seekers, all dedicated to free encounter, in which each would propound his hypothesis for the criticism of his colleagues, where each stood ready to convince or be convinced, truth would prevail. A further ingredient in this faith is that, "Truth crushed to earth will rise again." This second assertion is indeed a faith rather than a fact, and even the first does not admit of unexceptional verification. But it is the best method we have of arriving at truth, and it is the fundamental assumption of our universities.

The great religions claim that truth, though in some measure an object of a quest, in its most important phase (as it relates to the ultimate) is the subject of a deposit. Truth is given through a self-disclosure of God at definite times in the past and recorded in inspired sacred writings. The most unqualified form of this claim is made by the Roman Catholic church. Father van de Pol says:

Holy Scripture and the Church have always presented revelation as the making known by God of certain definite truths which before were hidden in the mind of God, but now, at the end of time, are announced and made known to all who believe. From the beginning, revelation, preaching, and faith have had a definite and unchangeable scope and content. These truths have always been proclaimed by divine authority, and it is precisely on account of this that they call for unconditional belief and unhesitating obedience on the part of man. The act of faith involves a complete surrender of man to the revelation of God, and to the authoritative teaching of the contents of this definite, final revelation.[1]

This is not to say that the revelation as given in scripture is explicit in every respect. Precisely because it is not, God has endowed the Church with the power of inerrant elucidation, and this power is focused on the pope. He is not an organ of revelation but only of explication. He is the unique recipient of that aid from the Holy Spirit which will so watch over his normal processes of reasoning that in making deductions from the revelation already given in the areas of faith and morals, when and only when he makes a pronouncement binding upon all Catholics, will he then be infallibly preserved from error.

The Catholic church claims, then, to be the custodian of the revelation given through Christ and recorded in the Scriptures, capable of formulation in doctrinal propositions and susceptible of further elaboration by inerrant deduction.

Is it possible, apart from religious diversity, to combine such a position with regard to the way to truth with that assumed by the modern university? It was done, of course, in the medieval university where theology was the queen of the sciences, and it was accomplished by a demarcation of sphere. Certain disciplines, such as physics, rest upon the inquiry of the human mind. Here the pagan Aristotle was regnant. Only theology proper dealt with revelation. Yet conflict arose even in the medieval university, and notably between philosophy and theology, when the philosophy in vogue came to be nominalism, which claims that reality consists of unrelated particulars, or more precisely, of particulars related only by contiguity in space and time. Difficulty arises when this view is applied to the doctrine of the Trinity, whose three persons transcend space and time. If, then, they have no relation save contiguity in space and time, the three persons in the Godhead become three unrelated absolutes, and the outcome in tritheism. The exponents of this view agreed that it did not comport with the theological teaching that the three are one. The solution was found in the doctrine if not of double truth at least of double logic.

The situation today is not vastly dissimilar. Catholic theology is compatible with natural science on the basis of a division of spheres, and many distinguished scientists are Catholic. In the area of philosophy only the Thomist's position is congruous with Catholic theology, and even in the natural sciences conflicts may arise and have arisen as in the case of Genesis versus geology and evolution. The pope has ruled that Adam was a real person from whom the human race is descended, an assumption with which no non-Catholic biologist would be ready to commence. One may wonder whether Catholicism can be genuinely at home in any university other than in a Catholic university. In any university whatever, Catholic theology could be taught but only by declaring itself to be at variance with some or at least an aspect of some of the other disciplines.

With regard to non-Catholics the case is different, and here it is that religious pluralism injects a difficulty at the most central point, the very concept of revelation. The Fundamentalist Christian and presumably the Orthodox Jew—as to Judaism I am less well informed than as to Christianity—find revelation in the Scriptures, which are taken to be entirely inerrant. Yet they do have to be interpreted, as the Roman Catholic church rightly insists, and what happens is that each Christian sect has its own scheme of interpretation. Once I sat in on an interchange between a Christadelphian and a Jehovah's Witness. They appeared to me to be of the same stripe, but they were quite unable to achieve common ground because of discrepant modes of interpretation. Fundamentalists are of course able in a university to do distinguished work in all of the disciplines not at variance with their own faith, and they may even fulfill the requirements of courses in a theology contrary to their own by mastering the body of information. A Fundamentalist can take a doctor's degree in religion in a liberal institution by being open to every fact and impervious to every idea. The purpose in so doing is to use the degree as a weapon with which to combat the point of view of the institution by which the degree was conferred. There may be some point in continuing such a situation because it does mean that in a measure a channel of possible communication is kept open. Yet one cannot but regard the case as sad if in religion the meeting of minds and hearts cannot go beyond the factual.

Those who belong to the liberal group among the non-Catholics entertain a view of revelation distinctly different from that both of the Catholics and of the conservatives in their own bodies. The term liberal is here used for those who have accepted the methods of historical criticism as applied to the sacred books and are not disposed in any case to think of revelation in terms that can be reduced to neat proposition. In this sense Barth, who has lavished so much criticism on Protestant Liberalism, is himself in many respects in the liberal camp.

Three examples may serve to illustrate differing views of revelation. The first is that of Berdyaev, a representative of the Russian Orthodox Church. He may be considered because he has been much read in American Protestant seminaries and because his point of view has its parallels in some phases of Protestant Liberalism as it did also in Catholic Modernism. "Revelation," says Berdyaev, "is not something which drops into a man's lap from outside and in which he has nothing but an entirely passive part to play." Berdyaev is the heir of that mysticism of the Eastern Church, not unknown to the Western, which finds the goal of religion in the union of man with God so that man himself is made divine. In the experience of union the distinction between faith and reason disappears because this belongs to the world of objectification. Revelation cannot be objectified. It cannot be formulated into propositions which in themselves are true or false. Revelation is a spiritual event. The truth which it communicates must be grasped integrally. Unless truth takes place in a man truth is not obtained. Revelation makes use of historical facts as symbols. "The Christian conception of the divine Incarnation ought not to mean the deification of historical facts. Christian truth cannot be made to depend upon historical facts, which cannot be fully attested nor ingenuously accepted as reality."[2]

This statement leaves one wondering as to the relation of faith and history. Is revelation the continuous self-disclosure of God in mystical experience for which the records of history provide only a garment of symbol or are we capable of receiving revelation in personal experience only because of the unique self-disclosure of God in the past? Berdyaev might respond to this question as he did to another: "There is," said he, "a question which is put by people who are wholly submerged in objectification and consequently in the spirit of authoritarianism. It is, 'Where then is there a fixed and abiding standard of truth?' And to that question I decline to give my answer."[3]

The second example is that of a Protestant layman, a Congregationalist and a natural scientist, Edmund Sinnott, who in his work *Two Roads to Truth* describes the one as the way of intellect, reason, science; the other as a way of insight, intuition, unreasoned assurance, instinctive feeling. The second way is strongly akin to aesthetic sensibility.

Beauty is a subtle, indefinable thing. Great art and poetry and music, nature's innumerable and radiant beauties—these set man's spirit singing. They warm his heart and wake within him a sense of glory and delight, lifting him to such ecstasy that, like the religious mystic, he becomes for a little while a higher sort of being, in tune with mysterious harmonies.[4]

The insight of the individual is incalculably indebted to the past—to the Hebrew and Christian past—yet is not to be restricted by the past. He continues:

Where all things thus are on the march it seems to the scientist the height of folly to try to tie up truth within the limits of a dogma, either philosophical or religious, and to deny the possibility of fuller understanding even of spiritual matters. Reverence for the past should never become a strait jacket for the present. Insistence on a truth that is certain and perfect, never to be changed, science repudiates. . . . Science respects the past, but builds upon it for a greater future. Why, one asks, should we not expect religion to have the same expansiveness, the same splendidly growing vision of the truth, as it explores mysteries deeper than science can ever probe? . . . He who told Simon to launch out into the deep would never counsel timid conservatism in such matters or seek to pour the truth's new wine into bottles of dogmatic certainty. "The worship of God," says Whitehead, "is not a rule of safety—it is an adventure of the spirit, a flight after the unattainable. The death of religion comes with the repression of the high hope of adventure."[5]

With this view of revelation the conflict between truth as a deposit and truth as a quest disappears. The difference lies between truth as sight and truth as insight.

The third example is afforded by Richard Niebuhr, a Protestant theologian, a liberal as to historical criticism, but with a much deeper feeling for revelation in history than one finds in Berdyaev's questing for obliteration of objective distinctions through union with the divine. Richard Niebuhr understands revelation as the disclosure of meaning in history and in life. The prophets by revelation illumined the history of Israel and gave to the men of their day an understanding of the memories of their people. Jesus, born in the fullness of time, brought to life the meaning of the convergence of the religion of the Hebrews and the philosophy of the Greeks.

Revelation continues ... The work has not been completed, for the past is infinite, and thought, even with the aid of revelation, is painful, and doubt assails the human heart. But for the Christian church the whole past is potentially a single epic. In the presence of the revelatory occasion it can and must remember in tranquillity the long story of human ascent from the dust, of descent into the sloughs of brutality and sin, the nameless sufferings of untold numbers of generations, the groaning and travailing of creation until now—all that otherwise is remembered only with despair. There is no part of that past that can be ignored or regarded as beyond possibility of redemption from meaninglessness. And it is the ability of the revelation to save all the past from senselessness that is one of the marks of its revelatory character.[6]

Such revelation cannot be set forth in a set of articles true or false. One does not assent to revelation as true simply by agreeing that it is so. The discovery of meaningfulness in life and history has to be felt, not simply believed, and it will not be felt unless there is first an inner transformation. "The response to revelation is quite as much a confession of sin as a confession of faith." What revelation

means for us cannot be expressed in the impersonal ways of creeds or other propositions but only in responsive acts of a personal character. We acknowledge revelation by no third person proposition, such as that there is a God, but only in the direct confession of the heart, "Thou art my God." We can state the convincement given in the revelatory moment only in a prayer saying, "Our Father." Revelation as the self-disclosure of the infinite person is realized in us only through the faith which is a personal act of commitment, of confidence and trust, not a belief about the nature of things.[7]

Such a view of revelation does not involve the discrepancy of the Catholic and Fundamentalist view as against the scientific, but it raises a much more profound question as to whether revelation can be taught at all. What will one do in a university with a course which must start with a confession of sin, and cannot the most untutored man make such a confession and receive the answer that gives meaning to his life and all that he knows of life? What then will one do with revelation in a university? The answer is that one can study the records of religious experience, the Bible as religious experience, religious biography as experience of religion. One can discover how others were brought to these moments of insight. An artist told me that he had no feeling for El Greco, but he looked and studied and observed and exposed himself until there burst on him an awed response to the clouds brooding over Toledo. It is the same with poetry and music. They can be studied by way of exposure. They will never be known until the spirit lists to blow.

If then there are differences so deep between the three religions and between varieties within these religions, how can religion be presented in a university where all three and more are present? Reconciliation of their divergent viewpoints is at present out of the question. Father van de Pol says that Protestants and Catholics must regard each other as heretics. He does not attach to the word all of the old invidious connotations. He is not issuing a summons for an auto-da-fé. He uses heretic in its primitive sense as one who is in error. Catholics hold out to Protestants no hope of reunion save by way of submission on our part, and we find the claims of Rome altogether untenable. The doctrine of papal infallibility is a great hinderance. We realize that the pope is claimed to be infallible only when he speaks on faith and morals, only when he elucidates previous revelation, and only when he speaks officially and makes his pronouncement binding upon all Catholics. He may in an unofficial statement be guilty of heresy as was Pope Honorius. Again Leo XIII pronounced the text in I John 5, which reads, "And there are three in heaven that witness, the Father, the Spirit and Son," to be an authentic part of this epistle, though not discoverable in any manuscript prior to the fifteenth century. Thirty years later another pope reversed this judgment. But this did not invalidate the infallibility of Leo in Catholic eyes, because he was not speaking officially. The distinction appears to Protestants very tenuous. Will the Spirit which bloweth where listeth so submit itself to that which is official? Even more repugnant to us is the claim that infallibility has no relation to the character of the pope. We can understand that a man does not need to be perfect in order to speak the truth, but that he should not only be immoral but even indifferent to religion and yet able to speak infallibly about religion taxes all credence. Leo X, for example, was a flippant pope more interested in hunting, gambling, and art than in religion. Yet the *Dictionnaire de Theologie E Catholique* reckons his bull, *Exsurge Domine,* as among the infallible pronouncements.

Even more grave is the preoccupation of liberal Protestantism with demythologizing, that is to say the endeavor to extract the religious core from the Scriptures while discarding the outmoded scientific thought forms of the first century, whereas Catholicism is occupied in making more mythology at variance we think both with history and with science, as for example the declaration of the Assumption of the Virgin. But this is not the place to air all of our differences. The point is that they are deep and not easily to be bridged. And they are lamentable because the very revelation which might bring balm to the world is discredited if the religions which profess to have received it are so at variance as to what it is. All of which is not to say that there are not great areas of agreement, and one is inclined to believe that the man who dishes out the hamburgers may be right in saying, "at bottom we are all the same, we believe in God, we believe in goodness, the rest does not matter." Yet it is easier for a Protestant to say this than for a Catholic, because for a Protestant what matters is not so much precise belief as interior piety and the Protestant is glad to testify that the Catholic has it. But interior piety or spirituality though esteemed by the Catholic is not sufficient without dogmatic rectitude. The gulf is still there. Happily some are striving to bridge it. Father Tavard, who has written a very understanding book about Protestantism, is seeking to make Catholicism more acceptable by a revival of the Augustinianism of the late Middle Ages as exemplified in

Saint Bonaventura, for whom the conflict of faith and knowledge was resolved in the vision of God.

Richard Niebuhr remarks:

There will be no union of Catholics and Protestants until through the common memory of Jesus Christ the former repent of the sin of Peter and the latter of the sin of Luther, until Protestants acknowledge Thomas Aquinas as one of their fathers, the Inquisition as their own sin and Ignatius Loyola as one of their own Reformers, until Catholics have canonized Luther and Calvin, done repentance for Protestant nationalism, and appropriated Schleiermacher and Barth as their theologians.[8]

The time for this has not yet come and until it does we shall not be able to organize a joint department of religion in a university. The only possibility is that a department of religion should offer courses given by Protestants, by Catholics, and by Jews working quite independently. They would be inculcating their own faiths. But this is impossible in a state institution because of the limitations imposed on education by the separation of church and state. What can be done is that religious bodies at their own expense may set up faculties of theology on the university campus and offer courses open to election by all students, for which the university will grant credits toward its own degree. In some places this is being done.

Yet this in itself is not enough, and no one of the faiths is content simply to give instruction. The impression must not be given that Catholics, because they can state revelation in propositions to be believed or rejected, are any less disposed than Protestants or Jews to say that belief must be more than intellectual assent if it is to be a saving faith. All of the three religions are concerned for the practice of religion alike in acts of worship and of social concern. The latter presents no problem. Fortunately, all three faiths experience no difficulty whatever in collaboration on such matters as social justice, opposition to racial discrimination, political immorality, and the like. This most important area does not require discussion here because pluralism offers no difficulty.

But worship does, and much more so for the Catholic than for the Protestant and the Jew. Because the Catholic feels that right worship requires right doctrine, and a liturgy acceptable to a non-Catholic cannot be satisfactory to a Catholic. The liberal Protestant and the liberal Jew place much greater stress on attitudes—reverence, awe, contrition, humility, adoration —and are willing to worship together with those who express these attitudes in other dogmatic terms. For us the dogmas have value more as symbols than as precise formulations of ultimate truth. That is why when I was in France with a Quaker unit of the Red Cross during World War I whenever we were in a village where there was no Protestant church I went to mass. Even on Catholic assumptions I cannot see why an occasional joint service of worship could not be worked out which would contain no dogmatic assertion unacceptable to any of the three. It could not possibly contain a full statement of the faith of each of the three; but it might center on common elements. As a Protestant I should have no difficulty in sharing with a Jew in a service drawn entirely from the Old Testament. He would have more difficulty in joining with me in a service including passages from the New Testament, but they might be so chosen that a liberal Jew would not feel obligated to withdraw. As a Protestant I could share with a Catholic in a service made up of scripture passages, of prayers from Saint Chrysostom, Saint Augustine, and John Henry Newman, hymns from Saint Ambrose, Jacopone da Todi, Saint Francis Xavier, and Gilbert Chesterton, and of meditations from Saint Francis, Saint Bernard, and Saint François de Sales. And I cannot see why a Catholic could not share in a service taken from the classics of Protestant devotional literature. I once gave a talk, by the way, on such literature over a Catholic radio program. Father Tavard says that: "Luther ranks among the most delicate devotional writers with his essay on *Christian Liberty* and his very devout commentary on Mary's *Magnificat*."[9]

A Catholic chaplain of one of our state universities tells us that it cannot be and warns us not to embarrass Catholics by inviting them to do what they must refuse. A Catholic he says can pray with anyone save an atheist (that he thinks would be tough)[10] privately, but not officially. One would like to know, in the first place, whether this is a universal ruling. There are regional differences in such matters. The Bishop of Syracuse, for example, has forbidden Catholic students to participate in a Religious Emphasis program. But the bishops in other areas permit it. The present bishop of Connecticut has reversed the practice of his predecessors in permitting a priest in New Haven to take part on the platform in a public service of Thanksgiving with scripture, hymns, prayer, and sermon. But I am told that such joint services continue in other places. Here is a point on which we should be glad to be more precisely informed. If the bishop says, "No," we should not embarrass the priest, but there is no reason why we should not address ourselves to the bishop.

Admittedly, however, joint worship could be only occasional. Christians would not be satisfied with a chapel service all the year through which did not go beyond the Old Testament, and Catholics would not be willing to be continuously reserved in references to the Blessed Virgin and to the Saints. But if we can do so there is a point in holding joint services, because God is one and truth is one, and if we are sincere in our desire to worship the one God in truth, though manifestly since we disagree some of us must be in error, nevertheless we cannot go astray in joining in common adoration and petition for forgiveness and illumination from the Father of Lights, with whom there is no shadow of turning.

Neither should it be impossible to discuss our differences. Some of the interfaith movements have insisted that in all joint endeavors reference to dogma should be avoided and in no case should there be debate. This means getting together by avoiding fundamentals. But let us remember that students do not leave these matters alone. In private bull sessions no knuckles are gloved and no friendships are broken. Discussion on a public platform might indeed lead to acrimony, but what could be the objection to interchanges between representatives of the three faiths among small student groups? On the same level why might there not be informal unofficial services of worship in areas where bishops have forbidden collaboration in public worship? The chaplain mentioned above said that he could pray privately with anyone. Did he mean only with one, or might not a group of half a dozen, a cell in other words, engage together in meditation and prayer? Every avenue of collaboration at every level should be explored.

WALTON E. BEAN

What Is the State University?

CHAPTER IV

The position of religion in the American state university is a position of tacit compromise. On the one hand, there is the principle of separation of church and state. On the other, there is the fact that religion is inseparable from large areas of human thought and feeling and thus from higher learning. The resulting adjustment is perfectly appropriate to the general nature and circumstances of the state university itself, and typical of it. For like most American democratic institutions, the state university is a complex and ingenious product of the diversity, freedom, and flexibility of American society, and consequently it works in an atmosphere of healthy compromise.

Perhaps the supreme adjustment which the American state university has had to make is the adjustment between the proper nature of a university as an institution devoted to the free advance of the human mind, and the proper nature of a public institution, created by government and supported by taxation. This adjustment, though still imperfect, has fairly steadily improved. American state constitution makers and legislators have been substantially successful in devising a system which protects public universities from both the special dogmas of religious sectarianism and the special group interests of political partisanship. In America both religious beliefs and material group interests are indeed extraordinarily "pluralistic"; and a state university belongs to the whole people of an American state. It should be noticed that the high purpose of protecting such an institution from religious sectarianism no more implies the complete exclusion of religion as such than the necessity of excluding politics in the sense of partisanship means that it is desirable or even possible to make the state university other than an instrument of public policy, a major developmental agency of the state.

At the same time it should also be noted that balance and co-operation between public and private enterprise has been preserved in American higher education, just as in other aspects of American society. The similarities between state universities and private ones in America are much more numerous and important than the differences. Public and private universities share inseparably in the community of knowledge. So far as many of the major aspects of American higher education are concerned, the differences between public and private universities can even be ignored entirely, as in fact these differences quite properly are ignored in a number of the chapters in this book. It is widely supposed that different conditions governing the treatment and status of religion are among the essential distinctions between public and private higher education in America. It is true, in general, that private universities have schools or departments of religion and public ones do not, but there are major exceptions even to this generalization. The exceptions include both of the public universities of Iowa. There is a School of Religion at the State University of Iowa at Iowa City, and a department of Religious Education in Iowa State College at Ames.[1]

An attempt at definition or rather at classification of American universities is no easy matter. When Richard H. Ostheimber prepared his *Statistical Analysis of Higher Education in the United States,* as of 1949, he discovered that "if one attempts to get perfectly homogeneous classifications, one approaches the absurdity of finding that the number of classifications equals the number of institutions to be classified." The wide discretion left to the states by the federal government has permitted considerable diversity among "universities" both in name and in fact. At present, however, we may say that there are roughly sixty state universities in the United States and about the same number of private ones. Each of

the forty-eight states has what it officially calls a state university. More than half of these institutions are "land-grant
universities." That is, the land-grant agricultural college was
made an integral part of a general state university. Moreover,
in eleven of the states that maintain their land-grant colleges
as separate institutions, these "state colleges" have now diversified their functions to the point at which they meet a reasonable
definition of a second state university, and one of them,
Michigan's, has recently received that official title. Any attempt
at an exact census is further complicated by hybrid public-
private institutions like "Rutgers University, the State University of New Jersey"; and by the fact that some states, most
obviously California, include more than one full-scale university in a single state university system. There is also the
question of whether some of the smaller state universities are
truly of "university" scope, but here we can only give full faith
and credit to the acts of each state.

A brief summary of the historical background is essential
to an understanding of the present situation, for the story of
the origins and development of American state universities
does much to explain their characteristic adaptability to special
needs and changing circumstances in American society.

The first American state universities were founded after the
Revolution in the southeastern seaboard states, largely because
no private colleges had been established there during the
colonial period. In the region between the Appalachians and
the Mississippi, state universities owed their original foundation largely to the fact that the federal government in 1787
had set the precedent of offering grants of one or more town-
ships of federal public land for "seminaries of learning" in
new states. The early "state universities" differed very little
from the many private denominational institutions that were
also founded on the pattern of the colonial colleges. The early
American college curriculum, with its core in the classics of
Greek, Latin, and Hebrew literature, had been designed for
the training of ministers and gentlemen in an aristocratic
society. The early state universities simply imitated this
"literary" and "classical" college pattern, which remained

almost static until after the middle of the nineteenth century. Neither public nor private institutions had succeeded in providing a system of education, let alone of research, which the American people could put to practical use, or which captured their imagination. College enrollments were actually declining in proportion to the population of college age.

The great potentialities of the state university first began to be apparent at Michigan in the eighteen-fifties under the brilliant presidency of Henry Philip Tappan, an admirer of the scientific achievements of the German universities. During the same period came the agitation that led to the Morrill Act of 1862, endowing state colleges of "agriculture and the mechanic arts" through federal land grants to the states. (These are the "land grant" institutions we speak of today, the earlier federal "seminary township" grants having now been largely forgotten.) Of the approximately sixty institutions that are reasonably classified as state universities at present, more than half owed their original organization to the stimulus of the Morrill Act agricultural college land grants. In the New England and middle Atlantic regions, where well-established private colleges and universities had pre-empted the field, the state university idea was resisted until well into the twentieth century, but in recent decades nearly all of the land-grant agricultural colleges in that area have become general-purpose state universities.

The American state university of today is intended to provide advanced general, professional, and technical education for the greatest practicable number of young men and women, largely at public expense. The proportion of students enrolled in public higher education in general is now larger than the enrollment in privately supported institutions, and this proportion, as well as that of college and university students in the general population, is virtually certain to continue a steady and rapid growth. Some of the implications and problems of this situation are certain to be of increasingly critical importance. College enrollments during the nineteen-sixties may be more than double those of the early fifties, mainly because in 1932 there were only about two million registered births in the United States; in 1943 about three million; and in 1950 nearly four million. Obviously, only the public purse can provide for the bulk of the enormous institutional expansion that will be required in the next decade. Where we shall find either the taxes or the teachers is an interesting question.

But find them we must and shall. For the role of public higher education as a central part of democracy, through its function as an avenue to greater achievement, service, and reward for the children of the common man is so familiar a fact of life in America that it is easy to forget its real meaning and importance. No one, perhaps, can truly comprehend the significance of mass public higher education until he has experienced the breath-taking contrasts between a society that has it and a society that does not. In this perspective the phrase "mass education" takes on an entirely new depth of meaning. For it becomes clear that the unprecedented and unparalleled achievement of mass public higher education in America has been not merely a result or a luxurious byproduct of the success of American society. It is rather one of the most essential causes of that success. The very heart of the plight of the underdeveloped nations lies in the limited number of their people who receive advanced general, professional, and technical education or are likely to receive it in the near future.

In the structure and the functions of the American state university a spirit of salutary compromise is everywhere apparent. In terms of structure and organization, there is constant compromise among the state university's constituent elements: faculties, administrations, governing boards, state officials, the public, students, and alumni. In terms of function, the state university performs simultaneously a maze of different services that are sometimes interrelated and complementary, but also sometimes in competition with each other. Thus there must be perpetual compromise, implicit and explicit, in the allocation of its energies and resources among the functions of teaching, research, and an infinite variety of services to the general public.

Although the state university functions as a human community rather than as a legal entity, an understanding of its special structure and form of organization under American state law is important not only as a part of its definition, but also for an understanding of the degree of freedom and flexibility that it has attained. Under the laws or constitutions of nearly every state, the state university is a semi-independent public corporation governed legally and to a considerable extent actually by a board of distinguished citizens, mostly appointed by the governor or elected by the people. This system, like the self-perpetuating governing board system of American private colleges and universities, is virtually unique and peculiar to the United States. In part, it grew out of quite accidental circumstances in early American history. No other country has entrusted its universities to the full legal responsibility and authority of external governing boards of "laymen," that is of men who are not primarily experts in educational matters. But although American university governing boards are often criticized as mainly drawn from the business community rather than from the entire community, the fact that every state has adopted this system and that none has seriously considered changing it indicates that in general it serves American purposes fairly well.

The governing board represents the interest of the public in the university, and it represents the university to the public. It has the duty both of keeping the university responsible to the public and of serving as a buffer to protect the university from unwise pressures. This is especially true in several states which, following the example of Michigan, have provided an important degree of corporate independence for their universities in their state constitutions. Theoretically such an institution is a kind of fourth branch of government, independent of and co-ordinate with the legislative, executive, and judicial branches, and this type of constitutional-corporation university was once defined by the Michigan Supreme Court as "the highest form of juristic person known to the law." Actually, of course, constitutional independence is somewhat compromised by financial dependence on the state legislature. But even in the states whose universities do not enjoy the protection of constitutional status, the institutions are coming to be regarded as a lofty and noble form of public trust, symbolized by the corporate governing board but shared also by the administration, the faculty, the students, and indeed by the whole body of citizens.

Several states define their universities for legal purposes as "the corporation known as the Regents," and an occasional regent may be found who seems to feel that he and his colleagues truly *are* the university in fact as well as in law. But even this extreme feeling is an understandable if not a pardonable form of pride. And moreover, similar feelings may be discovered among university administrators, professors, students, and even alumni.

In practice, governing boards have long since delegated much of their responsibilities to university presidents—a race of beings who must attempt to approximate superman. In the nineteenth century and the early twentieth, there was a critical stage in the evolution of American state universities when the development of the quality of each institution depended primarily on the wisdom and luck of the regents in selecting a chief executive. The net work of relationships, functions, and interests was becoming so complex that it was desirable to centralize responsibility in one man, and the "strong president" system was another American adaptation to special circumstances. In that stage, the American system of university administration was well described as "absolute dictatorship tempered by occasional assassination." Later, of course, as knowledge became more and more specialized and the number of university departments between art and zoology proliferated to about fifty (not including the number of departments within the professional schools), the president in turn had to delegate more and more of his authority and to rely much more heavily upon the advice of deans, department heads, and faculty committees. At present the list of administrative officers and faculty committees in the largest state university fills sixteen closely printed pages. It is difficult to keep the administrative camel from crowding the intellectual pilgrim out of his tent.

Even in this situation, however, the president remains a key figure. He must constantly mediate among all the diverse interests in an institution that is becoming almost as complex as the society it serves. For example, he must mediate between the values and viewpoints of professors and businessmen—between the scientist, the intellectual, the academic man on the one hand, and on the other the corporation presidents, bankers, lawyers, newspaper publishers, and farmers who make up the governing board. This function is so delicate that many state universities have a rule requiring all communications between regents and professors to be channeled through the president.

Thus the state university president has been rather accurately defined as "a man who makes compromises for a living." Yet he cannot succeed unless all his compromises are made on a high level of principle.

In describing the state university as an institution, a social structure, there is a tendency to overemphasize the relatively external elements in its organization and control. Its most essential components, of course, are not regents and administrators but teachers and students. A state university partakes of the familiar definition of a university as such: "a community of scholars." But even this definition is too narrow if it overemphasizes the idea of the faculty as an academic guild, if it implies that research is more important than teaching in the process of "scholarship," or if it forgets that a university is a place in which youth forms its purposes in life.

Between its primary function of teaching and its corollary function of research, the state university has in general achieved a healthy interrelationship, a healthy balance and cross-fertilization. A university has at its center an undergraduate college providing broad general education in the first two years and a partial specialization in the "upper division." In a university, the "college" may be compared to the palm of a hand from which extend the fingers of the graduate school and the professional schools. In all of these areas the process of research constantly vitalizes the process of teaching.

A description of the life and work of the state university must include the manifold services that it renders directly to the public, as well as the public service that it renders indirectly through teaching and research within its own walls. Through university extension, agricultural extension, and other activities,

it has come to regard the whole state as its campus, and sometimes the nation and the world as well. There is a massive
and constant interaction between the state universities and the
whole complex of American economic and cultural life, and
in several foreign countries teams of American professors are
introducing or reorganizing instruction in such fields as public
and business administration.

The intellectual freedom of the American state university
has in general been fairly well protected against the damage
it might receive from the constant stress upon practical service
to the public. The effectiveness of this service has led the
people's representatives in the legislatures of nearly all of the
states to regard appropriations for state universities as venture
capital of a remarkably valuable kind, for they are likely to
produce anything from the Babcock process for testing milk,
which revolutionized the dairy industry, to the atomic bomb,
which revolutionized a great deal more. The practical results
of university research are generally received with gratitude
and sometimes with a kind of awe. They have made the public
willing to allow universities a great deal of freedom to perform
their more mysterious and abstract functions.

The majority of the public still does regard universities as
rather mysterious, and professors often complain that the
public does not understand what a university is. Occasionally,
some wave of public emotion leads to drastic legislative interference in university affairs. Questions like those of "loyalty"
oaths, or of the current attempts of several state legislatures to
prevent racial desegregation, sometimes confront administrations and faculties with the delicate problem of whether they
should oppose and seek to change an emotionally aroused
public opinion on some major issue of state university policy.
This can present a serious dilemma. As a distinguished professor of philosophy at a southern state university has recently
pointed out, such a course may have the effect of inflaming
instead of changing public opinion on the particular question;
and it may also damage the general welfare by destroying that
degree of detachment which makes the university's highest

functions possible and which should therefore be preserved throughout all of its contacts with its various publics.

President Pusey of Harvard recently found it necessary to emphasize that the function of his university was that of "service without servility" to its constituents. This needs emphasis in state universities at least as much as in private ones. In American democracy the state university has become an important part of the mind of the state. To serve the state well it must be a free mind.

The constant proliferation of knowledge as well as the emphasis on its application to practical life have inevitably created real problems in the preservation of the values of broad, general, and liberal education. When, as someone has said, "the golden bowl of classicism was broken"—when the old homogeneous classical curriculum (in which religion was central) was replaced by one which recognized the demands of science, industry, and the professions, hundreds of new university courses were created. With the rise of the large university the total enrollment in the professional schools often exceeded enrollment in the liberal arts college, and even within that college the curriculum became increasingly complex. Many observers of American state universities, and many of the participants in them, feel that their curricula have become overspecialized and departmentalized. Some feel that they offer too many subjects that would be better left to technical and vocational institutions of lesser grade. Ezra Cornell expressed the intention of founding an institution "in which any student may find instruction in any subject." Cornell University is a private institution to which the state of New York entrusted its land-grant college, in an ingenious compromise between public and private enterprise.

Here again we see that there are few of the problems and shortcomings of American universities, just as there are few of their achievements, for which the blame or credit can be clearly ascribed to public or private institutions as such. The free elective system that permitted the student in the liberal arts college to browse at will among an ever-growing number of subjects, and under which the college tended to lose control of the curriculum to the departments, received its first great impetus not from the utilitarian demands upon public educational institutions but from President Eliot of Harvard.

In state universities as well as in private ones, a predominant recent tendency in reorganizing the curriculum has stressed efforts to reintegrate the knowledge that has been amassed in so many special fields. Private universities and colleges have more often taken the lead in this "general education" movement, but state institutions are making comparable efforts in it. It may be hoped that the reconciliation of specialism and generalism will be the foremost achievement, as it is perhaps the foremost need, in the next great epoch of higher education in America. It may well be that we are entering an age of reintegration in higher learning, and the various questions regarding the proper place of religion may well be considered in this context.

PAUL G. KAUPER

Law and Public Opinion

CHAPTER V

Writing to the Danbury Baptists Association in 1802, Thomas Jefferson stated that the Constitution built "a wall of separation between Church and State." Whether the "wall" metaphor was well chosen and whether government and religion can be as neatly and completely separated as this statement suggested, it is true that Jefferson expressed a fundamental idea that is generally accepted in American thinking and now regarded as a key feature of our constitutional system.[1]

The handy phrase "separation of church and state" symbolizes an important facet of American pluralism; namely, that church and state are to function side by side in American society, that each is to pursue its own sphere of competence and responsibility, and that neither has legal authority to interfere with or control the other's operations. An implicit result of this division is that the state, the politically organized community, alone can exercise coercive power whereas the institutions of religion must rest on a voluntaristic basis.

But the separation principle rests on something more than an attempt to allocate spheres of responsibility in the interests of efficiency and special competence. It acquires its substance as a limitation in the interest of human freedom. Separation of church and state as a jurisdictional principle can be restated in terms of private liberty to mean that the state may not execute its coercive power either to compel adherence to any religious faith or creed, interfere with the free expression of religion, or use its resources and powers either to prefer or to discriminate against any religious group or organization. It is our conception that the religious life, as expressed both privately and corporately, flourishes best when divorced from both the compulsion and the restraint of political force.

Any discussion of the place of religion at the state university, both in terms of curricular considerations and the relationship of the university to the primary religious groups, must necessarily meet the issue posed by the separation principle. Is it even appropriate for a state university, admittedly an agent or division of the state, to provide opportunities both for instruction in religion and for primary religious groups to function more effectively on the campus?[2]

Before attempting any concrete answer to these questions by reference to explicit constitutional limitations that furnish positive grounds for legal application of the separation principle, it is appropriate to mention some basic considerations relevant to the constitutional aspects of the problem.

In the first place, it should be noted that the term "separation of church and state" symbolizes a generalized concept or principle and not a specific rule. Indeed, to the best of the writer's knowledge, this term does not occur in any American constitution. Insofar as the separation principle has been recognized as a legal limitation, it represents a judicial interpretation and synthesis of empiric provisions found in written constitutions. But legal limitations did not create the separation principle. They reflect the principle that has grown out of the experience and understanding of our people.

Viewed as a legal proposition, the separation principle lacks the historical depth and perspective that may give a solid core of meaning to such constitutional language as "due process of law." Moreover, when we look at American history and the practices sanctioned by history, some of which are now repudiated in the name of the separation principle while others continue unchallenged, all in the face of constitutional provisions that have remained unchanged, it is evident that we are dealing with an idea that in its application at any one time has no fixed or precise meaning. This idea, nonetheless, is sufficiently elastic to accommodate itself to new concepts and trends in American life and the popular understanding. It is true of law generally that to maintain its vitality it must be responsive to the needs of the day. And constitutional law even when fortified by judicial review under a written constitution has proved to be no exception to this. The whole history of constitutional interpretation makes clear that the Constitution is a malleable document, that the important limitations of the Constitution that rest on implication or on broad phrasings in the text do not lend themselves to precise technical rules or doctrinal absolutes, and that the judicial appraisal of underlying policy considerations and the pragmatic weighing of competing interests that deserve constitutional recognition become critical elements in the decisional process. In turn the current of historical movement and the climate of public opinion give life and meaning to the underlying values that either expressly or implicitly shape the course of judicial interpretation.

Turning now to the empiric constitutional provisions and their significance in respect to religion in the state university, we are faced at the outset by the pluralism within our constitutional system. In the continental United States we have forty-nine written constitutions, the Constitution of the United States and the constitutions of each of the several states. Plans and programs that may conform to limitations of a state constitution as defined by the state's supreme court may still be held to run afoul of the federal constitution as interpreted by the U. S. Supreme Court. In turn, it is also true that a plan or program may be held invalid under the state constitution even though found to be consistent with the federal constitution.

The variety of state constitutional provisions adds complexity to our study. And yet they go to the heart of our problem. State universities are instruments of state authority, policy, and power. They represent one of the proprietary enterprises of the state. The function, policy, and purpose of the state university are matters which should be determined by reference to the constitution and educational policy of the state, all responsive in turn to the forces of informed opinion within the state. Moreover, provisions of state constitutions that provide the legal scaffolding for the separation principle are usually stated with more precision and definiteness than the broad limitations in the First Amendment. Finally, it may be noted that these specific provisions of state constitutions have a long history. The results reached under them whether by judicial interpretation or by general acquiescence and understanding may be in the end a more reliable index to the meaning of separation as authenticated in American experience than what has been said by the U. S. Supreme Court in recent years in the few cases interpreting the First Amendment's brief and ambiguous language forbidding laws respecting an establishment of religion.

The state constitutions, as stated above, exhibit the greatest variety in the provisions relating to religious freedom and the use of public monies or appropriations of public property for religious purposes.[3] In general it may be said that the least restrictive provisions are found in the old constitutions of the states in the east, which simply affirm the general principle of religious freedom and freedom of conscience and worship.[4] But the constitutions of many of the states, in addition to affirming the principle of religious freedom, embody provisions forbidding appropriations of tax monies or public property for any church or sectarian purposes, and in many instances expressly prohibiting the use of public funds to support sectarian schools or sectarian instruction or to support a teacher of religion.[5] In some states the constitution prohibits sectarian instruction in the state's schools without relating this prohibition to the use of tax funds.[6] Although the usual provision is directed against "sectarian" education, it should be noted that the constitutions of the states of Washington, Arizona, and Utah prohibit the use of public funds "for any religious worship, exercise or instruction."[7]

Apart from these differences, the state constitutional provisions, while showing considerable uniformity in many respects, display diversities of other kinds.[8] Space does not permit a complete cataloguing of these variations, and it is hazardous to attempt to classify them or to base any generalizations upon them. The important point to be observed is that each state is master of its own house in this matter, and that the questions respecting the place of religion at a given state university must necessarily take into account the specific provisions of that state's constitution.

The state constitutional provisions have given rise to numerous cases involving public schools. The decisions are not very helpful in answering concrete questions raised with respect to the place of religion at a state university, but they shed some illumination on the general area under discussion and furnish some clue to what state courts understand "separation of church and state" to mean in the context of the positive limitations found in state constitutions. Bible-reading in public schools has frequently been challenged on the ground that this is a form of forbidden sectarian instruction since the Bible, depending on the particular version and the parts read, offends the religious or nonreligious scruples of some children and parents. The state courts have divided on this question. The majority of decisions, including some decided at a relatively early date, have held that Bible-reading is not constitutionally objectionable, particularly if objecting or dissenting students are excused from participation.[9] According to these decisions the Bible is not a sectarian book—its reading does not make the school a sectarian school and does not make the teacher a "teacher of religion" within the meaning of constitutional prohibitions. Other courts have reached the opposite result, and it may be noted that these contrary decisions have for the most part come at a later date. The reasoning in these cases is that the Bible is by its nature sectarian, and that the effect of reading it in school is to coerce the consciences of those who do not accept it as authoritative.

Programs whereby students are released from public school classes one hour a week in order to attend religious education classes conducted by representatives of the primary religious groups have also come under attack on the ground that the public school system was being used as a means of recruiting children for sectarian instruction and that the effect of the program was to place children under compulsion to attend these classes. But the few authoritative state court decisions dealing with the matter have upheld the released time program on the ground that attendance at the religious education classes was optional and that it was not inappropriate for the state to co-operate with religious groups in this way in the interests of religious education.[10]

Although it is futile to attempt to extract from the numerous state court decisions any commonly accepted definition of the term "sectarian instruction," a review of the opinions indicates that the courts in giving meaning to the term have been concerned with two primary considerations; namely, (1) that the public school classrooms shall not be identified with any type of religious instruction whereby the state in effect establishes an official creed and gives a preference to one religious faith over another, and (2) that the public school system shall not be used as a means of compelling students to accept religious instruction. Whether a given type of instruction or exercise does constitute an attempt at indoctrination in a particular religious faith and whether a given practice operates as a restraint on conscience are questions on which they have disagreed.

We turn now to limitations derived from the federal constitution. The First Amendment states that Congress shall make no law respecting an establishment of religion or prohibiting the free exercise thereof. In the *Everson* case (330 U. S. 1 [1947]), decided in 1947, the U. S. Supreme Court for the first time held that the effect of the Fourteenth Amendment, adopted in 1868, was to make this language of the First Amendment, adopted in 1791, equally applicable to the states and that the nonestablishment phrase ordains the separation of church and state. This in turn means, according to Justice Black's opinion in the *Everson* case, not only that government must respect freedom of conscience and worship, that it cannot prescribe official creeds or punish the dissenter and unbeliever, and that government cannot establish an official state church, but it means also that the state cannot give aid to religion even on a nonpreferential basis. "No tax in any amount, large or small, can be levied to support any religious activities or institutions, whatever they may be called or whatever form they may adopt to teach or practice religion."

One year later in the *McCollum* case (333 U. S. 203 [1948]) the Court, with only Justice Reed dissenting, held that the system of released time followed in Champaign, Illinois, whereby school children were released one hour a week for religious instruction given on the school premises by teachers supplied by the primary religious groups, violated the separation principle since in the Court's view the public school system was being used as a means of recruiting children for religious education purposes. Yet only four years later in the *Zorach* case (343 U. S. 306 [1952]) the Court by a five to four vote sustained the New York system of released time, which in its objectives and general features could not be distinguished from the Champaign system, except for the one circumstance that in the New York system the released-time religious instruction took place off the school premises. But even more remarkable than the slender ground on which the *McCollum* case was distinguished was Justice Douglas' majority opinion, noteworthy for its repudiation of the absolutism expressed by Mr. Justice Black in his prior opinions in the *Everson* and *McCollum* cases.

Space does not permit the extensive quotation from Justice Douglas' opinion needed to catch the full flavor of its thought. After pointing out that the First Amendment does not say that in every and all respects there shall be a separation of church and state, he asserted that in its provisions respecting nonestablishment of religion and the free exercise thereof, it studiously defines the manner in which there shall be "no concert or union or dependency one on the other." The problem like many other problems in constitutional law is one of degree. In short, according to Mr. Justice Douglas, in applying the separation concept the Court must follow the balance-of-interests technique and must engage in the familiar pragmatic process of weighing constitutional limitations against permissive ends within the range of legislative power. The state and its agencies may appropriately express a concern for religious education in view of the place that religion has occupied in the country's history. "When the state encourages religious instruction or cooperates with religious authorities by adjusting the schedule of public events to sectarian needs, it follows the best of our traditions. For it then respects the religious nature of our people and accommodates the public service to their spiritual needs. To hold that it may not would be to find in the Constitution a requirement that the government show a callous indifference to religious groups. That would be preferring those who believe in no religion over those who do believe."

The majority opinion in the *Zorach* case restored what appeared to many to be a sound perspective and judgment in the interpretation of the separation principle regarded as a constitutional mandate. The matter of separation cannot be approached in terms of verbal absolutes. Nor can a metaphor such as "the wall of separation" serve as an aid to analysis. The truth is that religion and government have been and continue to be interrelated, and that by hypothesis it is impossible to describe this situation in terms of "absolute and complete separation." Religious groups often exert a forceful influence in shaping governmental policy, and the spiritual and moral influences generated by religious forces have an important impact upon our national character and public life. In turn government has contributed much to religion. Our history bears witness to the numerous ways in which government has employed its powers and processes to provide more favorable opportunities for the exercise of religious freedom and the pursuit of religious interests without impinging upon the freedom of the nonbeliever and without giving a preference to a single religious group. The idea that the separation principle means that government cannot "aid" religion, if stated as a universal and absolute proposition, is not supported by precedent, history, or the common understanding.

The foregoing discussion, designed to give us the flavor of the federal and state constitutional limitations and the principal ideas that have emerged in their interpretation, furnishes the background for a consideration of the problems raised respecting religion at the state university.

At the outset, it should be noted that there is very little judicial authority dealing with these problems. Indeed, the only case directly in point is the decision of the Illinois Supreme Court upholding compulsory chapel services at the University of Illinois.[11] Possibly other suits have been brought to challenge certain practices at state universities but were not taken to the highest court of the state. No case involving religion in a state university has ever come before the U. S. Supreme Court for consideration and decision. The attorney generals of the states have on a few occasions given opinions on questions of this nature, but even these are scattered and for our purposes do not add much to the discussion. This picture is all the more surprising both because of the amount of litigation that has been brought regarding religion at the public school level and the extent to which our state universities over the years have offered instructional and other programs directly or indirectly concerning religion.

Indeed, if our constitutions require complete separation of church and state, and if, in turn, this means that the state university cannot take account of religion as a curriculum and teaching factor and that it cannot otherwise do anything to foster an interest in religious matters or afford opportunities to students for the cultivation of religious faith, it becomes extraordinarily remarkable to what extent our state universities for almost a century have engaged in unconstitutional practices. Or perhaps the more sensible conclusion can be drawn that these practices have given us a practical interpretation, founded on public approval and understanding and consistent with an understanding of the university's function, which is more vital and authoritative than logical conclusions drawn from abstract propositions. Here is a case where a page of history is worth a volume of logic, to use Justice Holmes's pithy observation. A brief look at history is here warranted.

We do well to remind ourselves that in the United States higher education was first instituted under religious auspices, and that our oldest colleges and universities owe their origin to denominational groups. And, when the tax-supported state university came into being, the religious influence was strong there too and this, notwithstanding state constitutional limitations. Compulsory chapel services were the rule rather than the exception in the early days of the state universities, and attendance at Sunday worship services was often required. Indeed, a number of state institutions continue to hold chapel services at the present time. So far as the curriculum and teaching programs were concerned, it is interesting to note that state universities at an earlier day taught courses in such subjects as Biblical Hebrew, New Testament Greek, and Evidences of Christianity.[12]

Then came the movement that resulted in de-emphasis of religion at the state university. Chapel services were abandoned after a while at a number of state institutions. The courses distinctively religious were dropped from the curriculum. Compulsory attendance at worship services was generally abandoned. In view of the practices previously followed, it can hardly be assumed that these changes were in deference to constitutional mandates. (The relevancy of the Fourteenth Amendment in regard to some of these practices did not become apparent until 1947!) On the contrary, it appears that these changes were attributable to a growing secularization of society, the adoption of the elective system in institutions of higher learning, the unpopularity of chapel services with students, and the lessened intellectual respectability of religion as the result of the new sciences.

But, in turn, the recent decades have witnessed a new burgeoning of interest in religion at the state university.[13] Novel, interesting, and diverse patterns have emerged and continue to develop in attestation of the state university's sympathetic concern for the religious understanding and religious life of its students. New courses have been added dealing with the intellectual and historical aspects of religion. Credit courses in specific religions, often taught by scholars committed to the religion they teach, are not uncommon. Or credit may be given for courses taught by religious scholars off the campus. A department of religion has been added by some universities. Indeed, a School of Religions functions as a regular department at the University of Iowa. A number of universities have created the office of chaplain or co-ordinator of religion to assist in the formulation of the university's academic program respecting religion, to co-ordinate the university's program with those of the primary religious groups, and to counsel students. Student religious groups are in many cases permitted access to university buildings for meetings, and in a few cases chapels are maintained on university campuses for use by these groups.

During the course of the development briefly outlined above, the relevant provisions of state constitutions have for the most part remained unchanged. It is fair to infer, therefore, that constitutional limitations relating to separation of church and state have not been the primary factor in determining the role of religion at the state university.

What accounts for the apparent acquiescence in these programs at state universities despite the frequency of the objections raised when public schools interest themselves in religious matters?

Obviously, there are important differences between state-supported education at the public school level and state-supported education at the university level. Parents are compelled to send their children to some school, whether public, parochial, or nonparochial private. A child attending any of these schools may be said to be attending under compulsion of law. Moreover, the typical public school course, at least at the lower levels, is a required course in that all students are expected to take part in the same program. Even if dissenting children are excused from participating in religious exercises or instruction, they may find it embarrassing to state their objections and to find themselves separated from the other students because of this factor. Also, children at the public school level have impressionable minds and are more likely to accept as true what is told them, with the result that religious instruction of any kind is more vulnerable to the charge that it leads to indoctrination.

The foregoing arguments, usually advanced by those who oppose either any kind of religious instruction in the public schools or even that which affords some opportunity for religious instruction during the school week by means of the released time system, lose their force when we deal with religion at the state university level. Attendance at the state university is wholly voluntary, courses in religion in conformity with the general elective program are optional, the element of divisiveness is dissipated in view of the nature and size of the institution, and the maturity of students at this level, coupled with the general atmosphere of free and critical inquiry at the university, minimizes the risk of indoctrination as an incident of religious instruction.

The considerations mentioned above are adequate to demonstrate that the state university is in a totally different position from that of the public school in regard to religious matters, and that these differentiating factors are adequate to explain the paucity of litigation respecting religion at the state university, despite practices both past and present that show considerable involvement by state universities in matters of religious interest. In the end, however, the question whether the state university can properly teach religion and furnish opportunity for cultivation of the religious life must be answered by reference to positive considerations that are relevant to an appraisal of the university's function. What grounds may the university advance in support of such a program? Attention may be concentrated briefly on two primary considerations.

In view of the place that religion has occupied and continues to occupy in the life and history of man, its influence in the shaping of moral ideas, its impact on culture, and its significance as a unifying and integrating force that provides a high sense of purpose and motivation and opens up new vistas of truth, goodness, and beauty, religion must of necessity command some attention at any academic institution both as an intellectual discipline and as a way of life. This is especially true if it fulfills the role of a university in creating the educational milieu that evokes awareness and understanding of the ideas, values, and avenues to truth that are man's heritage. The university may well take the position that it is derelict to the high purposes for which it was created if it fails to deal in a positive way with religion as a vital force in the life and history of man. Indeed, it is fair to assert that for a university deliberately to exclude from its curriculum all courses with a positive religious content is not simply to fail to teach religion but in itself becomes a telling witness that religion is irrelevant to that process of cultivating the mind and spirit that we call higher education.

A second and corollary consideration is that by hypothesis it is impossible to exclude all consideration of religion, religious ideas, and religious institutions from any course of study at the university level, whether this course centers in the natural sciences, the social sciences, philosophy, literature, or art. Religion has played too large a part in man's history and thinking to be completely excised from academic consideration. Religious beliefs, theological formulations, and ecclesiastical institutions are frequently the subject of critical inquiry and discussion in university classes. Moreover, it has never been supposed that it was in any way inappropriate for a state university to teach such courses as Comparative Religion and Psychology of Religion. The real question then is not whether religion may be studied at the state university, but whether it deserves treatment in courses with a primary religious orientation. If, as the Supreme Court has said, the Constitution does not require the state to be hostile or even indifferent to religion, and if equality and evenhandedness are important facets of the separation principle, the university may well decide that in order to balance the scales and to afford religion an equal opportunity to be heard, it is necessary or at least proper that students have the opportunity to study religion, not simply obliquely or as a marginal adjunct to other courses, but in courses with a primary religious orientation and designed to afford opportunity for knowledge and understanding.

What conclusions may be stated then with respect to the limits on the university's freedom to teach religion and to afford opportunities for student religious groups to cultivate the life of the spirit? Some limitations are obvious. State universities may not discriminate against students because of religious or nonreligious beliefs. Adherence to an official creed may not be made a condition of admission or continued enrollment. Students should not be obliged to attend religious services. Even though the Illinois Supreme Court as late as 1891 (North v. Board of Trustees of University of Illinois, 137 Ill. 296 [1891]) upheld the validity of compulsory chapel services at the University of Illinois, it is safe to assert that such a practice would generally be condemned by courts today, unless excuses were granted to objecting students.

But to offer courses with a positive religious content should lie within the permissible range of the university's discretion in determining its total program. In deference to the separation principle, important limitations should be respected. Such courses, while properly given for credit, should be offered as electives so that the student's participation is wholly voluntary. Secondly, the principle of equality of opportunity should be observed. The state university should deal in a fair and even-handed way with all religious groups. If courses are offered to enhance understanding of specific religious doctrines and institutions, discrimination should be avoided. If opportunities are offered for various religious groups to supply teachers for courses in specific religious faiths, this opportunity should be open to all who are prepared to meet the university's academic standards. A third consideration is that the distinction should be observed between the teaching of religion to promote knowledge and understanding and that type aimed deliberately at indoctrination and commitment to religious faith. The teaching of religious ideas in an objective and fair way is appropriately a state university function. To win converts and seek commitment is outside its function and violates the separation principle. But in view of the intellectual climate that prevails at the university level, there is no compelling reason why a specific religious faith, whether it be Christianity (either in its general aspects or by reference to the various denominations and movements within it), Judaism, Islam, or Hinduism, cannot be taught fairly, objectively, and temperately for the purpose of presenting the doctrines, history, and nature of the ecclesiastical organization in the same way that the university may properly offer courses in the history, platforms, and organization of political parties without being subject to the charge that it has involved itself in partisan politics.

Whether the courses with a definite religious content are (1) offered as part of a definite program in religion, (2) given by several departments, (3) offered in a department or school of religion, or (4) taught for credit by regular members of the faculty or by teachers supplied by religious groups, the separation principle should not stand in the way of a state university's adoption of a program in any of these forms as long as the principles of voluntarism and equality are observed and the courses are taught to promote understanding rather than to indoctrinate and seek commitment. At least it appears that the First Amendment should present no obstacles.[14] To be sure, the Supreme Court has said that the state may not teach religion. But these statements were made in the context of cases dealing with the public schools and indicate that the Court's concern was with attempts to indoctrinate children with an officially sponsored religion. And it is worth remembering that the Court has said that the state may properly show an interest in religious education and accommodate its program to further this interest (Zorach v. Clauson, 343 U. S. 306 [1952]).

Substantially the same considerations apply in respect to most of the state constitutional limitations. Here the most acute question under many state constitutions is whether tax-raised funds are used for purposes of "sectarian instruction." This question is peculiarly relevant with respect to courses taught in specific faiths by teachers representative of the various religious bodies. Courts have not had occasion to define the meaning of "sectarian instruction" in the context of the state university teaching program. Historically, the term acquired its chief significance as part of the movement to keep the public schools free from control by religious bodies and to avoid use of public school classes as a means of compelling indoctrination in the religious tenets of a specific religious faith. To the extent that state constitutions extend the "sectarian instruction" prohibition to the state's institutions of higher learning, its significance must be determined by reference to the evils to be avoided. The principal considerations arising from the operation of the public school system in regard to this problem are irrelevant in the context of the university situation. As long as courses in religion are optional with the student, preference is not given to any single religious faith, the instruction is aimed at understanding and not indoctrination or commitment, and the university insists on observance of its usual academic and scholastic standards with respect to the teachers giving the courses, a persuasive case may be made that this program does not fall within the "sectarian education" category.

Certainly the term is irrelevant to courses taught by university professors aimed at study of religion in its central features. In any event the arrangement whereby religious groups pay the salaries of teachers offering courses in specific religious faiths seems to meet the type of constitutional objection which is directed against the use of tax funds, even if it is conceded that this is the kind of sectarian instruction embraced by the constitutional limitation. In the few states that prohibit use of public monies for any religious instruction, the breadth of this limitation may mean that no courses with a definite religious orientation may be given by teachers on the university staff, but here again it may be permissible for the university to give credit for courses taught by teachers supplied and paid by church groups. On the other hand, the constitutions of some of the older states in the eastern part of the country appear to place no limitations whatever on the teaching of religion at tax-supported institutions of higher learning as long as there is no compulsion that results in coercion of conscience and preference is not given to any particular religious faith or faiths.

Apart from courses in religion, a state university may also pursue a program designed to enlarge opportunities for cultivation of the religious life on the part of its students. The primary responsibility here, of course, is centered in the various religious groups that often maintain chapels and centers off the campus. But not all groups have such facilities. Again it appears to be a distortion of the separation principle to suggest that the university may not make its regular facilities available for use by voluntary student religious foundations or guilds provided that no preference or discrimination is practiced. Here the "aid" is not substantial and no appreciable out-of-pocket costs at the expense of tax-raised funds are involved.[15] Moreover, since a university usually makes such facilities available for various types of student activities, it is hardly warranted in discriminating against a particular student group because its interests extend to religious matters.

A more substantial question is raised if the university provides chapel facilities or a center to house the activities of student religious groups. A principal requirement is that the use of the chapel or of the center be open to all groups on a nondiscriminatory basis. A real problem is raised here, however, respecting the use of tax-raised funds. The provisions of many state constitutions forbid the use of such funds for purpose of a place of worship. It appears, therefore, that consistent with these provisions, the university will have to look to special funds to finance the construction of chapels, although it is not clear that these constitutional provisions bar the use of tax-raised funds to build student religious centers to house student extracurricular activities so long as they do not come within the "place of worship" definition.[16]

In summary then, we may fairly say that consistent with the First Amendment a state university in the exercise of its discretionary authority may make a substantial contribution to religious education and to the furtherance of the religious life of its students, once it is recognized that the separation principle states no absolute rule, that the university in response to the felt needs of the time may accommodate its program to meet the student's total needs, and that the problem is one of a wise, fair, and sensible reconciliation of a legitimate and sympathetic concern for religion in the total educational process with the underlying values at stake in the separation concept. The same conclusion may be stated with respect to most of the state constitutions, although specific provisions of some constitutions may present real obstacles.

Granted that a state university has considerable freedom and a wide latitude in determining the place of religion in its total program, it must also be recognized that the determination of a concrete program concerned with the teaching of religion and the futherance of student religious activities is a matter within the discretionary authority of the administration and faculty. The university is under no duty to go as far in this matter as constitutional limitations permit. The constitutional considerations are important and the university must necessarily be guided by them. But first the university must determine what is its responsibility in this matter in terms of the university's total educational program and the demands properly made upon it. A number of considerations may lead the university to decide that it will not be wise or feasible to further the teaching of religion to the extent allowed by legal limitations. In case of serious doubt as to the propriety of a given type of program, the university as an institution which is expected to exercise a high degree of moral leadership and to show honest regard for the substantive values underlying the separation concept may well decide to resolve the doubt in deference to this principle. Likewise, with respect to certain types of plans that call for the teaching of courses by teachers supplied by the primary religious groups, the university may reach the conclusion that the risks entailed by way of possible contention or controversy between the various groups, exploitation of such teaching opportunities for indoctrination purposes, and weakening of the university's authority in control of its educational program are not worth taking. But on the other hand a fair consideration of the place of religion at the state university should not be obscured by an uncritical and dogmatic invocation of the separation principle. The problem in its total dimensions deserves careful and discerning study unhindered by a doctrinaire absolutism that ignores history, common understanding, and the public interest. We do well to remind ourselves that the life of the law, as Justice Holmes admonished, has not been logic but experience.

Religion and University Education

HELEN C. WHITE

What Place Has Religion in State University Education?

CHAPTER VI

Religion is of inescapable interest to any university no matter what the limitation of its faculties may be. Theology, the systematic study of religion, is one of the historical branches of learning, with its own distinctive field of inquiry, its own body of knowledge, its own techniques and methods, and its own objectives. But this fact has been obscured by the actual circumstances of the universities in which most of us live, and it is therefore easy for us to forget it.

Even in those private universities that have always had a faculty of theology, there has been a tendency to view the School of Divinity as something beyond and removed from the preoccupations of the ordinary faculty. Not long ago one of the great Protestant theologians of our day told me how he had challenged his university colleagues on their lack of curiosity concerning his field. It was assumed that the Divinity School professor would be interested in biology and psychology, for example, but the biologist and the psychologist on their side seemed to regard themselves as emancipated from any concern about the professional preoccupations of their colleague in theology. Much as many of us may regret it, the fact is that today in most intellectual circles theology is not regarded as the queen of the sciences.

There is, of course, a historical reason for this. Like so many other things in our American picture, it is part of a reaction to the period of theological controversy in the sixteenth and seventeenth centuries that nearly engulfed religion in Europe. The danger that the very life of religion might be destroyed in the theological battles that then rent Christendom was perceived by sensitive and thoughtful men at the time, but the fighting went on at every level until there were a good many people who came to feel that any concern about theology was a danger to the peace, and any extended consideration of theological issues a hazard to the higher life of religion. Such a reaction is quite understandable to anybody familiar with the extremes of oversimplification and vituperation to which sixteenth- and seventeenth-century religious controversy too often went.

But I suspect that there was another reason, too, for the popular reaction against theology, and that was the preoccupation with verbal expression that leads to jargon. The substantively preoccupied effort to define terms is, of course, one of the most important phases of human intellectual endeavor and one of the great instruments for the advance of human thought. But when the battle of words becomes a substitute for the battle of thought, and in itself an instrument of warfare, then all too often men take refuge in a jargon that removes the whole enterprise from the realities of ordinary life; and the average man, when he ceases to be awed by the incomprehensible words of the expert, tends to reject the claims of expertness. This is the more likely to happen when the issues do involve common human experiences with unavoidable opportunities for testing the relevance of the words. This phenomenon of jargon is, of course, not peculiar to theology. Many of those who have too easily rejected the realities of what is behind the jargon in the case of theology have not been equally alert to draw the lesson in their own fields.

But however understandable the common reaction to theological controversy and its battle of words, the results have been unfortunately narrowing for both religious and secular inquiry. We still have in intellectual circles a widespread suspicion of theology with an equally widespread ignorance of what it is all about. Yet those very sections of society that are the immediate concern of the university have still a great interest in what are essentially theological questions. This is especially apparent to anyone who has anything to do with young people.

Our age is an age of planning, and that fact is reflected in the findings of some of the surveys that have recently been made of student thought about the future. Some older people have been surprised at the materialistic vision of the future uncovered in these surveys. People who can recall the day-dreams of a more romantic youth are sometimes appalled at what seem the imaginative limitations of the new generation's planning. And yet every so often the shiny suburban surface of these plans gives way and one catches a glimpse of a very deep uneasiness, a fear that in the planning itself there may lurk an unsuspected booby trap. There is military service, for one thing, and afterward there is always the possibility of the never-quite-forgotten war of the nuclear giants.

Nowhere is the paradox of the modern world more apparent than here. In this society, so ingenious in eluding so many of the implications of man's mortality, there is everywhere a resolute disregard of the grimmer possibilities of life. And yet there is an uneasy awareness that, however morbid attention to them may be, they are still there. The immemorial wonders concerning the nature and destiny of man and the meaning of his life are no less inescapable because they are fenced off with plans that are more immediately engaging. The imaginations of the young are not calloused enough to shut them out forever.

This pervasive, even if unacknowledged, theological pre-occupation is particularly characteristic of the university. Whether or not there is a theological faculty on a particular campus, religion in the less specialized sense is certainly in the university because it is one of the great humanities to which the modern university is dedicated in its devotion to the study of man and his world. Religion is essential to any understanding of human nature that reaches beyond the most restricted laboratory experiment. Even the man who wishes to avoid religion on the contemporary scene cannot escape it in any approach to the past. The question of religious observance is one of the first to emerge from the very kitchen middens of lost peoples, and the names of the gods are often among the earliest words identified in the inventories of forgotten scripts. No secular enterprise but presently leads the investigator to religion in its not too remote antecedents. And many aspects of the latest developments on the contemporary scene are without meaning to one unaware of the religious elements in their genesis. Indeed, analysts of the present are not wanting who insist that the basic issues of our day are in their essence theological.

Certainly religion is necessary to any understanding of the works that are most expressive of man's nature—literature, the dance, music, the visual arts. They express religious conceptions, but what is even more important, they rest on religious assumptions and implications. Milton's *Paradise Lost,* to invoke one of the great poems of our language, is an obvious example; but the religious premises of Chaucer and Shakespeare, Wordsworth and Shelly, and even Swinburne are quite as essential to the understanding of their work. And religion must be reckoned with no less in our approach to contemporary literature. There is no escaping the necessity of an appreciation and an understanding of the fact of religion for the understanding of man and his history, the thoughts of his mind, and the work of his hands.

To some people, of course, all this may seem a chronicle of illusion and aberration. But then for them, a lot of human history must be a history of aberration, and much of what has most concerned man, illusion. Religion is simply a fact inescapable in any approach to man and the human world.

Yet religion is a good deal more than a humanity, a branch of study. Religion is something to be experienced. It engages not only the reason but the will and the imagination and the emotions. It involves not only the flash of insight, the decision, the conclusion, but also discipline and habit with its building of contexts. For religious life is dependent not only upon the individual insight but upon group support, not only upon the electric flash of momentary discovery and reaction but upon all the sustaining rhythms of the dear and the familiar. In short, religion is not only a matter of knowing but of living. Obviously, knowledge about religion is not enough.

It is not religion as a branch of knowledge that arouses the varying types and the varying depths of solicitude with which we are all familiar. It is not religion as a branch of knowledge that is worrying the parent at home who fears that his child in the university is not only drifting away from the religious life and observance of his family but is losing any contact with the whole moral and intellectual atmosphere in which he was brought up. What such a parent dreads is that it will not be possible for his child ever to come back home with any sympathy for the world in which his family lives. And so with the various religious advisers and guides. It isn't knowledge about religion that is the main concern of the Catholic priest who observes that a student is airily dismissing the claims of religion because his elementary-school command of religious ideas is inadequate to confront even his sophomore command of scientific ideas. Or the Protestant minister who, viewing with some understandable misgivings the bunch of cheerful heathen in the fraternity house next to his church, wonders how he'll ever get a little Christian influence into his incredibly inaccessible neighbors. Or the Jewish rabbi who sees a young man putting the rich tradition of his fathers behind him as something foreign and primitive to be forgotten in his rush for modernity. It is not knowledge about religion that is troubling all these. And one can sympathize with their desire to find some help in reaching the young people about whom they are so movingly concerned.

But this business of reaching another human being is a very delicate and complicated business at any age, and it is especially so at the university age. It is very often precisely those students whose parents are most concerned about their holding to family beliefs who are most eager to escape. It is precisely the type of young person who is apt to be swept off his feet by any new experience who is most enamored of the freedom the university offers. And here we must not forget that the basic principle of a university is freedom. Very much is offered at a university, often a bewildering array of possibilities. But the acceptance

of these offerings is dependent upon the individual. It is the
essence of the educational process as distinct from certain
other human operations that the objects of educational attention can be influenced and led and guided and helped; but in
the last analysis acceptance or rejection is up to the individual.
The success or failure of the whole enterprise is at his mercy.
No young man can be made wise or good in spite of himself.

On the other hand, the anxious elders should never forget
the other side of the picture. The university age is an impressionable one and normally a generous one. As anyone who
recalls his own youth remembers, a hint or a suggestion may
count for a good deal. I still remember how a very wise man
once received an outrageously glib and oversimplified historical
summary which, I may hasten to add, was by no means original
with me. He didn't waste any time trying to argue with some
rather widespread illusions of that period. He merely said very
thoughtfully with a tone of sympathetic speculation, "I wonder
if you will always think that," and dropped the matter there.
But I didn't. That was the beginning of a lifelong endeavor to
understand certain historical relations which, I may add, has
helped me to face the world in which I have lived better than
that old and now quite outworn formula. One must never discount the ability of youth to take a hint nor forget that in a
good many areas time is on the side of wisdom—if only the
young man has not shut the doors of his mind too soon.

But religion is a good deal more than one interest among
many. For a religious man it pervades and informs all his undertakings. It is the very air he breathes. It is the strength by which
he lives. Particularly is this true of the higher intellectual life.
No believer can think of that as alien to his basic preoccupation.
And nowhere is the aid of supreme wisdom needed more than
here. One might add, too, that nowhere is the worship through
the exercise of the gifts which God has given more appropriate.
When it is a matter of attempting to understand the natural
universe around him, the structure of the society in which he
finds himself, the community or the want of community among
the peoples of the earth, and so on, then certainly the religious
man relies on the Spirit of God within him; and in the exercise

of his highest endeavors for the discovery of truth, he pays supreme Truth his highest tribute of honor.

This permeation of all the activities of the religious spirit is not, of course, confined to the scientific. Whether in the Platonic tradition or not, the worship of God has always been thought of as involving all the faculties of man, the love of goodness, and the enjoyment of beauty, as well as the pursuit of truth. It is at this point of the permeation of all life by the religious spirit that the church college, whatever its cost from other points of view, has an indisputable advantage. And it is at this point that the state university must admit its limitations. This is something that by the very terms of its relation to the state it cannot compass. It is at this point that we face, and might as well admit that we face, a very complicated situation.

Religion involves the individual in the most intimate fashion and, because it does, religion must take account of the tremendous range of individual differences. There are great variations in delicacy and range of sensitivity to things religious as to everything else. Individuals differ greatly in the intensity of their needs and responses and in the drive of their pursuit of an objective in this area as elsewhere. It is very easy for us here in America in the middle of the twentieth century with its middle-of-the-road atmosphere on problems of adjustment and balance to underestimate the wide range of human variation and by that underestimation to concentrate on the mythical center and forget about the rest. People who take up art, religion, or politics too enthusiastically for the prevailing temper may be great nuisances to others and very uncomfortable themselves. But we owe a great deal to their prototypes in the past, and we would lose a lot if we eliminated the possibility of their recurrence in the future. We are all safer in camp if there are at least a few scouts out in No Man's Land, and this is no less true of religion than of any other major field.

For the individual does not develop his distinctive tastes in a vacuum, even the most independent of individuals. And especially is this true of the balanced human being to whose production we seem to be dedicated today. Here it is well for us at the university to remember that there are other institutions—the family, the church, the synagogue, and a variety of societies that perform similar functions. Here, as in other fields of our society, we have an intersection of several institutions that are concerned with the same individual, but these institutions have a different character. The state, for example, is neutral to the various religious societies. But the family and the church or the synagogue are not neutral at all—in fact, they are highly demanding. In an age when great emphasis is put upon individual personal development—individual comfort, individual convenience, or what might be called accommodation to the individual—both family and church make demands upon the individual that are considerable. Both the egotism and the laziness that are catered to by other agencies of our society are here called upon to make great sacrifices. Indeed, so pressing are these demands that their fulfillment is possible only on the basis of a strongly consolidated personal preference —what may be defined as a genuine commitment.

The co-operation of the university and the church or synagogue or religious society must be thoughtfully planned for. That does not mean that it should be cramped by red tape or anxiety about jurisdictional jealousy. But thought should be given to certain principles, respect for which will facilitate co-operation. The two institutions can take pains to express their respect for each other. The recognition of church and synagogue in certain types of university functions is traditional. The participation of representatives of the local clergy in prayer and scripture reading on such occasions as commencement is a widespread, probably universal, example. The university can take pains to give recognition to religious leaders and establishments on other appropriate occasions, but all such recognition should not only avoid suggestion of preference but any hint of discrimination against the uncommitted. The university roof is a broad one, and no one who has a right to be under it because of his intellectual competence and scholarly commitment should be made to feel out of place because of any other consideration.

But while this recognition is important, it should never be

forgotten that the church or other religious body does not depend upon the university for the recognition of its status. It has its own dignity and methods, its own sphere, actually much larger than that of the university. And conversely, the university has its own mission and sphere and way of working—its own dignity, which the religious interests should take pains to respect.

There are a good many practical ways in which this co-operation can be implemented. The first and the most obvious is where the state university can find some place in its regular curriculum for the direct course in religion among courses in literature, history, and so on. Various types of general courses in religion are found in state university curricula. Some of those are long established, going back to a period when most of the clientele of the university shared a common religious outlook. Where such courses tacitly assume a common approach, they do not, as a rule, make much appeal to those who do not share that approach; and there is on all sides a considerable doubt as to whether such a solution is entirely adequate in an age when a good deal of emphasis is being put on the pluralist character of our culture. Nor is the "essentials of religion" or any type of least-common-denominator approach likely to be satisfactory to very many people.

After all, we get more from each other when we meet at our fullest and best. So there would seem to be much more scope for an approach that emphasizes common fields of concern in varying traditions and possibilities of co-operation between them on the basis of common interests. Expository courses in the religions of the world certainly have their place. In such courses it is possible to let the various religious traditions speak for themselves through their great books. They probably are easiest to manage when they deal with religious traditions that are more remote from our own. For it is easier to be objective in areas where one does not think that any of one's own commitments are threatened. There is no reason why an American citizen might not be a Moslem or a Buddhist. Indeed, some are, but they are still too few to elicit much response beyond friendly curiosity; so in the average American university community there will probably be less self-consciousness about an approach to oriental religions than to Christianity. Objectivity is something that the university is always working for, and it would be fatal if the university ever gave up that endeavor. But the difficulties of objectivity should never be minimized. It is easy to be blind or self-deceived here, as anywhere else, if we fail to take account of human limitations and the difficulties of transcending those limitations.

The field of religion is one in which the problem is especially acute. Any man who holds a position with regard to the tradition he is presenting is quite aware of the fact that the history of religion, for example, involves a very complex business of attention and interpretation. Two perfectly sincere inquirers may survey the same situation and find their attention riveted on quite different aspects of it. Two scholars on opposite sides may agree as to certain facts that have played a part in religious history—say, loss of original zeal or lack of contact with changing social conditions—and yet draw very different conclusions because of the different degrees of importance attached to various elements in the situation. It is only possible to handle this problem with great humility as to the limitations of any one man's approach and with great candor as to differences of perspective and value.

One does not have to give up the struggle for objectivity in this area to recognize that a man who believes in the religious tradition he is presenting will communicate a warmer and richer experience to his students than one who does not. It is for this reason that the arrangement which would probably be most satisfactory to the various religious groups concerned would be a system whereby each group offered its own instruction in the university with its own representative on the faculty, giving courses in its tradition which would be treated like any other courses. There is no question that such an arrangement would reassure the parent as to the university's concern about religion and as to the possibility of his child's having continuing access to his tradition and opportunity to mature in religious understanding as in other aspects of his intellectual relation to the world. There is no question either that such an arrangement would make it easier to persuade the indifferent or pre-occupied young man that the acquisition of religious knowledge is to be regarded as important. There would, of course, be problems of joint appointment. To draw attention to this is not in any way to suggest that the professional religious representative is not as intellectually competent and as well trained as the usual faculty member. In many cases he has undergone an even more extensive period of training. But the objectives of that training may be different as the criteria of selection in the first place may well be different. Justice would have to be done to two sets of standards.

The problem of judgment of work done would not always be an easy matter. The university has a responsibility for standards in any credit-giving, and its attitude toward and its concentration on values is somewhat different from that of the religious society. Moreover, if this pattern were developed, the great variety of religious commitments in this country would have to be taken into account. Particularly is this true with the groups who are usually rather summarily lumped together under the heading "Protestant." Any very high degree of specialization in these curricular offerings would inevitably lead to problems of representation. And the more seriously the whole thing were taken, the more considerable these would probably be. It is very doubtful if this arrangement would be possible in many places because of legal problems of separation of church and state and restrictions on denominational activities in the public institutions. But it has been possible to do this sort of thing successfully at an institution like Michigan State University in East Lansing.

There is also a possibility of co-operation between the university and religious bodies in the form of the School of Religion set up within the university. Here the university and the church and other religious institutions co-operate in maintaining an organization to which both can contribute and which both recognize. One such arrangement is the Bible College at the University of Missouri—an arrangement probably possible only where there is a relative preponderance of one religious orientation in the population. A more inclusive and more widely applicable pattern is that of the School of Religion at the University of Iowa, which has for some thirty years now aroused great interest over the country. Here courses for the three major divisions of the American religious population, Protestant, Catholic, and Jewish, are offered by representatives of those traditions on the campus for full credit as university work. The success of the School of Religion at Iowa shows what can be accomplished where no legal or social barriers are raised and where the problems of representation and co-operation can be patiently worked out.

The University of Michigan, contemplating at present neither a School of Religion nor Department, sponsors activity in this area through an Office of Religious Affairs under the Vice-President of Student Affairs, and a faculty committee of professors from the College of Literature, Science, and the Arts. These two are roughly divided into that area of religion which is experience and that which is knowledge: the first co-ordinates the twenty-two student religious foundations in the campus community and has responsibility for the religious counseling services of the university; the second works closely with curriculum and the intellectual life. Needless to say, the Office and the Committee work in close harmony.

The Committee, responsible to the Dean of the College, is active in six main areas: (1) the degree program which, through requiring 18 hours of approved courses in religion in various departments and 18 hours in a single discipline, such as philosophy, history, anthropology, etc., provides a "major" in religion and ethics; (2) the securing of appointments to the faculty in particular departments to strengthen the program and enrich the intellectual life of the University; (3) the lecture program —in 1956-57, with a generous College appropriation, the Committee co-sponsored with appropriate departments eleven outstanding lecturers who expounded authoritatively the beliefs and values of various religions, represented stimulating points of view about religion to sizable lay audiences, and described significant research in the area; (4) encouragement of interdisciplinary thinking about religion among interested faculty members through monthly meetings of the "Faculty Colloquium in Religion"; (5) increasing the possessions of the general library in religion; and (6) co-operation on the university level with other agencies on the curriculum in religion in the state university.

The Office of Religious Affairs, newly established in May of 1956, is recognized as one of the Personnel Services of the University. Full attention is given to co-ordination, including such a program as may be necessary to the building of a climate in which co-ordination can be most effective. It also makes religious resources available in all the schools and colleges of the University and it emphasizes the relevance of religion to the educational process, moving toward the effective integration of the intellectual and the practical aspects of religion.

Another plan is the development of a number of credit programs in the various religious centers around the university—as at the University of Illinois and the University of North Dakota, where programs are well established and recognized. This makes possible wider representation of groups than the School of Religion and probably makes possible a freer hand for the religious group concerned. Such a program certainly demonstrates to parents and the community the regard of the university for religious instruction and leaves no doubt in the minds of students that from the point of view of the university this is as important as any other type of instruction. Such a program necessitates, of course, the maintenance at the religious center of a staff qualified for this additional work. There is the problem of maintenance of standards for work done in the atmosphere of other activities, and the problem of credit for work not under the university's control.

It is not, of course, always possible. Sometimes there is an explicit legal barrier; sometimes it is established custom and a prevailing climate of opinion that suggest caution. But barriers that are referred to as explicitly legal often have been revised by custom and public opinion. Where for various reasons these more direct provisions are not possible, the strong religious center—especially one that provides for both student and faculty participation—seems to be the most widely available solution. The religious center maintained by the church or other religious group at the university offers, of course, a full experience of religion as both material for study and a way of life. But there are problems of staffing. The ideal youth leader or the ideal counselor may not always be the ideal professor. And even when he is, he may be torn between the demands on his time. There are problems, too, of facilities, secretarial help, libraries, and student and faculty time. The student with a full schedule of university work, earning his way through school, may not have many hours left over for noncredit study. There are problems of contact with the university community. A good deal of the day-to-day administration of the university is carried on quite informally, even casually and incidentally. In such a situation, being in the middle of things is of great value. Anybody who lives in a university community knows how important the factor of constant communication is, so that it would not be surprising if the professional worker at the student center feels that he is left out on the sidelines. On the other hand, the student who has learned to pursue his religious education at the church center in a voluntary class is likely to keep up that process of self-education upon which the religious groups rely for the continuation of their lay leadership.

But whatever the possible situation on any particular campus, there is no question that the university and the religious groups can and do co-operate in the interest of the individual student. This co-operation between the faculty and administrative officers, especially those charged with counseling and guidance responsibilities, and the student pastors is a valuable thing on the campus of the state university and, I suspect, pretty generally appreciated. It is my experience that university officers are very glad to be able to call upon student pastors for help in individual problems, especially when they lie beyond the resources of the academic staff. And, on the other hand, the religious bodies look to university administrative authorities for understanding of special problems of students whose religious commitments bring them into conflict with university regulations and requirements. The conscientious objector in the institution with required ROTC, the Christian Scientist, the Seventh Day Adventist, the orthodox Jew with dietary prob-

lems, and so on, can usually count on a sympathetic understanding of his problems and help for their solution.

As for the general student community, it is very important
that it should learn as early as possible that the respect for
the individual on which we pride ourselves is likely at times
to require some taking of pains for practical realization. More
could be done, certainly, to promote communication and
understanding. The contact of the student chaplain or rabbi
with the faculty members in his own congregation is probably,
day in and day out, the most reliable source of communication.
On the other hand, the individual professor on any large
campus is likely to be pretty much absorbed in his own academic and extracurricular obligations and not too much aware
of what is going on in other corners of the campus beside his
own. Any professor who travels at all has had the mortifying
experience of hearing for the first time on a distant campus of
something that's going on at home. Probably more formal
occasions and conferences would help here, if for nothing else
than to maintain contacts. Some central office on campus with
provision of office service would unquestionably be useful,
though on any campus there is a tendency for each new office
to develop its own distinct sphere of activity that might make
any administration hesitate about the expansion of claims on
an already overstrained budget.

Various types of co-operation between the university and
the church groups on common projects are found on different
campuses. The faculty-student committees for religious activities are one example. They offer a good deal of opportunity
for both understanding and co-operation. The religious sections in university libraries are another. The faculty member
who sees that first-class religious books find their way into the
library is performing a real service. Lectures give another
opportunity not only for interchange between the students in
the various religious bodies but for the university and the community around it. The visitor in a lecture series like that at
Wisconsin usually meets not only with student groups but
often with church groups in town, and the result is a very

widespread stimulation of religious interest. Such programs as occur during Religious Emphasis Week stress the importance of religion and stimulate serious consideration of religious problems among a variety of groups—fraternities and sororities and dormitories as well as churches. And there are the various intergroup activities—programs, committees, conferences, weekends, and so on. All of these have demonstrated very real values and possibilities. But, of course, there are problems of funds, staff, and so on. And student response is often incalculable. All education, however, is a sowing of seed of which the harvest is still some way off. Indeed, he who is not willing to cast his bread upon the waters should not embark on any educational enterprise, secular or religious.

There is no doubt that here, as usual in the vast possibilities of the state university, there is a good deal that we might do that we are not doing. Certain things should, I think, be kept in mind. There is a legal problem of state-church relationship in some states that stands in the way of explicit and formal inclusion of religion in the university curriculum. Even where there is some doubt as to the full extent of legal barriers, it must be asked whether the good desired is considerable or sure enough to justify the risk of strain in community relations. There are a good many situations where one may make more progress without forcing the issue. No palpable unfairness should stay unchallenged, but it would be a failure of traditional American enterprise to let any possibility of growth go unexplored.

Here we have a great variety of circumstances to consider, and it is characteristic of the human predicament that every set of circumstances has its disadvantages and its advantages. But the fact of difference of opinion is one that must be faced by young people in our society. They will need when they leave the university to know how to plunge into the varied common life of our time with quiet confidence in their own values but with respect for the different values of others.

Finally, from the point of view of the religious man or woman, student or faculty member, we should never forget that those human qualities which religion fosters—devotion to the things of the mind and spirit, respect for other people, love of justice, and charity—are things which are greatly needed in the university as in any other community. For these things the personal example is still the most potent witness, and that witness is not without power even in so large and so varied a community as that of the state university.

Academic Freedom

CHAPTER VII

The claims of academic freedom, while including the freedoms which should be the right of every citizen, go beyond these to freedoms that institutions of learning and the scholars therein must possess if they are to fulfill their functions in society. The freedom that should be accorded the individual faculty member perhaps has had fuller treatment than the freedom of the student or the freedom of the institution as a corporate body. I deal with this first.

The Association of American Colleges and the American Association of University Professors formulated a Statement of Principles, accepted by both in 1940. Although modifications of procedure are being considered, this statement is still the commonly accepted standard. I shall quote from it, omitting the material concerning academic tenure, which of course is closely involved with academic freedom. After stressing the importance of academic freedom, the statement attempts to define it.

(a) The teacher is entitled to full freedom in research and in the publication of the results, subject to the adequate performance of his other academic duties; but research for pecuniary return should be based upon an understanding with the authorities of the institution.

(b) The teacher is entitled to freedom in the classroom in discussing his subject, but he should be careful not to introduce into his teaching controversial matter which has no relation to his subject. Limitations of academic freedom because of religious or other aims of the institution should be clearly stated in writing at the time of the appointment.

(c) The college or university teacher is a citizen, a member of a learned profession, and an officer of an educational institution. When he speaks or writes as a citizen, he should be free from institutional censorship or discipline, but his special position in the community imposes special obligations. As a man of learning and an educational officer, he should remember that the public may judge his profession and his institution by his utterances. Hence he should at all times be accurate, should exercise appropriate restraint, should show respect for the opinions of others, and should make every effort to indicate that he is not an institutional spokesman.

It is clear from the above that the scholarly profession claims a freedom beyond that which the scholars have as citizens. There is no constitutional guarantee that a man will not lose his job because of his expression of opinions. This is one of the essential guarantees which should be given to the mature scholar. There is no expectation that the ordinary citizen would be furnished a captive audience and a platform from which he can proclaim his opinions. These privileges are not accorded for the pleasure of the teacher or investigator. Rather freedom is the necessary condition for his maximum usefulness, stemming from the proper function in society of the scholar and also from, in the case of the faculty member, the purpose of the institution he serves.

Yet this freedom is not a freedom beyond that of the ordinary citizen except in the areas of special competence of the scholar. It is not a freedom to discuss the irrelevant in class. It is a freedom that presupposes the essential progressive character of scholarly investigation, the constant improvement of the tools of investigation, and the honesty of the scholar.

The independence of the scholar is needed by society in somewhat the same sense and for kindred reasons as the independence of the judiciary. In terms of his knowledge of the law, not limited by executive pressures, not controlled by any legislative act which may be unconstitutional, nor swayed by the biased points of view of the parties concerned, the judge interprets the law in the interest of society. The law forms a standard, yet a changing and developing standard, above the self-interest of various groups or individuals. The scholar also, through his scholarship, may bring to bear upon societies an insight more complete and more impartial than that of others. His findings also form a standard, both changing and developing, which in the field of his competence should be above self-interest and prejudice. One could say he also has a judicial function in society that is best when it is freely fulfilled. Or perhaps it would be more accurate to say that the judge is a scholar who, in the realm of his competence, must have the same independence that all scholars need in order to be of maximum use.

Not only truth but also diversity should be cherished. The university that does not promote the understanding and the development of the arts falls short of its purpose. The skyscraper and the Parthenon, the sonnet and the epic, the abstract design and the genre painting, the Bartók concerto and the Gregorian chant, all contribute to the richness of humanity and to the heritage we bequeath our children. The university is an executor of the estate left to us by our fathers and augmented by ourselves for the enrichment of our children. The artist as a creator, the critic as an interpreter, require freedom as much as does the scholar as fact-finder and analyst.

Another aspect of academic freedom which should be borne in mind is distinction between freedom of thought and speech and freedom of action. Society, in its own interests, makes certain decisions as to how the individual shall act and legally enforces these through the police and through the courts. For instance, there may be a sixty-mile-per-hour speed limit for state highways. A driver going faster than this limit should be arrested and penalized. A driver driving with reasonable care within this limit should be exempt from penalty. It would be intolerable, however, if a citizen did not have a right to argue that this speed limit should be changed to fifty miles per hour or to seventy miles per hour. Academic freedom demands freedom of thought, investigation, and expression. The scholar's freedom of action is that of any other citizen.

Academic freedom is not all-inclusive; in particular it must be remembered, especially by the scholar, that it does not include freedom from criticism. The scholar who brings forward his own ideas in the hope that they will enlighten the subject matter of his field must expect them to be criticized not only by other scholars but frequently by the general public. Even an administrative officer, if he makes clear that he supports the scholar's freedom, should not be denied the privilege of criticizing the scholar's ideas.

The freedom that should be accorded the student in learning, in his organizations, in the speakers he listens to, and in his actions is a constant problem. In the classroom this is largely covered in connection with the freedom of his teacher. But this is not always the case. Unfortunately, there are teachers who, demanding freedom of their own to expound their subject, are grudging in allowing the student to form his own conclusions. Happily, such teachers are rare, but the students should be protected against them. However, it should also be remembered that students should be protected from the monopolizing of a class period by the persistent vociferation of the occasional exhibitionist in their own ranks.

The freedom of students and student organizations to bring speakers to the campus has been among the most discussed problems in academic circles. In general I believe that the limitations should be only those that state and federal legislation would impose upon all citizens and that we should strive to make this imposition light.

A community is something other than an aggregate, and the community of scholars that forms a university has a corporate identity and a corporate purpose. The university as a corporate body, especially the state university, is not free to define its own functions. It must be responsive to the needs of the state as expressed by its legislature; and, in general, the legislature determines the list of its component colleges. However, to agree that its function in society is largely determined by society does not mean that society should prescribe the means by which it fulfills its function. The state may determine that the university have a college of engineering. The university must determine the curriculum of this college, as well as the content of courses and the method of teaching. And if freedom is necessary in teaching, it is equally necessary in research. It is difficult to determine what portion of our knowledge best forms the content of a course. It is even more difficult to determine what paths we should follow when we explore the unknown. Within the broad limits, therefore, of areas of work that the state is willing to support, the university should have freedom of action.

Relevant to the freedom of the professor, of the student, and of the institution is a statement that those of us at the University of Wisconsin cherish, formulated by the Board of Regents in 1894 and now engraved in bronze of Bascom Hall, which proclaims that the University "should ever encourage that continual and fearless sifting and winnowing by which alone the truth can be found." Last fall this plaque was stolen, and just before its recovery, when it was expected that a new one would have to be cast, the Regents passed a resolution containing the following statement: "The search for truth is the central duty of the University, but truth will not be found if the scholar is not free, it will not be understood if the student is not free, it will not be used if the citizen is not free."

In respect to religion, however, the academic freedom of the faculty, students, and the university itself has been curtailed because most state universities are barred by constitutional provision from giving "sectarian" instruction. This is sometimes accompanied by a ban against "partisan" instruction. There is no question that such constitutional provisions limit academic freedom, but this limitation is probably wise.

It is now impossible to determine fully either the motivation that led to these restrictions or the meaning their authors would have attributed to them. I believe there was little antireligious sentiment involved. The doctrine of separation of church and state, as expounded by such men as Jefferson, must certainly have carried weight. Probably the zeal of each denomination and its jealous wariness of the others, as well as the desire to "keep peace in the family," were the major factors in barring sectarian instruction in both school and college.

In the state universities of the Midwest, for some time after the adoption of the state constitutions, compulsory attendance at chapel was the rule. This was succeeded by chapel services provided by the institution for those who wished to attend voluntarily. These chapel services were formed from the elements common to the dominant Protestant denominations. They were also a convenient vehicle for the expression of presidential opinions. The increase in the number of Catholic students as well as the number of students of faiths other than Christian would make any such services not supplemented by other types unacceptable at present. Such religious instruction, or at least religious exercises, were not considered unconstitutional. The constitutional provisions against sectarian instruction seem, in practice today, to be given a more narrow interpretation than immediately after they were adopted. It is almost certain that constitutional objections would be raised against any attempt to install compulsory chapel in state universities today. Even the provision of chapel with voluntary attendance probably would be subject to careful legal scrutiny.

These constitutional provisions chiefly restrict the program of an institution rather than the freedom of a faculty member. If medicine, for instance, is omitted from the list of colleges the legislature will support, this immediately limits the program of the university. To a large degree the barring of religious instruction is of the same nature. In at least two important respects, however, it differs from a determination not to support a medical school. In the first place, it is a constitutional provision that the legislature itself may not set aside. And, in the second place, it is a ban against a field that traditionally is a part of the liberal arts' curriculum while, at the same time, every state university contains a college of liberal arts. Thus it limits the freedom of the college in the choice of the relevant subject matter contained in its curriculum. (I still believe it might be disastrous to the support of the university and its relation to the public, if not to the curriculum, to remove this restriction.)

It is clearly recognized that the principles of academic freedom do not include the right of a professor to discuss at length in class materials irrelevant to his field. Yet in many fields the discussion of religion is essential. As it is integral to almost all history and central in the history of such periods as the Reformation, the teacher of history will inevitably discuss religion. The same is true of the philosopher, the anthropologist, the art critic, and a whole list of others. Although in practice wisdom, tact, and respect for the opinion of others is especially needed in dealing with religious topics, no scholar should be denied the right to give his own conclusions when they are relevant.

It is also clear, I believe, that state universities have the right to give courses in such subjects as the history of religion, the philosophy of religion, and comparative religions. If the treatment both as to exposition and as to emphasis of various doctrines is fair, one should not object to the students being told which of the many views discussed his instructor holds. There is no question, however, that the judicious handling of such material is more difficult than, for instance, the comparison of metrical forms. Instruction in these subjects is not sectarian. But neither does it fulfill the function of religious teaching.

Thus in law and in practice there are certain limitations on the freedom of the public college to develop a program of religious instruction. This is a major restriction on the corporate freedom of the institution. Since teachers of religion will not be employed under present constitutional provisions, these provisions are only a minor restriction on the freedom of the teachers at present on the staffs of the state universities. Unless religious instruction is supplied by other sources, especially the church, these constitutional provisions are an important restriction on the student.

Yet, despite this bar on sectarian teaching, religious groups have been actively interested in what takes place on the campus. It is very difficult to give the right balance to any discussion of the relation of religious groups to academic freedom, particularly in state universities. It would be easy to give the impression that there has been a constant struggle on the part of the state universities to protect their faculties from the undue pressure arising from religious sources to curtail their freedom. If one did this, one would be overlooking the fact that most of the defenders of academic freedom are themselves men of religious convictions and affiliations. Moreover, those who object on religious grounds to the statements or behavior of persons in the academic community seldom are speaking officially for any religious organization. Whether these persons are clerics or laymen, they are usually expressing convictions with which many in their own churches would differ. Nevertheless, it may be worthwhile to examine a few of the attacks that at times have been made in the name of religion on academic freedom.

Until shortly after World War I, one of the most frequent attacks upon the university has been in connection with the teaching of evolution. For those who believe in the literal interpretation of the Biblical story of creation, the teaching of the doctrine of evolution is the teaching of error; and because it throws doubt on the infallibility of the Bible, the error is important. This conflict of opinion was at its height during the formation and growth of our state universities. Our land-grant colleges, many of them parts of state universities, inevitably strongly emphasized the biological sciences. Practically all biologists, for well over half a century now, have been evolutionists. Attacks upon the freedom of public education through such laws as the antievolution laws in Tennessee and through such spokesmen as William Jennings Bryan lasted until the era of many of us still teaching. These attacks have to a large degree ceased—which is a triumph for the universities, particularly because it is a noiseless triumph. I believe they have ceased not chiefly because people have become convinced that all points of view should be fully taught but because the leaders in most churches have accepted the doctrine of evolution. In doing so they have discovered that the essence of their faith remains unchanged under the impact of biological science as under the impact of Biblical criticism.

Another area of attack has been upon outspoken agnostics in university faculties. Here the problem is somewhat more complicated. No one can possibly criticize churchmen for their own answers to agnosticism. They properly defend the creeds they believe and it is healthy that they do so. There is no reason why they should not criticize the points of view held by many of those who differ from them on the basic questions of religion. I believe it is unfortunate, however, when they criticize an institution for containing agnostics on its faculty who, in discussing philosophical problems, present their own points of view. When, as perhaps has occasionally been the case, this presentation becomes so insistent as to be essentially propaganda, one can understand how churchmen will declare that it is unfair in an institution which cannot give "sectarian" instruction to allow "antireligious" instruction. This is not an easy challenge to answer. I shall give my own reaction to it. A man who uses the classroom for propaganda purposes is acting improperly. I say this in spite of the fact that I believe a man, in trying to deal with all questions fairly, should not disguise his own beliefs and, if he is respected, those beliefs will carry weight beyond even the arguments given for them. This, however, is different from deliberate propaganda which, as I said above, is always improper.

There is much, however, that is improper that is not illegal; and the question always arises as to what degree should an institution use its authority to keep its own staff from acting improperly. This question has no absolute answer, for judgments of propriety are difficult to make and often dangerous to apply. I believe that universities should go a long way to refrain from institutional judgments that limit the freedom of the individual to act in accordance with his own judgment. The risk of limiting a scholar's freedom is so great that before any action is taken the administration should be convinced it is clearly necessary to step in. I have not myself experienced an abuse on the part of a faculty member in regard to a discussion of religion that I believed demanded administrative interference. Even so, I would not take the stand that such might not arise. For instance, a student's right to hold and express a particular religious point of view should be protected against the penalty of unfair grading or of ridicule. I also believe that in regard to occasional propaganda on the part of the faculty member, the greater danger is from its irrelevance rather than from the possibility of the unfortunate swaying of opinions. Most of our students are reasonably good at spotting propaganda, but they have no protection against the waste to their time that such propaganda represents.

The college-age period is often the last and sometimes the most painful in the long process of weaning. During this period independence of ideas and of action should be fully attained. As the uses of independence made at this time are sometimes rather foolish, the university is frequently attacked for not exercising more control over the behavior of its students. This is a different attack than the attack on the freedom of the scholar, although there are elements of the latter contained within it. For the university is often attacked for leading a student to doubt the precepts under which he was brought up by his parents and his church and for leading him to question social standards that are proclaimed, if not observed, by his elders. The university is also frequently criticized for being lax in the standards of behavior it permits. Again, the answer is one of degree—not an absolute.

The more strict institutions of the past seem to have had just as great difficulty with student discipline and individual student behavior as do the universities under the generally freer attitude of the present. I would not for a moment wish it to be thought that I am happy with the present situation. Cheating in university classes is prevalent and, to a large degree, uncontrolled by either discipline or student opinion. I believe that the moral standards of the university student community are somewhat above those of the general public. The difference, however, should be greater. To a large degree the blame must be shared by the home, the church, and the school. All of us must contemplate with reverence the possibilities of the human spirit but often be depressed by the actualities of the average. However, it would seem best, insofar as possible, to work toward higher standards within the framework of freedom rather than within the framework of restriction. We must remember that an enforced conformity will do little to improve the average and may do much to damage the ideal. Moreover, the conservative who criticizes youth without making distinction between standards of virtue and minor standards of good taste is inviting youth in its revolt against the latter to revolt also against the former. The university is in a very difficult situation in dealing with students on matters of conduct which we would not tolerate in the child nor interfere with in the adult. The home and the church can do more by intensifying their influences in the years before college and during college life than by asking the university to take a more restrictive attitude toward its students than the community in general takes toward its citizens.

I do not wish to be understood as advocating that the university should tolerate serious misbehavior. I do not! However, I believe the university should more consciously develop a sense of values in the students through example and through its faculty members being less reticent in presenting their own ideals and in showing their indignation with the selfish, the shoddy, and the dishonest. Many of us could usefully wear our hearts on our sleeves to a greater degree than we do now. I subscribe heartily to the faculty committee which wrote: "What are the qualities sought in a staff member? The first is integrity of character—the second, sound scholarship. Both must be present if a faculty member is to be useful to the University. Other qualities will enhance that usefulness."

Besides criticism of the university for explicit teaching in connection with such topics as evolution, or for agnosticism (which quite frequently has been confused with atheism), there is the vague charge that the state university is godless. I believe that traditionally this arose in the days when most private institutions were closely affiliated with particular churches. The degree of this affiliation frequently became somewhat more tenuous during the period when Carnegie pensions were being granted to persons in nonsectarian colleges. To a large extent the talk about the "ungodly" state universities died down. There is now a slight revival—particularly in terms of the appeal to wealth to give to private colleges, especially to church-related schools, rather than to public institutions. To only a certain degree this is connected with academic freedom in that it affects the ability of the institution to secure support for many of its programs from wealthy individuals, from corporations, and even to some extent from foundations. Moreover, at times it has been suggested that it was improper for a state institution even to solicit support for its work, especially its instructional program, from private sources. It is strange that the "godly" will sometimes use means to seek the dollar that the "ungodly" would shun.

We must make it clear that anyone has a right to state that he believes a professor in the university is mistaken and that the university policy in regard to teachers and even in regard to academic freedom is mistaken. Equally it is the obligation of the university and its administration to defend the academic freedom of the individual and of the institution and to try to persuade the public that attacks upon this freedom are—even if permissible—unfortunate, unwise, and mistaken.

There is no question that the state universities have been criticized, and I believe unwisely, by religious persons for the sciences they teach, for the opinions expressed by their faculties, and for the freedom they grant their students. It would be totally unfair to leave the impression that this was the only relation of religion to academic freedom. Religious groups have been among the staunchest defenders of academic freedom. An attack upon an institution by churchmen can generally be left for other churchmen to answer—frequently from the same denomination. And attacks also upon institutions' freedoms made by various political groups such as, for instance, veterans' organizations, are frequently offset by the strong defense that religious groups make. Let me give some illustrations.

Certain groups in the American Legion in Wisconsin urged the University not to allow student organizations on the Attorney General's subversive list to be registered at the University or to invite speakers from outside. There are many strong arguments for this point of view. I feel the strength of the case against it, however, is overwhelming. The University has not altered its original policy in this matter. Some of the strongest support the University received was from the groups of ministers within the State of Wisconsin. I quote, as typical of those received by the University from church groups or church men in support of its stand, a statement taken from the report of the Board of Social and Economic Relations of the Wisconsin Annual Conference of Methodist Churches:

"We commend the University of Wisconsin in its stand on freedom of expression. We maintain with pride our American heritage of freedom to study and express ourselves on even such a controversial subject as Communism."

A delightful experience that I had in regard to the attitude of churches toward academic freedom was soon after World War II, when the University was so crowded that we requested permission to give a course in political science in the local Congregational Church near the campus. This was granted when we assured the trustees that the University would be responsible for any damage to property and assured the minister that there would be "no limitation on the freedom of the teacher" in teaching this subject.

The history of the church would lead us to expect that religious groups would both limit and defend the freedom of the university and of the university scholar. The record of Christianity is an interesting mixture of conservatism and of revolution. An established organization such as the church is naturally conservative. Religious leaders—idealists, socially conscious, and frequently highly emotional by nature—are naturally reformers. This is why it is simple on the one hand to depict progress in western civilization as an expression of Christianity and on the other hand to have books written with such titles as "The Warfare of Science and Theology."

An established organization is also likely to be somewhat authoritarian. The reformer, religious or otherwise, naturally will break with authority. In some cases this break is merely an attempt to establish a new authority in the place of the old. The theocrats of New England did not wish to be under the authority of the King or the Church of England, but neither did they wish to give religious or intellectual freedom to the people of New England. On the other hand, such leaders as Roger Williams placed tolerance among the first of Christian virtues. Progress of freedom was first dependent on those who wished freedom for themselves without having generalized this to granting freedom for others, and then upon those who later saw that freedom as an underlying principle was even more important than any one of its individual uses. It is a mature social philosophy that accepts the principle of freedom as the first condition of change.

An institution must jealously guard those prerogatives without which it cannot fully serve society. The independence of the court, the church, and the university in each case is such a prerogative. The freedom of the scholar is another. Clearly among the pressures limiting the freedom of the state university and its faculty are those arising from religious sources. Yet I believe that at present these freedoms are to a far greater degree supported by religious influences. Today, as yesterday, much of the intellectual leadership and social conscience of the nation centers in the church and the university. Such leadership always seeks freedom for itself and latterly has come not only to grant it to others but to join in its defense. There must ever be a strong kinship between the university that seeks freedom in order to find the truth and the church that cherishes the text:

"Ye shall know the truth, and the truth shall make you free."

THEODORE M. GREENE

Religion and the Humanities

CHAPTER VIII

It is today a truism that the over-all purpose of education in this country is the enrichment of the life of the individual and the strengthening of our democratic way of life. The distinction between vocational and professional education, on the one hand, and "liberal" or "general" education, on the other, is no less obvious. We can assume that our school system will be expected to provide increasing facilities for the acquisition of specialized skills. The why and how of so-called "liberal" education, however, is much in dispute, not only among professional educators but also among liberal arts students and the general public. There is disagreement as to the kind of welfare which liberal education should seek to promote. If we approach this problem superficially, in terms of popular short-range objectives, present procedures seem reasonably efficient. The important controversial questions arise at the level of basic human needs and possibilities.

How today do most Americans conceive of the "good life"? Predominantly in "sensate" terms (to borrow Professor Sorokin's descriptive adjective), that is, in terms of physical health and comfort, passive entertainment, and economic and social security. Most of our fellow citizens seem to be willing to settle for a house equipped with the modern appliances, a car and a T.V. set, and the life of work and play that currently prevails in our big cities and their suburbs. Those who are more ambitious conceive of "success" in comparable terms, that is, in terms of a more responsible job at a higher salary which will make available a bigger house, a more expensive car, greater comfort, and greater local prestige. The type of person most respected and envied in our society is not the saint or the sage, not the scholar or even the brilliant scientist, not the military hero or the gifted athlete, not the great statesman, the powerful politician, the brilliant lawyer, or the shrewd financier, but rather the successful executive who is in a position to make "important" decisions and to control events within the framework of our competitive business-oriented institutions.

For this kind of life a minimal "general" education will suffice. Bare literacy and a slight knowledge of current events, national and international, make possible the casual reading of most newspapers and popular magazines. T.V. programs and the movies demand even less and so does most day-by-day social intercourse. American parents want the "best" for their children, and this "best" has come to include, wherever possible, a college education. But this education, insofar as it is general and not vocational, is chiefly valued by most parents and by most of their sons and daughters not for its potential enrichment of life but primarily because it provides useful social contacts, enlarges the field of marital selection, and thus opens a variety of doors to "success" in our society. When the value of general education is conceived of in these terms, it merits the half-hearted patronage which it presently receives from the American public. Small wonder that so many parents encourage their boys and girls in college to strive for athletic and social prestige, and that so many of our undergraduates exhibit little motivation for strenuous application to their non-vocational studies.

To take liberal education really seriously, we must raise our sights and define its objectives in a much more challenging way. We must envisage an ideal of human living which, though valid for all men in proportion to their capacity for response, will in fact capture the imaginations and enlist the loyalty of only a minority of our total student population. This may sound aristocratic. But only thus can we hope to safeguard our democracy and provide our abler youth with the enriching education to which they are entitled. It is in this realistic context that we shall discuss the proper role of the humanities and of religion in higher education today.

Let us start with the proper objectives of liberal education. These can best be defined in terms of basic human needs. What must we do and be, as human beings, not only to survive but to live a good life in the world as we know it today?

The answer is not far to seek. We are finite creatures living in an incredibly complex world not of our making to which we must adapt ourselves. Each of us is a composite being of body, mind, and soul (to use three vague but familiar terms) seeking to live in a composite total environment of nature, man, and God (to use three other familiar but ambiguous terms). Our total task in life is to know ourselves and our total environment as well as possible in order to discipline and develop ourselves for the most propitious response to the challenges and opportunities which objective reality actually offers us.

All men are also born into a society with a cultural legacy of language, customs, beliefs, institutions, and artifacts, both useful and aesthetically pleasing. We would be condemned to a primitive barbarism far closer to animal existence than obtains in the most savage human society were we not able to stand culturally on the shoulders of our predecessors and to benefit from their cumulative achievements. These achievements can be of great help to us in our response to the various impinging facets of our world. The richer the cultural heritage of a society, the greater are the opportunities for cultural assimilation and advance. A "primitive" society cannot provide its young people with the powerful linguistic instruments, the scientific procedures and knowledge, the technological skill, the wealth of artistic expression, the cumulative philosophical wisdom, and the enlightened religious beliefs of an "advanced" culture such as our own. We also have available to us today the cultures of other contemporary societies and the many great cultures which have arisen, flourished, and died.

What, then, are the chief attitudes and skills most conducive to our effective response to our total environment in the light of this cultural heritage? As regards attitudes, we need, first, an attitude of alert curiosity and wonder, a lively desire to discover all we can about nature, our fellow men, and the ultimate mysteries which have intrigued and haunted man since time immemorial. Equally important is what might be called the responsive attitude, that is, the cultivated impulse to get along with our natural, human, and Divine environment in the best possible way, through submission or accommodation or control. This responsive attitude finds its complement in an attitude of respect—the respect for nature which, until recently, was called "natural piety," a respect for ourselves as human beings and for our fellow men, and a respect, better entitled reverence, for the Ultimate as it reveals itself to us in philosophic wisdom and religious insight. An attitude of sincere respect tends, in turn, to arouse in us a sense of loyalty or obligation. Finally, the attitude which most perfectly complements a sense of spontaneous obligation is that disciplined abandon which characterizes human *creativity* in its myriad forms. These five general attitudes of curiosity, response, respect, obligation, and creativity, in combination, can put man into vital rapport with his environment. Without them he is unlikely to address himself to reality in the right spirit or to acquire the requisite insights.

There are four basic skills which together implement these five attitudes. The first can be entitled the logical-linguistic skill, that is, the ability to think clearly in one or more of the several languages, verbal and nonverbal, which man has invented to express and communicate his ideas. I couple the logical and the linguistic skills thus because of their absolute mutual dependence. We can think only as we articulate our thoughts linguistically; our use of language, in turn, makes sense only as it expresses clear thinking. The second basic skill can be labelled factual. This is man's ability to become factually informed and to distinguish between fact and fiction. The third generic skill is the normative, that is, the ability to discover and appreciate the value of whatever we encounter with informed and judicious sensitivity. The fourth and culminating skill is the synoptic, that is, the ability to rise above provincial prejudice, to widen our horizons, and thus to see life and reality more steadily and whole. We are well equipped for the task of human living in direct proportion as we approximate an ideal mastery of these four skills, that is, in proportion as we are literate, articulate and clear-headed in the several complementary languages of human discourse, as we are factually oriented and informed, as we are sensitive and mature in our normative responses, and as we acquire the capacity for synoptic vision.

These attitudes and skills are all prerequisite to an adequate apprehension of and response to our total environment. It is the responsibility of liberal education to cultivate these attitudes and skills as efficiently as possible.

But liberal education should also be focussed upon certain large distinguishable areas of reality and experience. To do so, it must be differentiated into several families of "disciplines" which differ in basic subject matter, that is, in the basic aspects of reality and human experience which man must systematically explore. These include the world of nature in all its complexity, human society with its multiple institutions, man's artistic artifacts, and, finally, the realm or dimension of ultimate mystery. The emergent disciplines are the natural sciences, the social sciences, the study of the arts and letters, and the systematic study of religion. These are the basic subject-matter disciplines of scholarship and of liberal education.

In addition to these four subject-matter disciplines there are two other types of discipline of major importance. The first of these embraces man's systematic studies of his own logical processes and of the various languages of human discourse, primarily the verbal languages. These studies include logic in its various forms and linguistics in all its ramifications. They can be entitled "skill" disciplines because it is these complex skills which are here the subject matter of orderly inquiry. The whole field of pure mathematics should be included in this family of disciplines.

The second type of discipline is oriented to synoptic vision. Scope and perspective can be developed along the two complementary axes of time and logic. The discipline whose basic frame of reference is time is, of course, history; the intensive study of reality as a whole in terms of its basic similarities and contrasts, and of the whole gamut of human experience, is philosophy. These can be called the "synoptic" disciplines. Neither of them has a unique subject matter of its own; both deal with what, as subject matter, is of equal concern to one or more of the "subject-matter" disciplines. What distinguishes them is their primary concern for inclusiveness or wide perspective, either temporal or logical.

A well balanced liberal education can best be defined in terms of these long-range objectives and these basic skills, attitudes, and disciplines.

Which of these disciplines constitute the "humanities"? The term "humanities" is very ambiguous today in academic circles. It is always, I think, made to include the study of literature and the fine arts. It often but not always includes philosophy, and, less often, history. It is usually distinguished from the social sciences and is always differentiated from the natural sciences. This usage is, I believe, largely indefensible but this is not the place to argue the matter. For convenience, we may list as humanistic disciplines the study of literature and the arts, history, and philosophy on the ground that they all deal specifically with human values and with man's attempts to express and assess these values. Let us now consider the proper role of the humanities, so defined, in a balanced liberal arts education, and how can they most effectively be taught.

Why is a meaningful introduction to literature *and* the fine arts an essential component of a liberal education? To answer this question adequately would involve a thorough analysis of art as such, of its value to mankind, and of the distinctive elements of strength and limitation in each of the arts, including literature. Here we must content ourselves with a bare enumeration of certain crucial facts. There is, first, the fact of sheer aesthetic enjoyment which, though always spontaneous, can also be cultivated by appropriate study. Secondly, it is a fact that the art of any culture and period is the most vivid expression of the ethos or temper of that period and culture. Thirdly, art at its best, and even at the level of honest competence, gives us the most poignant and immediate understanding of how the individual artist saw and assessed life and the world about him. Finally, these insights of unusually sensitive human beings into man's hopes and fears, triumphs and defeats, conveyed to us as they are with such moving eloquence in the successfully expressive work of art, can, in conjunction, give us an unrivalled comprehension of the values, secular and religious, which men cherish. Philosophers discuss values abstractly; the clergy and the moralists preach values; social scientists and doctors tell us by what means to realize many important values; the artist not only creates works of beauty but, in and through them, helps us to encounter the values which men prize and thus "brings them home" to us with unparalleled imaginative power. There is no study more conducive to the sensitive appreciation of human values than the study of the arts and letters.

It is important to add the study of the fine arts to the study of literature because each of the fine arts is unique and deserves to be studied in its own right. The medium of literature differs so greatly from the other artistic media that literary studies cannot serve as an adequate introduction to the nonliterary arts. The visual arts of sculpture and painting are most closely allied and both have much in common with architecture; these three arts can be studied together with profit in their historical context. They too, however, differ radically from music which, in turn, is most closely affiliated with the theater and the dance but which is, of course, an infinitely rich and unique art in its own right.

History as it unfolds is the concrete context of all cultures and human events. There is a history of everything and nothing can be understood apart from its history. Each of the disciplines should see itself and its subject matter in historical perspective. But only the professional historian weaves these specialized historical strands together—the artistic and scientific, and economic, political, and social, the military and technological, the philosophical and religious—and thus recaptures, in some measure, the concrete actualities of the past.

Philosophy is the systematic analysis and interpretation of all human experience and the assessment of all human beliefs regarding reality as a whole. The philosopher stands on the shoulders of his more empirically oriented colleagues. He studies their methods and inquires into their tacit presuppositions. He accepts and interprets these findings and tries to answer, as cogently as he can, the perennial questions of mankind concerning appearance and reality, the secular and the holy, the nature and criteria of beauty, truth, and goodness. Every reflective specialist is, of necessity, a lay philosopher, but it is the philosopher's task to help the specialist and the thoughtful laymen to see the innumerable details of human knowledge and experience in larger systematic perspective and to speculate as wisely as possible about life's ultimate enigmas.

History and philosophy, as disciplines, also need each other. The historian must select and appraise, and without philosophy his basic standards of selection and appraisal are bound to be naïve. Similarly, the philosopher who is unaware of his own place in history and of the fact of cultural conditioning is bound to speculate *in vacuo* and to imagine that he can indeed apprehend reality *sub specie aeternitatis*. There is a history of philosophy as there is a philosophy of history; each is an essential component of its sister discipline.

How can our undergraduates best be introduced to these two complementary synoptic disciplines? There are two approaches, both of which are feasible and profitable. The first is the "dispersive" approach whereby each specialist is, so far as he is able, his own philosopher and historian. The great merit of this approach is that the specialized studies are kept, for the student, in illuminating historical and philosophical perspective and are not sealed off from one another in insulated compartments. The other approach, which might be labelled "intensive," involves heavy reliance on courses in history and philosophy. This approach has the merit of giving the student a more concrete and unified account of specific periods and a sense of the continuous flow of history; it also more effectively introduces the student to the scope and the rigor of philosophical analysis and synthesis. These approaches complement each other and should, if possible, both be exploited.

We can now consider the vexatious problem of the place of religion in the college or university in the context of a balanced liberal curriculum and with due regard to the relation of religion to the humanities.

The first distinction to be made is that between religion as belief and worship, on the one hand, and the study of religion, on the other. The institution charged with responsibility for the former is the church; the chief responsibility of an educational institution in this area is for the study of religion. Much harm can be done by confusing the proper roles of these two complementary institutions.

A university or college does have a responsibility for the religious education of its students. But this responsibility cannot be restricted to scholarship and formal instruction for two reasons. Higher education, as we conceive of it in this country, though of course primarily concerned with its students' minds, cannot remain indifferent to their multiple needs and their total welfare. It should make appropriate provision on or near the campus for whatever religious activities are judged to satisfy a real religious need. Moreover, genuine religious insight and understanding cannot be achieved in a purely intellectual way, i.e., in formal study, but depend also on primary religious experience. Opportunities for religious worship and for religiously oriented activities should therefore be regarded as a kind of "laboratory" equivalent for the scientific laboratory, the art or music studio, or the practical social science project.

The importance of religious study is evident from the preceding account of the total goal and proper scope of liberal education. If a student is to be helped to explore all the facets of reality which impinge upon him so that he may properly adjust himself to them, the mysterious depths of reality which religion seeks to plumb cannot be ignored. Even if it be argued that man's age-old religious quest is based upon a gigantic illusion and that there are no such divine depths to explore, the student of human culture is still confronted by the undeniable fact that men in every human culture have, however mistakenly, taken religion seriously and that this religious concern has expressed itself in many fascinating ways and has profoundly affected their beliefs and their behavior. The most religiously skeptical anthropologist, sociologist, and historian must take religion, as a cultural phenomenon, seriously. So must the philosopher take seriously the problem of the validity (or invalidity) of religious belief. Similarly, the art and the literary historian cannot possibly ignore the whole body of religious art and religious literature and their great cultural importance. In short, religion must be accepted as an important part of the total subject matter of liberal inquiry.

Even if this be granted, however, the question must still be answered as to how religion can best be taught and studied in a university. Two alternatives suggest themselves: (a) The study of religion can be left to the several fields into which it intrudes itself in one way or another. If this is done, work will be offered by historians in the history of religion, by philosophers in the philosophy of religion, by psychologists in the psychology of religion, and so on through the whole list of germane disciplines. The value of such a multiple approach to a crucial subject is indubitable, and every well-balanced university is today, at least to some degree, already committed to this approach. The question is, is this sufficient? (b) That it is not sufficient should be evident at once from our current conception of what a responsible study of other major subjects involves. No one alert to the demands of historical study would tolerate the farming out of history to the other disciplines, despite the fact that all these disciplines do, or should, be concerned with the history of their own progressive inquiry and of its subject matter. Full-time professionally competent historians are needed to pull together the specialized strands of history into a total unified historical account of historical periods and of the whole sweep of history in all its complex concreteness. Similarly, a major phenomenon, like religion, calls for a discipline of its own and for teachers and scholars who, in conjunction, can provide competent instruction in it. In short, a "department" of religion is as imperative, from a strictly scholarly point of view and without regard for creedal commitment, as is a "department" of history or philosophy, or art or literature.

This still leaves unsolved three crucial problems. The first

of these relates to the chief areas of, or approaches to, religion
for which a well-equipped department of religion should hold
itself responsible. On this controversial question I can only
express my considered opinion.

1. I would strongly urge that undergraduates be introduced
first to their own great religious tradition, that is, the Judaic-
Christian. The present almost universal ignorance of this tradition on the part of our undergraduates today is a byword on
every faculty and a great source of embarrassment to teachers
in many areas such as art and literature. Courses should be
made available on the Old and New Testaments and on the
historical development of Christian and Judaic thought and
practice.

2. A department of religion should also offer courses devoted
to the systematic study of the psychology of religion, the
philosophy of religion, and ethics in Judaic-Christian focus.
These courses should provide thoughtful students the opportunity to raise and explore, in a disciplined manner, the many
controversial problems relating to the nature and validity of
religious insight and religious faith.

3. It is also highly desirable that undergraduates be given
an opportunity to study primitive religion in at least some of
its concrete manifestations and also to learn something about
the other great religions of mankind such as Buddhism, Hinduism, and Islam. Without such study they can hardly hope to
see and assess their own religious heritage in historical perspective and with philosophical objectivity. They should also
have every encouragement to compare a religious approach to
life with a secular or humanistic approach at its powerful
best; indeed, every effort should be made to avoid the "special
pleading" involved in the neglect of vital options or a narrow,
provincial approach.

4. Students seriously interested in the study of religion
should, finally, be encouraged to relate these intensive inquiries
to the multiple expressions of the religious consciousness in
art and literature. They should also explore the role of religious
institutions, beliefs, and practices in various cultures and historical periods, as well as the impact upon religious belief, in-

formed and uninformed, of modern science and contemporary social studies.

The second problem which must be faced concerns the spirit in which religious phenomena are taught and studied. Here again the issue is highly controversial. There are those who believe that only the unbeliever is able to study religion objectively and without warping prejudice. Others argue, with equal conviction, that only the believer is in a position really to understand religion because it can be truly comprehended only "from within," by the committed participant, that is, only by the "agent" rather than the "observer." Finally, there are those who insist that the whole enterprise of teaching religion in a college or university dedicated to liberal studies and cultural scholarship is hopeless because religion is, in its very essence, dogmatic and illiberal and because it cannot therefore be taught in an open-minded liberal manner.

It would be most unrealistic to minimize these difficulties, both at the level of theory and of practice. I cannot, however, believe that the problem is insoluble. In principle it seems clear that the only way really to "encounter" and grasp any subject is to approach it with initial sympathy and involvement. To know what science is "all about" one must surely adopt the creedal point of view of the scientist and be willing to go with him, at least imaginatively, into his laboratory, interest oneself, at least vicariously, in his tried and tested scientific method, and thus see his problems, experiments, and findings through his eyes. The same spirit and approach, *mutatis mutandis*, are surely important for a true understanding of art and literature and of man's basic social and moral problems. It would indeed be strange if an illuminating approach to religion were less dependent upon real involvement or, at least initially, on a very sympathetic and concerned attitude.

But this is, of course, only half the story. For anyone who restricts himself solely to the sympathetic approach, especially if it includes genuine involvement and commitment, is doomed to prejudice and provincialism. The only escape is to combine the approach of the "agent" with that of the detached cultural "observer" who can dispassionately relate the subject in ques-

tion to other subjects and judicially assess conflicting inter-
pretations and appraisals. Man can hope to approximate to
authentic "objectivity" only by combining these two approaches
and by keeping them in fruitful dialectical tension. Either
approach alone is bound to be inadequate for real understanding. That it is difficult to combine these approaches must be
granted, and it may well be particularly difficult to do so in
the study of religion. But the outstanding scholars and teachers
of religion in our day and in the past prove by their work that
it is possible. A university should therefore try its best to
secure the services of scholar-teachers of this temper and
caliber.

The third problem which we dare not ignore concerns the
art of teaching in any controversial area and therefore the art
of teaching religion. We can assume that anyone of mature
stature will have definite convictions on matters of great human
concern, be they political or economic, moral or religious.
Should such a person, as a teacher of undergraduates, be
careful to conceal his relevant convictions, whether they be
affirmative or negative, in order not to prejudice the relatively
immature minds of his students, or should he express his convictions freely and openly? Many noted teachers still insist
on the first-mentioned policy as alone compatible with proper
academic "objectivity." I would myself plead strongly for the
second policy, both on the score of honesty and in the interest
of pedagogical effectiveness.

If one has real convictions on important issues germane to
the subject of a course and to one's own discipline it is, it
seems to me, only honest to reveal them and indeed defend
them to one's students, provided that one expresses these convictions not as dogmas or self-evident truths but with proper
humility and a lively sense of human fallibility. Such frankness,
in turn, has great pedagogical value for it not only helps the
student to sense the importance of the issues at stake; it also
enables him to discount the teacher's interpretation as much
as he sees fit in the light of what he feels, rightly or wrongly,
to be his "prejudice." But a teacher is also, of course, obligated
to try his best to do full justice to opposing views and thus to
exemplify the truly liberal attitude, particularly when he has

his own deep convictions on controversial issues. If he is successful, he will give his students an invaluable example (worth more than endless exhortation) of that reflective and open-minded yet sincere commitment which is the very essence of the spirit of liberalism. Our American undergraduates need, above all, to learn how to be both convinced and open-minded on vital human issues. If they can learn with our help how to have real convictions coupled with real respect for the opposite convictions of others in all the great controversial areas of our culture, they will indeed have benefited from their liberal education.

If religion is taught and studied in this spirit and manner, the resultant discipline surely deserves to be included among the great subject-matter disciplines of a liberal arts curriculum. It can also serve as one of the major synoptic disciplines because, as here envisaged, it includes careful consideration of such synoptic problems as the relation of time to eternity, of the infinite to the finite, of God to man, and the holy to the sinful, of the religious to all secular perspectives, and many other problems of comparable scope. Indeed, an exhaustive study of religion in all its ramifications would be a liberal education in itself. It is a sad commentary upon our contemporary culture that so many of our young men and women graduate from college with no inkling of the nature and value of this rich discipline and in almost complete ignorance of its subject matter.

Paul Tillich has said that religion is the substance of a culture, culture the form of religion. This is true only in proportion as both religion and culture are vital in a society. Our prime responsibility as educators is to help our students achieve a lively sense of religion as a vital force and of culture as a vital expression of the human spirit. A grudging study of religion and the "humanities" will not benefit our honest realistically minded undergraduates. What they need is inspired teaching by dedicated teachers. We must learn how to quicken their imaginations, challenge their will, arouse their curiosity, and evoke a passion for integrity, a real social concern, and genuine humility. This is the crucial task of all liberal education and of all the basic liberal disciplines. Only in this context can the distinctive values of the study of religion, and also the humanities, be properly appreciated and actualized.

I have deliberately avoided, in the foregoing analysis of religion and the humanities, all special pleading for the humanities or for religion. Such one-sided appeals are still prevalent, but they do more harm than good. They merely encourage an aestheticism which belies the power of authentic art and an artificial piety which is essentially irreligious. If we would be realistic and mature as human beings we must orient ourselves primarily to the whole of life and to reality as a whole. If education is to be vital it must be truly liberal; it must liberate us from ignorance, insensitivity, and provincialism. If any of the humanities are to perform their proper function they must, from first to last, do what they are uniquely qualified to do, that is, help to make man more truly human, more humane. No religion is worthy of our respect and allegiance which fails to provide us with a valid central objective, an "ultimate concern for the Ultimate."[1] Every human being has some sort of ultimate concern, but in most cases it reflects an idolatrous veneration for something merely finite. It is our prime responsibility in the university to direct our student's attention to the truly Ultimate and to help him to make his concern for the Ultimate as sincere, profound, and enlightened as possible. We can do so only in proportion as we help him to make his religion the vital core of his life and to relate it, both intellectually and existentially, to all of man's major inquiries and pursuits. The study of religion in a university is bound to lack the significance it should have unless it is made an integral part of the total curriculum and of the total life of the undergraduate.

The study of religion, so conceived, should make an essential contribution to each of the liberal disciplines; each of these, in turn, has its own unique value for religion. This is particularly true of the humanities. A great work of art in any medium is great because the insights it expresses are profound, and profundity depends upon the humility, scope, and deep involvement that characterize man's religious quests at their authentic best. This is no plea for any religious orthodoxy in art and literature or for an explicitly religious "subject matter." It is, rather, a reminder that all significant art reflects, in one way or another, man's "ultimate concern for the Ultimate." Truly significant art is thus absolutely dependent upon a religious orientation. But religion is equally dependent on significant art and literature. They are, par excellence, the most precise and eloquent vehicles for the expression and communication of man's religious insights and the necessary vehicles for his religious worship.[2]

A similar case can be made for the mutual dependence of the study of religion and the disciplines of philosophy and history. The study of religion is bound to be dogmatic, uninformed, and provincial if it is divorced from the historical record of evolving cultures and from judicious philosophical interpretation and appraisal. History, in turn, cannot with impunity ignore or minimize man's recurrent and manifold religious search and the rise and impact of religious beliefs in the course of human events. A dogmatic secularism and an exclusive focus upon religious beliefs and practices are equally one-sided and provincial. The discipline of history is significant in direct proportion as it avoids these extremes and studies the march of history with the realization that religion is indeed the essence of every culture, and culture the form of religion. Similarly, philosophy dooms itself to triviality when it limits itself to the sophisticated puzzles—logical, epistemological, and metaphysical—of the philosopher who has lost contact with life and with man's deepest anxieties and needs. Significant philosophy is focussed upon man's most vital problems, and these can never be divorced from his predicament as a finite mortal. In this sense, which contains no plea for any species of religious orthodoxy, philosophy at its best must be profoundly religious in its ultimate orientation.

All these sweeping generalizations are, of course, highly controversial and call for extensive development and defense. They must suffice, however, to indicate my own conception of the proper roles, and the supreme importance, of religion and the humanities in liberal education on every college campus, including the state university.

KENNETH E. BOULDING

Religion and the Social Sciences

CHAPTER IX

The great drama of man's history has a long and continuous main plot in which the principal theme is the tension between the sacred and the secular aspects of life. This struggle is not a simple dialetic in which, for instance, the secular enlightenment gradually overthrows the sacred gloom, but a complex web of interacting strands as first one, then the other aspect of life rises to dominance in constantly changing forms—priest over peasant, king over priest, prophet over king, priest over prophet, emperor over priest, pope over emperor, princes over pope, people over princes, preachers over people, professors over preachers. The development of man's whole image of the universe can be interpreted in terms of a tension between the heroic vision—the wild leap of the poetic imagination, the awe in the presence of Revelation—and the prudential vision—the common-sense view of things, the wisdom of practical men. On the whole this tension between the secular and the sacred has been a creative tension, each constantly reproving the excesses of the other, though there have been times when it has become excessive and destructive.

We are now contemplating a single scene in this enormous drama. The set is the campus of a state university in the United States; the time is A.D. 1957. (It is interesting to note that the number 1957 is part of a series with a sacred origin.) We have come late to the play, as inevitably we must; we find our seats— no, worse, we find ourselves pushed onto the stage from the wings, for we are not spectators but actors. We fumble for our programs: What has gone before? How much do we have to know of what has gone before, and of what is still going on in other theaters, in order to get the hang of the plot and to know what is going on now?

Our first clue is the set itself. The architecture is strangely miscellaneous; surely an amorphous mixture of the sacred and the secular. If there is an emotional center to the campus it is likely to be a bell tower with no church attached. This is deeply symbolic: the sterile phallus. There is likely to be some Gothic or quasi-Gothic architecture, recognizably a sacred type. The building, however, that looks like a cathedral turns out to be a library, and the one that looks like a chapel turns out to be a gymnasium. Detailed inspection reveals no building on the campus used primarily for religious purposes, except perhaps something called, enigmatically, a Y. The conclusion seems to be that we have here an institution in which the secular is completely dominant, and in which the sacred is present only in vestigial forms and organs. We must be careful, however. On the edge of the campus, pressing in on all sides, are buildings that are quite clearly sacred, both in form and in use. We count at least a dozen churches and perhaps two or three building. Furthermore, we find them crowded and prosperous, bursting with activity. Looking at the matter in some detail, we find that on one or two campuses there are even chapels, just built or projected. On other campuses there remains a certain hostility to religion; this, however, is diminishing, and the prevailing attitude toward religion might be described as a slightly bewildered friendliness. We might conclude that we are here witnessing a turn-of-the-tide phenomenon; that a high watermark of secularism has been reached somewhat earlier and that the tide of religion is once more coming in.

Now we must look at some of the previous scenes. The idea of a university itself comes from the previous high watermark of the Sacred, the thirteenth century. If we visit the older universities of Europe, we shall find them occupying the sets of the previous act, and at the center of the set is always a large chapel. The medieval university was primarily a religious institution, modeled on the monastery, and the monastic flavor lingers in the architecture and in some of the customs. Today, however, the chapel is little more than a tourist attraction— students rarely visit it, and it plays little or no part in the life of the college. Between the thirteenth and the twentieth century a great tide of secularism has washed over the whole world. The story is a familiar one—the Reformation, which broke the unity of Christendom and yet renewed the vigor of the society; the Renaissance, which was an infusion of a strong current of ancient secularism; the Discoveries, which brought the whole world into a geographical unity; the Enlightenment; the rise of nationalism and democracy, and finally the enormous enlargement of man's view of the universe and of his power over it through science. The American state university is a monument to nationalism, to democracy, to the separation of church and state, and to science and technology. Its saints are Copernicus, Galileo, Kepler, Newton, Adam Smith, Dalton, Darwin, Freud, and Einstein, and perhaps Washington and Jefferson.

Here again, however, the plot is not so simple as it seems. The tide of secularism is full of strange eddies; it not only draws its springs from sacred waters but carries them on its surface far and wide. Medieval Europe, which we westerners parochially think of as the then known world, was in fact a tiny peninsula on the edge of the great world of Islam, sprawling across the hemisphere from Spain to the Philippines. The cultural explosion that carried Europe to a position of world dominance by the ninteenth century is a good illustration of the creative tension between the sacred and the secular. It can be argued that it was a revival of religion in the Reformation and Counter Reformation that set it off—a revival fed continuously by the rise of new sects in Protestantism and new orders and movements in Catholicism. Even the saints of secularism are strangely religious; both Galileo and Copernicus were unmistakably Catholic Christians, Newton was obsessed by theology, Dalton was a devout Quaker, Faraday was a Sandemanian preacher, Priestley was a Unitarian minister, Darwin was a man of natural piety, Einstein a mystic. The apparent breakup of the medieval religious unity was in fact the

beginning of the great age of world expansion of Christianity—
to all the Americas, to important missionary enclaves in Asia
and Africa. Coming closer to the present scene we find that one
of the most striking long-run trends in the history of the United
States has been the rise of organized religion. The United States
was founded at the height of the Enlightenment; the founding
fathers were almost to a man deists and rationalists. I have seen
one estimate that at the time of the Revolution not more than
4 per cent of the people of the American colonies were actively
associated with any organized church. This figure may be un-
duly small; however, there seems to be evidence for a very
steady rise in the proportion of church members in the population from a rather small figure in the mid-eighteenth century
to about 60 per cent today.

Where then—to come to the main topic of this chapter—do
the social sciences stand in this complex historical pattern? The
rise of social science is one of the most striking, and perhaps
one of the most far-reaching, movements of the twentieth century. Its origins, of course, go far back into social thought and
philosophy. The peculiar characteristics of the movement that
enable it to qualify for the holy name of "science," however, are
quite recent. I would argue that Adam Smith developed the
first over-all "system" of social science in his theory of the
equilibrium of a price system. Quantification comes even later.
The modern census began in the eighteenth century, but it is
not really until the twentieth century that the collection of
social information becomes deliberate and massive. Statistics
owes a great deal to, and has done a great deal for, the social
sciences, but this, too, mostly in the twentieth century. Sociology, anthropology, and psychology, as organized professions
and departments of learning, are creations of the second half of
the nineteenth century. The twentieth century has also seen the
rise of applied social sciences into professions with professional
schools in the universities to propagate them. Schools of public
administration, business administration, journalism, and social
work, and institutes of human relations, labor relations, and
international relations can all be regarded as applied social
science institutions, much as schools of engineering are mostly

applied physical science and schools of medicine and dentistry are applied biological science. Social science is even creeping into professions and professional schools that previously had little to do with it. Industrial engineering tends to become less and less distinguishable from business administration; schools of medicine get interested in social medicine, in public health, in psychosomatic and psychiatric medicine. Nursing is presumably at least half applied social science.

I think it must be argued that the social sciences historically ride firmly on the secular side of the secular-sacred seesaw, even more so than the natural sciences. It is extremely hard to think of antireligious persons or even nonreligious persons among the great names in the natural sciences. This is perhaps because the natural sciences compete with religion only at its periphery. Religions, especially those which rest on sacred books, have always tended to give sacred sanction to the ideas of the physical world which were prevalent at the time of their founding. These ideas of the physical world, however, are the accidents of religion—they rarely form its central core. Thus, while Copernicus and Galileo are upsetting to the church, in that they destroy the literal validity of much of the physical imagery of the Bible, they upset the imagery rather than the image, and insofar as the new ideas of the physical universe inspire awe and wonder at its grandeur, they are actually friendly to some of the deepest religious emotions. The extension of the universe, both in time and in space, away from the cozy three-storied, four- or five-thousand-year-old universe of the Bible into the billion-galaxied, four-billion-year-old universe of today's image should make man more, not less, ready to fall on his knees in wonder and adoration at such great majesty and splendor. As we penetrate more deeply into the intricate machinery of life, here again a sense of awe is neither unseemly nor unnatural.

The great object of study of the social sciences, however, is man. (A sociologist has recently described his science as the improper study of mankind!) The subject matter of the social sciences lies closer to the heart of religion than does the material of the natural sciences. The views which religion holds of the nature of man are not peripheral, for all religion concerns itself deeply with the regeneration, improvement, or salvation of man, and consequently its views as to what should be done about him must be rooted firmly in certain views about his nature. The possibility therefore arises of competitive relations between the views held on the nature of man by religion and by social science. A further possibility for competition arises because in their applications both religion and social science conceive themselves as performing a therapeutic role not only on the individual but on society as a whole. A church that lays down the law on usury runs into disagreement with the economist; a church that lays down the law on divorce runs into disagreement with the sociologist; a church that claims divine right for kings runs into disagreement with the political scientist, and a church that claims to divide human actions sharply into sins and virtues may run into disagreement with the psychoanalyst.

In view of the potential competition, therefore, between religion and social science, it is not surprising to find that on the whole the great figures in the social sciences have been frequently indifferent or even hostile to religion. Adam Smith, like his friend Hume, might be classified as a deist, but his attitude toward religion was at best quizzical. He looks at the church as a kind of spiritual business, meeting certain human needs which no doubt need to be met, but always in danger of creating an artificial demand for its products by arousing enthusiasm. His recipe for "that pure and rational religion, free from every mixture of absurdity, imposture, or fanaticism, such as wise men have in all ages of the world wished to see established"[1] is, as we might expect, free competition among sects so that each has to moderate its doctrines in the direction of sweet reasonableness in order to attract adherents from the others. I have never been able to detect the slightest interest in religion in Ricardo's writings. Malthus, it is true, was a clergyman, and this fact seems to have given him some slight qualms about birth control, but apart from this, religion seems to have made singularly little impact on his thought. Keynes was a thoroughly secular character. Marx, of course, like Freud, was actively hostile to religion.

The sociologists have been more interested in religion than

the economists, as one might expect, but apart from Max Weber[2] and Durkheim,[3] it is hard to think of outstanding figures who have paid much attention to it, and I doubt if there are more than a dozen sociologists in the United States today who regard themselves as specialists in the sociology of religion. The one sociologist who has taken religion very seriously is Sorokin, and perhaps partly because of that very fact he is looked upon with a good deal of suspicion by his professional colleagues. In psychology, likewise, there has been little attention paid to religious experience except when it takes pathological forms. There was very little follow-up from the pioneering work of William James's *Varieties of Religious Experience*, and apart from Allport's study of student religion,[4] there seems to be little interest in the matter among modern psychologists. Yet in spite of all this, religion flourishes as it has not done perhaps since the seventeenth century!

Anthropologists, by reason of their very subject matter, have been much interested in primitive religion, for religion, as one of the earliest parts of the intellectual life to develop, forms a large part of the culture of primitive peoples. With some exceptions, however, anthropologists have been also indifferent or hostile to the religion of their own culture—perhaps because of a certain habit of nonparticipation in the cultures which they have investigated and a not wholly justified identification of advanced with primitive religion.

The aversion or indifference of many social scientists toward religion may arise in part because of the difficulty of transferring from one abstract role to another when the subject matter with which the two roles are concerned exhibit so many similarities. The role of the scientist is marked by aloofness from the subject matter which he investigates and an assumption of an ideal of objectivity. By contrast, the role of the religious person is marked by deep involvement with the subject matter, by commitment and dedication to it, by reverence and obedience. The role of the scientist is like that of the musicologist and critic—a questioning, inquiring attitude, holding nothing sacred, approaching the object of inquiry as an "outsider." The role of the religious person is like that of the artist, identifying himself with his material, willing of course to use objective knowledge, but always being willing to transcend it in the act of identification. It is not surprising, therefore, that there seem to be few people who are capable of sustaining both roles, as they seem to involve contradictory values. Nevertheless, tolerance of apparently contradictory roles may be one of the principal sources of creativity in the individual.

My main thesis is that the traditional hostility or indifference of social scientists to religion is a historical accident, arising from the peculiar circumstances of the period when the social sciences developed, and that, if certain misconceptions can be overcome, we should be able to enter a period of mutually beneficial interaction between these two great areas of human life and experience. We can think of these two areas as slightly overlapping regions of our social space. Each consists of a "core" of more or less professional, full-time practitioners, with a penumbra of persons affected in greater or less degree by the web of interaction within the region. At present the "cores" of the two regions overlap little; there are a few Catholic social scientists; there is some interaction among social scientists and professional churchmen, both in the denominations and in such bodies as the departments of the National Council of Churches. There are also certain strong currents of ideas which permeate our whole society—the ideas of Marx, Freud, and Keynes, for instance, exercise influence on many who have never read them or who do not even know their names, and similarly the influence of Barth, Niebuhr, and Tillich spread out far beyond the relatively narrow circle of their own readers. On the whole, however, the overlap is small; economists, psychologists, sociologists, and anthropologists pursue their professions, teaching, reading, writing, meeting, without being much aware of what is going on in the world of religion (or even of what is going on in neighboring sciences). Similarly, the religiously minded go on their own way, preaching, teaching, writing, worshipping, conferring, without much regard to what goes on in the little world of the social scientists. The two areas differ in that religion has a very large penumbra, reaching out in varying degrees of involvement and interaction into almost the whole society, touching all classes, poor and rich, intellectuals and laborers, whereas the penumbra of social science is much smaller, reaching beyond the intellectual classes only in a very attenuated form, and consisting mainly of students, most of whom have only a very casual contact. The difference may be stated in the form that religion is sustained by a general, non-specialized community (the church); social science is sustained by a specialized community of academics and intellectuals. Social scientists have classes, social workers have clients, but only preachers have congregations!

Let us then explore some conditions under which a greater degree of interaction between these two social regions would be mutually beneficial. The most essential condition of such inter-course is a widely shared belief in the complementary, or at least noncompetitive, nature of the two areas. As long as even one side visualizes the other as a "threat," interaction will be discouraged, and defense will be sought in isolation. Important in this connection also is whether one party visualizes itself as a threat to the other. Here is an area where few or no studies have been made and where a little social-scientific inquiry might be very fruitful. One may venture a tentative hypothesis that on the whole the churches do not see themselves either as threatened by, or as a threat to, social sciences, either at the core or at the penumbra, whereas many social scientists visualize social science as something of a threat to the churches; hence, expect the churches to see social science as a threat and, hence, see the churches as at least potentially hostile to social science. Both the complacency of the churches and the arrogance of the social scientists may, of course, be due to ignorance; at the present stage of this interaction, however, one suspects that the obstacles lie more on the side of the social scientists than on the side of the churches. This may not last. As the churches become more aware of the "threat" of social science, their attitudes may harden.

In situations of this kind a clear delimitation of boundaries can lessen tension and prepare the ground for interaction. As long as each does not feel secure within a certain "home base," there will be mutual suspicions. This delimitation would take the form of a recognition of the different levels of abstraction at which the two processes operate. Social science on the whole is an attempt to apply mechanical and mathematical models to the behavior of men and societies. This is a useful abstraction, and the power of social science lies precisely in its ability to abstract from the immense complexity of the human organism those elements that permit the construction of rather simple mechanical models. The danger of abstraction, of course, is the danger of mistaking the abstraction for the reality and hence elevating the model into a metaphysic.

Religion on the other hand is not an abstraction, but a practicum—an area of human life, experience, and practice in all its complexity, both present, past, and to come. To revert to a previous analogy, that of music: there is a "science" of music, which includes both its physical mechanics and its social mechanics. There is a physics of sound and a sociology of the symphony. Both these are necessary to the full understanding of the phenomenon; neither are strictly necessary to the practice or the enjoyment of music. Religion similarly encompasses an area of experience—in prayer, in worship, in liturgy, in revival meetings, in meditation and devotion, and so on. This likewise requires a mechanics—in this case a mechanics of communication and emotion, of social involvement and individual values. The practice and enjoyment of religion, however, like that of music, is not necessarily dependent on the underlying mechanics. This is not to say that in both cases understanding may not lead to enrichment of the experience, though I have known cases where an overintellectual understanding destroyed the enjoyment of music, and there are even more cases where an obsession with the mechanics of religion has prevented the enjoyment of its practice. Where this happens, however, it is because of a failure to appreciate the difference between abstraction and reality, or because of a fear of reality which prevents a person from plunging into it and giving himself to it, and which leads to the substitution of the safe abstraction for the dangerous reality. To use still another figure, it is no doubt useful for a swimmer to know the mechanics of swimming, but nobody ever learns to swim by just studying the mechanics. To learn to swim, we have to get in the water.

There is here a very interesting problem of the relation of science to practice which might be described as the relation of explicit to implicit knowledge. The swimmer swims largely because of implicit knowledge. He could not formulate his knowledge of hydrodynamics in terms of differential equations, and it would not help him to swim better even if he could, in spite of the fact that his actions depend on the implicit solutions of some very complex equation systems. On the other hand, airplanes fly and submarines swim because of explicit knowledge; an airplane does not fly like a bird, nor does a submarine swim like a fish. This is because we have discovered that by the application of much simpler systems than are generally present in living organisms, it is possible to do simple things better than the living organism. Because living organisms have to do such enormously complex things as growing and reproducing, they have to have an immensely complex machinery, and because they then have to use this complex machinery for doing simple things like locomotion, they do these simple things rather badly. Hence, no living organism uses the wheel, the piston, and the screw as part of its biological apparatus mainly because devices which require a high degree of mechanical accuracy can only be made, they cannot be grown.

The business of science is explicit knowledge; the power which comes from this kind of knowledge arises out of the possibility of applying it at its own system level—that is, its own level of simplicity. Mechanics is very useful for making machines, but if we are ever to duplicate living organisms—as one day I expect we will—we will have to have explicit knowledge about the processes of life which we do not have at present. Art and skill, on the other hand, involve implicit knowledge—the application of unconscious systems in which the organism is able to control parts of its environment because of an elaborate system of information fed out from and back into the system. Thus, the potter who throws a pot on a wheel adjusts the pressure of his fingers to the feel of the clay by a complex "cybernetic" process in which deviations of the performance of the clay from the "ideal" in the mind of the potter are perceived and almost instantly corrected by movements of the hand.

One of the great difficulties in the application of the social sciences is that the subject matter of the social sciences largely consists of behavior involving the use of implicit knowledge of social systems. These systems, however, are immensely complex—quite beyond, in their complexity, the ability of simple mechanical systems to describe. On the whole, however, social science has not risen much above the level of simple mechanical systems in its theoretical models. The explicit systems of the social scientist, therefore, are very imperfect substitutes for the implicit systems on which most human behavior is based.

The church, like all social organizations, tends to operate with implicit rather than explicit knowledge of its social environment. The question as to what use can the social sciences be to the church then resolves into the question, whether there are any areas in which an explicit knowledge of social fact or relationship derived from the peculiar techniques of the social sciences can improve upon the implicit knowledge which comes out of common-sense experience and casual observation. The answer to this question would certainly seem to be "yes" in some limited areas. The survey method, for instance, can be applied to derive explicit information about the population of the area which is served by a church or a group of churches— information which may be of great importance in planning the work of a church, in visitation, in planning buildings or new locations, in identifying its "constituency," in pointing the way to needs which it might serve and which it is not now serving. These things may sound trivial, and perhaps they are. Whatever else a church is, however, it is also an organization, existing in a certain environment, drawing its sustenance from the fact that it meets certain human needs and is therefore able to attract resources to itself. There seems to be no loss in becoming more self-conscious of the nature and environment of the organization, even though all these matters may properly be regarded as secondary in the minds of the "core group" of the church.

The question of explicit knowledge of the internal functioning of a church organization is perhaps more delicate. In every organization there is a formal hierarchy of some kind, but also an informal system of communication and influence, and the two systems do not usually coincide. A skilled social anthropologist should be able to go into any organization, such as a church, and by studying the patterns of communication and influence, develop a picture of the organization as an explicit role structure. It might be doubtful whether he would find out more than a well-placed individual within the organization would know; on the other hand, it might well be that much more goes on than any single individual is aware of.

Another point at which the social sciences can be—and are —helpful to the church is in the field that might be called applied religious ethics. All religions include some kind of an ethic, and in the advanced religions the development and inculcation of the ethic is conceived as a major task of the church. Religion is thought of as containing a set of general ethical principles which have to be applied in the situations of daily life as well as in the observance of specifically religious ordinances. As the world changes around us, however, so do these applications of the religious ethic change—new techniques, new products, new ways of life constantly pose new ethical problems, and if the church is to remain in touch with the life of its people, it must help them to solve these new problems. This is perhaps less pressing in churches whose life consists mainly in ritualistic pursuits and otherworldly hopes, but for most American churches, the problem of social ethics has been one of substantial interest. It is interesting to note that the interest in this problem in the Roman Catholic church has closely paralleled the development of the "social gospel" in the Protestant churches, and also that a common interest in the social applications of Christian ethics has been one of the main sources of the ecumenical movement in Protestantism.

If the ethical judgment is to be mature and informed, it must be based on a firm knowledge of the consequences of various kinds of human action or political policy. It is one of the objectives of social science, however, to increase explicit knowledge of social systems and relationships, and this increased knowledge cannot fail to have an effect on the ethical judgment. As an illustration of this point, we might observe the change in the social doctrines, especially of Protestant churches, which has come about as the result of increasing sophistication in regard to economics. In the middle of the nineteenth century, the prevailing social doctrine was one of classical laissez faire; preachers united with economists to laud the benefits of free trade and the magic of property. Toward the end of the nineteenth century, "Christian Socialism" in various forms became popular. The roots of this are to be found not so much in Marx as in the "romantic" revolt against the coldbloodedness and calculatingness of capitalism—as represented, for instance, by Ruskin and Carlyle, William Morris, and Charles Kingsley. It is the contrast between the mechanical coldness of laissez faire market capitalism and the warm, familistic love ethic of the New Testament that really produces this revolt. By the end of the nineteenth century, this had produced the "social gospel" as represented by preachers like Gladden and Rauschenbusch, and by the various social action agencies of the churches. The British Labour party and the American "New Deal" owe much to this "social gospel" movement—British socialism has been described as Methodist rather than Marxist socialism, and the New Deal owes a great deal intellectually to a group of reforming economists of the early twentieth century (H. C. Adams, Ely, Commons), who in turn were much affected by the movement for "social Christianity."

In the mid-twentieth century again, the "social gospel," as represented, say, by the pronouncements of the Department of Church and Economic Life of the National Council of Churches or by the writings of leading Christian social philosophers like Reinhold Niebuhr and John Bennett, has become more sophisticated, partly of course under the impact of the momentous events of the times, such as the rise of Hitler and Stalin, but also under the impact of criticism from professional social scientists. Christian social thinkers have come more and more to realize that familistic forms of organization may not be suitable for large groups, that there is a real and difficult problem of power and responsibility in society, that a "profit system" does not necessarily imply Scrooge-like behavior, and that all problems are not solved by turning them over to co-operatives, labor unions, or the benevolent mother-state. The rise of the Keynesian economics has opened up the possibility of remedying the major defects of an unregulated market economy by the fairly simple means of government policies that do not involve serious loss of individual freedoms or the manipulation of men. Such a movement in social science inevitably has a profound impact on the judgments and preachments of social ethics.

In other areas also, a wider knowledge of the social field inevitably leads to modifications of the ethical judgment. In their teaching on sexual ethics and family life, for instance, the churches can hardly fail to be affected by Malthusian and Freudian theories, even though they would be under no necessity to swallow them whole. They can also hardly fail to be affected by the growth of explicit knowledge of the facts of sexual behavior as represented, for instance (however imperfectly), by the Kinsey studies. Ethical judgments on race relations, both inside and outside of the churches, have likewise been profoundly affected by the work of social scientists. Insofar as prejudice might almost be defined as judgments in social ethics derived from highly limited and restricted fields of experience, the expansion of the field of experience which the methods of social science opens up inevitably has a corroding effect on prejudice. The churches have to make their own adjustments to this widening of the field of knowledge. As it is hard for the church to move much ahead of its members, these adjustments are often difficult. They are, however, necessary and creative.

I now come to the very delicate and difficult problem of the contribution that religion can make to social science. The very suggestion that religion might make some contributions to social science will be resented by many social scientists, especially by those whose vocational drive into the social sciences arose out of a rejection of the religion in which they were brought up. It must be admitted also at the start that many excellent and creative social scientists have been indifferent or even hostile to religion. There is no law which says that a man must be religious in order to be a good social scientist. Indeed, there might well be cases in which devotion to religion actually stood in the way of that objectivity of mind and devotion to truth at all costs which is supposed to be—and sometimes is—the mark of scientific inquiry. This problem, however, is not peculiar to religion. If any ideology is held in such a way that a threat to the ideological system is perceived—even subconsciously—as a threat, either external or internal, to the person holding it, devotion to the ideology will be a handicap in the discovery of truth. This is true of the communist ideology; it is true also of materialist or atheist ideologies, as well as of religious ideologies. The strait jacket into which scientific inquiry is forced by the ideology of dialectical materialism is well known—the destruction of free scientific inquiry in Russia has been one of the most shocking fruits of communism. It is not so easy for us to see that we may have a strait jacket of our own—a kind of secular, nationalist materialism which likewise sets limits to scientific inquiry that does not follow the established high roads. There is a quasi religion of "scientism" which by rejecting all psychic or spiritual phenomena severely limits the scope of scientific inquiry.

Religion differs sharply, however, from these atheistic and materialistic "faiths" in that it consists not merely in an ideology but in a set of practices and special experiences. There is really no equivalent, for instance, either in communism, national secularism, or scientism for the practices of prayer and worship. These represent one of the worlds of human experience, just as music or art or science itself is a world of human experience. If this is rejected out of hand as invalid or uninteresting, this rejection severely limits the field of social-scientific study. We may say, therefore, that one important contribution of religion to the social sciences is to give it a field of study and inquiry. For reasons which may be found in the sociology of the social sciences themselves, this is perhaps the most neglected field in the whole subject matter of social sciences. Psychologists make very little attempt to study religion as an aspect of human behavior; sociologists have done very little work on the church as a social organization. A world of fascinating subcultures within the framework of American society awaits the social anthropologist, and religion, as an outgrowth of small group interaction, has been shockingly neglected by the social psychologist. Even the economist might find it profitable to look at the influence of the churches on economic behavior.

This neglect of an important field of study is merely one facet of a serious problem in the sociology of the social sciences, arising out of the narrow field of personal experience of the social scientist himself. Social scientists, like any other occupational group, form a subculture within the larger society. They are, moreover, a rather small and narrow subculture —not quite so narrow as that of the Amish, perhaps, but almost comparable. This subculture has its own sublanguage, its own rituals, such as the publication of articles in quasi-liturgical form (coefficients of correlation and statistical tests of significance are nice examples of social science liturgies), and its communications are very largely internal to the group —even casual and social communications. Furthermore, this subculture is middle class, academic, largely cut off from contact with wageworkers or farmers, and is transmitted from the old to the young through the power which the old have over the promotion and professional advancement of the young. As a result of this, the social scientist tends to have less and less firsthand, intimate, face-to-face contact with people in the other subcultures around him. He consequently tends to concentrate his investigations within his own or closely related groups—experimental human psychology and social psychology, for instance, is almost wholly confined to the behavior of college sophomores—or his contacts with other groups are made on the basis of such an impersonal relationship as the questionnaire or the interview. This inevitably leads to a narrowing of his field of social vision, and it becomes very hard for him to escape the prison of his own subculture. Of all the social scientists, anthropologists live most intimately with other cultures. Here, however, there has been a strong tradition of studying remote cultures, so that while we know a great deal about the Ubangi, we know very little about

Jehovah's Witnesses. Also, one wonders whether the limitations of the intimate personal experience of the anthropologist in the cultures of his own civilization do not at times blind him to certain qualities of richness and depth in more primitive cultures.

Few social scientists will quarrel with the proposition that religion should provide subject matter for social science investigations. Many will not follow me in the assertion that for the healthy growth of social science we need maturely religious social scientists. I base this assertion, however, on two grounds. The first is that, as religion is part of the whole experience of mankind, the social scientist who does not participate in it is cut off from a deep and meaningful area of human experience and is in this sense maimed. Now, of course, a maimed person may be a very good scientist; the blind and the halt also serve, and these deficiencies can be overcome. But who would argue that they are an advantage! Similarly, the social scientist who is deaf to music and blind to art may be excellently skilled in his profession, but there will be something lacking in his person. Not that I would press the argument too far—otherwise, we might find ourselves arguing that we must sin the more that knowledge may abound! But where a large area of human experience is rejected or neglected, surely it can be argued that there is a deficiency.

The other argument is that as social science develops, the problem of the ends of human activity become increasingly pressing, even for social scientists. Knowledge, we write over our schoolroom doors, is power, and power is power unto salvation or unto damnation, depending on how we use it. As long as man is relatively impotent, the problem of what to do with the power he does not possess remains academic. With the growth of power, the problem of its use becomes of increasing importance. We see this in the physical sciences, where the question of the use of the powers which knowledge has unleashed has become perhaps the most critical question of our age. The power which the social sciences may unleash, however, may be ever more terrible—power to control the minds and actions of men, both individually and in the mass;

the power of indefinite corruption of the integrity and individuality of sovereign man. We cannot therefore rest neutrally with the question, "How do people get what they want?" We cannot even assume that it is ethically neutral to help people to get what they want. As social science develops, the critique of ends becomes ever more important, and the question, "Do I (or does anybody) want the right things?" becomes insistent and inescapable. It is precisely this critique of ends, however, which is the great moral task of religion. The future of science, and especially of social science, may depend on our getting better answers than we now have to the question of when ignorance is bliss—or, as a matter of fact, what bliss is anyway! And bliss, curiously enough, is one of the great subjects of religion.

I am not, of course, advocating religious tests for the employment of professors of social science—religious tests, like so many others, test the test rather than the testee, and even from the point of view of the health and vigor of religion itself, the secularization of academic (and political) institutions has been a great gain. We have only to compare, for instance, the remarkable vigor of the Lutheran churches in this country with their debility in Scandinavia to see the futility of trying to impose religion by external sanctions. One does not make people musical by forcing them to go to concerts, nor does one make people religious by forcing them to profess religion. Religion must make its own way and be judged on its own merits; the very breath of coercion will destroy it. It is not necessarily a bad thing to have a few atheists around a university, even if it is only to prove that there is religious freedom (a few communists, incidentally, might also be used to prove that there is political freedom). But there is a great opportunity today for fruitful intercourse between religion and social science, and if the university should not force this, at least it should be able to provide some facilities.

The application of religion to the social sciences must be left to the social scientists themselves. With the application of social science to religion, however, the university might well be positively concerned. One can visualize, for instance, a research institute in this area, somewhat analogous, shall we say, to institutes of industrial relations, which would bring together social scientists from different fields for the development of both theoretical and empirical research in the area of religious experience, practices, and institutions. Such an institute would be difficult to staff at present, and it would run into some difficult problems of public relations, both inside and outside the university, for its members would have to deserve the confidence of both the academic and the religious communities. The development of such a research center would do much to encourage the kind of interaction which I have argued is desirable; it would also bring the university closer to its ideal of studying the universe.

G. E. HUTCHINSON

Religion and the Natural Sciences

CHAPTER X

In this chapter I shall explore what appears to me to be the most important aspect of the relationship of science and religion. Inevitably I write from the standpoint of one brought up in the tradition of Western Christianity, but I shall consider no dogmatic aspects of religion; the particular kind of problem discussed is presumably of equal importance to analytically minded people educated in various faiths.

No question of the traditional encounter between nineteenth-century science and nineteenth-century religion is discussed; we do not now live in that period, and its problems, however instructive in retrospect, are not those that we have to solve. The problem of the conflict between the account of creation in Genesis and that implied by palaeontology may still occasionally arise in the classroom, but it is not an important educational issue today. The problem of the nature of the human soul and its survival after bodily death, which in the past has frequently been an area of debate between primarily scientific and primarily religious people, is likewise not considered explicitly, though it is a source of anxiety to some. All such questions will be regarded as special cases of a much more pervasive and educationally significant problem: namely, to what extent does the method that we call scientific investigation give a true and a complete picture of existence?

The attempt to answer this question leads to the conclusion, firstly, that in studying increasingly large and increasingly small aspects of the universe, we probably have before us two fields of investigation that can never be completely known. Science is probably in this way inexhaustible. It is secondly also possible that science is inexhaustible in the same sense as mathematics is inexhaustible owing to the existence of unprovable propositions in mathematics, which could have physical models in nature. It is evident thirdly that, when we study human behavior by the ordinary technique of building conceptual models of various isolated processes, we run into difficulties of an epistemological sort owing to the fact that some of the conceptual models can actually be physically realized. The question whether an electronic brain thinks cannot be solved except by denying any kind of intuitively significant meaning to the word think, so that we have to admit that we do not know what we are. Fourthly, the only region so far encountered in the whole of empirical science which seems to bear on this last problem leads to such paradoxical results that it is not accepted at all by many scientists, and, if accepted, is admittedly at the mercy of a kind of uncertainty principle due to inevitable interference by the experimenter with the results of the experiment.

It is concluded that scientific investigation, though it leads to results that are convergently true, is certainly and probably permanently an incomplete mode of knowledge. Since we live in the universe which is incompletely known and probably incompletely knowable, we must live our lives using everything at our disposal and not merely the scientifically mapped part of reality. Statements outside the scientific body of knowledge are inevitably made in a language which is formally derived as metaphor from language describing the investigable world. Yet words will have different meanings in the scientific and theological languages.

It is obviously impossible to give, in a few paragraphs, an account of the present state of scientific knowledge as a whole. The aspects of the known external world to be presented are chosen because they appear to be relevant to the present discussion.

The universe accessible to investigation is, even by terrestrial standards, immense, of radius of the order of 10^{21} or 10^{22} miles.

It is uncertain whether it is better regarded as part of an open infinite system or whether it is closed though unbounded.[1]

The major, more or less discrete, objects in the universe are galaxies or enormous collections of stars and clouds of dust. The number of these systems in the accessible universe is of the order of billions. There is evidence of some sort of an irregular pattern in their distribution. They appear in general to be moving away from each other, giving the impression of an "expanding universe." This effect has often suggested that, initially, all the matter in the universe was collected together. Such a state would imply a creation at a specific time, or it could imply an excessively unlikely random collection of matter achieved in the course of infinite time. Dates for creation can be derived from other phenomena and are in general of the order of 6,000,000,000 years ago. It has, however, recently been widely held that such dates are specious. In an infinite universe which was apparently expanding locally, matter would seem to be disappearing. In order to maintain a steady state, matter would have to be continually created locally. This view has appealed to certain investigators on the ground that it permits the postulate that at any time and at any place the general large-scale features of the external world are the same. It does so at the price of introducing an entirely unexplained random creation of matter at an arbitrary rate, which is, however, so small that it is most unlikely that it could be directly detected instrumentally in the foreseeable future.

One galaxy, known to us as The Galaxy or Milky Way, has a moderate-sized star about halfway from its center and edge, which we know as the sun. Around the sun, a number of planets revolve and on one of them we live. It is very probable that on one other planet, namely Mars, there is a low form of life, which, if we could examine it, we should probably regard as vegetable. It is quite likely that several species of such organisms exist on Mars; their physiology must be most peculiar. The evidence for their existence is primarily the changing color of certain areas of the planet's surface in circumstances suggesting growth. The observed existence of life on earth, the probable presence of life on Mars, and the fact that, when a mixture of gases comparable to those likely to have formed an early atmosphere of a planet is subjected to a silent electric discharge or other source of high energy, a vast number of organic compounds is formed, all suggest that, given a suitable environment, living matter evolves spontaneously. That it is not observed to evolve in nature today is due to the fact that the earth is already populated with bacteria which would decompose the initial organic compounds, and to the fact that the oxygen of the air itself, largely a biological product, screens the surface of the earth from the short-wave radiation of the sun, which would be the required source of energy.

Once life has started, it appears to evolve by a process of variation followed by natural selection or survival of the more favored varieties. The variation process appears, within the limits available to an organism, to be essentially random. When we attempt to analyze the ordinary physiological behavior of organisms, in every known case an analysis in terms of the process of physics and chemistry appears to be possible.

In some of the less complicated physiological processes, such as that by which the energy in a molecule of glucose is converted into mechanical work by the contraction of a muscle, we now have a fairly complete account of what is happening. Though this is one of the simpler biological events, its physico-chemical description is extremely complicated. It involves at least twenty chemical changes in relatively simple organic compounds and a set of changes in the much more complex fibrous protein system of the muscle fiber which lead to those changes in position of the parts of the molecule that appear macroscopically as shortening of the muscle fiber. Though these changes in position are visually understandable in terms of models, when we inquire into the actual processes involving the forces binding together the constituent atoms, we enter a world in which visual macroscopic models are less and less significant. As soon as we want an analysis not in molecular terms, but in terms of subatomic phenomena, ordinary macroscopic modes of presentation become useless. Entities which are particles at one moment are waves at another, energy is no longer transferable in a continuous stream but only in discontinuous packets, and we can only make statements about the probability of an event and not its definite occurrence. There is nothing surprising in this. Our senses have evolved to deal with phenomena in a world of great size compared even with the largest molecules. What we regard as the true visual appearance of objects is determined by this. When we look at things we ask about phenomena which initially can be sensed directly. Later in the analysis, we reach a state when the properties of the smaller and smaller entities become increasingly unfamiliar. This is true of the nonliving as well as the living parts of the world. The results of the application of scientific method is to produce a series of explanations of increasing generality, in terms of well-defined relationships between increasingly abstract entities. Anyone who doubts this has merely to sit in the sun with a copy of the *Astrophysical Journal*.

In view of the fact that the methods of investigation available to us do not give us absolute and certain truth, it is legitimate to inquire how true the current scientific view of the world is likely to be. The answer is, I think, that over the field that is being considered something very like our world picture must be in a certain sense largely true. Quantitative details will certainly be revised, but in general such revision will tend to make the universe older, larger, and containing more subsystems. It is exceedingly unlikely that the apparent age of the earth or of any of the major systems used to determine "ages of the universe," would prove to be much less than the figure given. An age as low as 600,000,000 years is so improbable as to be hardly worth considering. An age for the earth as great as 60,000,000,000 years seems intuitively rather less improbable, but nevertheless is not at all probable. This is a matter of importance in the present context, because there has sometimes been a tendency to conclude that, since scientists are always changing their minds, their conclusions are of little general interest. Scientists certainly are always changing their minds, but within very definite limits; in any science developing healthily, the limits moreover tend to decrease.

Apart from the ordinary epistemological difficulties, such as the sense-data problem, it is evident that there are at least two major barriers, or at least areas of increasing difficulty, namely the study of the very large and that of the very small. In both cases the conceptual procedures become difficult, and there is no certain guarantee that they can be developed indefinitely. In the intermediate region it is usually supposed that the main difficulties are in matters of technique. I have, however, a very strong suspicion that there are really three main areas of increasing difficulty, the third being the study of events that are commonly spoken of as mental or psychological. The ordinary method of procedure in this area nowadays is to build theoretical models embodying sets of relationships between entities which are either unanalyzed or are believed to be reducible to physicochemical terms. In such models, the boundaries are regarded as spatiotemporal of an ordinary kind, so that whatever may enter or leave the system is considered to be a signal or series of signals bearing information, which at any moment is describable in any desired degree of detail in terms of ordinary physics. This method of procedure has proved extraordinarily successful. A monistic system accepting no postulates save those of the laws of physics as now known has sufficed, it is often claimed, to provide explanations of phenomena wherever they have been sufficiently analyzed. It is illegitimate according to the rule of procedure known as the principle of parsimony, or the simplicity postulate, or Occam's razor, to introduce any entity into a theory where it is not needed. It is, therefore, argued that, since nothing has been shown to be needed so far, apparent demonstrations of additional needs in limited areas are likely to prove specious. The whole position is of some interest in the present context because it is a special case of an argument also used to deny any validity to religion.

The most cogent argument that has been brought against religious ideas by scientists is that such ideas add unnecessary terms to scientific theory. The idea of God is held to be an unnecessary addition, either because, as to Laplace,[2] it adds nothing to an analytical explanation, or because it can be used to provide an unlimited number of *ad hoc* pseudo explanations. For this reason, it is important to consider as carefully as possible the simplicity postulate, or Occam's razor. The idea is certainly an old one. Occam (*de Corpore Christi,* 28) uses it quite casually in the form *non est necesse ponere*

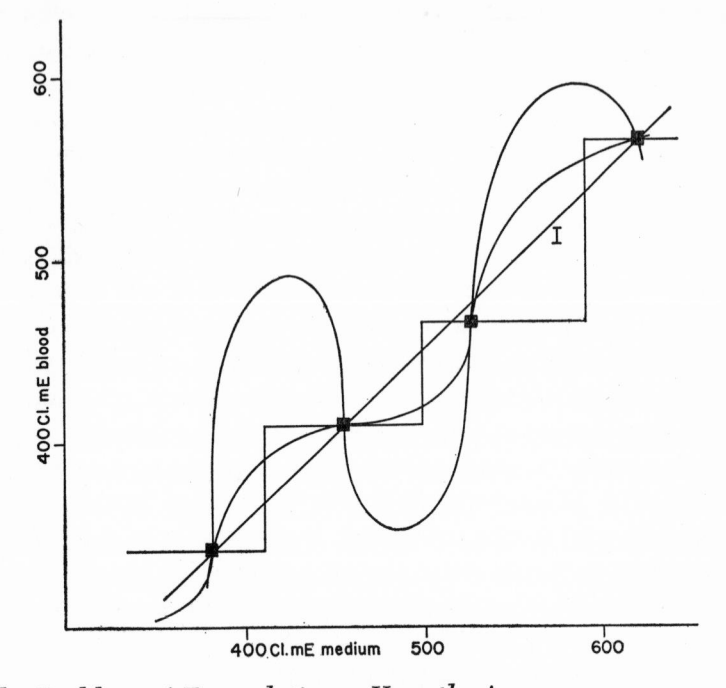

The Problem of Formulating a Hypothesis

Diagram illustrating the problem of decision in formulating a hypothesis to account for a set of facts. The actual data, which are irrelevant to the discussion, are the blood chloride concentrations of hagfishes in sea water of varying chlorinity.

talem . . . et ita frustra poneretur. Occam would have been horrified to have known that God was what it is not necessary to postulate, but very many people, apart from Laplace, have held such a view in discussing the universe. It will, however, be best to begin on a less grandiose scale.

Suppose we have a set of observations of two variables determined simultaneously in an experiment, which can be plotted as on the figure. It is possible to draw through these points an indefinite number of curves. Some of these curves have been drawn in the figure. The problem that arises is what criterion have we for deciding on any particular curve. Practically everyone would choose the straight line (*I*) and would be fairly confident that, if further observations were to be made, their choice would be vindicated. Since the straight line can be described by the minimum number of coefficients and involves only the first power of the independent variable, departure from it is equivalent to adding unnecessary postulates, which according to the rule must not be done.

If the rule is a valid one, it therefore appears that, before we have actually proceeded to construct any hypothesis, there is a certain prior probability that hypotheses of a certain kind, namely those with few terms, are more likely to be verified than those with many terms.

It would seem extremely odd if the universe actually were constructed in this way, and much more likely that the apparent high probability of the simple hypothesis is introduced into the argument surreptitiously by the investigator. If we suppose, given a body of confirmed theory T_n and a new set of observations relating to the subject matter of T_n, there is a infinite number of ways of proceeding to an increased body of theory T_{n+1} it is obvious that there must be a priori a distribution of probabilities so that some methods of proceeding are more probable than others. If this were not the case, since there is an indefinite number of ways of proceeding, each would have an indefinitely small probability of being true and we should never find a reasonable hypothesis. Actually, unless T_n gives us a lot of hints as to what the new data may mean, we should probably have to be content with a rather unsatisfactory empirical statement that the two variables look as though they are related in simple proportionality. The somewhat more complex hypotheses such as:

$$Y = k\left[(1-e^{-x}) - \frac{1}{15}(1-e^{-9x}) + \frac{1}{45}(1-e^{-25x}) \; . \; . \; . \right]$$

which would give for small values of x a graph hardly different from the straight line, are likely not to be tried, unless T_n predicted that this was the sort of relationship likely to be found in material of the kind treated in the theory. For example, if we are dealing with growth, a proportionality to a logarithm of some observable parameter would be the most reasonable simple expectation.

What the simplicity postulate really says is that early in an investigation we know less than when we have made further advances, and that the terms must be added one by one, if we want to keep erroneous theory to a minimum. The simplest hypothesis is to be preferred, because it makes the minimum number of statements and so reduces the chance that the whole hypothesis is wrong. At any given stage in the development of science, there will be regions of such great difficulty that no hypothesis of any predictive power can yet be invented. These may be approached stepwise often over a long period of time. The whole distance early in the investigation will seem impossible; the last step will probably, when all preceding steps have been taken, appear reasonably simple. There is no evidence that the whole of the universe can be investigated, merely experience that we can build up a body of generated information dealing with increasingly more of the universe. Occam's razor therefore merely clears the most practical path immediately ahead of us.[3]

This does not mean that, when we are confronted with the whole of experience, and must live our lives in conformity with such experience, the simplicity postulate is necessarily a good rule to follow. We can in fact be confident that what we cannot deal with analytically is likely to be as complex as what we can. Occam's razor, unless used discreetly and stepwise, certainly would let us down in the study of the investigable parts of the universe; how far it can help in facing what cannot be stated in the form of cognitive propositions, only experience can tell. It is certainly an abuse of the principle to use it to exclude the whole field of experience not so describable, or to attempt to use it to limit what we may try to think about.

I am here using the word "investigable" to indicate everything which can be described in a series of propositions constituting the language of science, S, publicly verifiable in principle, which may be either analytic or synthetic. The question of the existence of noninvestigable existents is obviously a difficult one because no constructive definition in S can be given of any such things if they exist. I am inclined, however, to regard all directly known sensations and images as at least containing uninvestigable elements, such as the quality yellow as it is perceived, as distinct from the publicly defined color of light of wave length about 5890 Å, or the electrophysiological changes that might be studied in the perception of such light. It will be apparent from the argument of the next two sections that the existence of such uninvestigable aspects of sensation is not as trivial or unimportant a matter as many modern philosophers appear to have thought. All statements that attempt to refer specifically to such uninvestigable subjective aspects of experience fall outside the S language, even though they make up a large part of what we attempt to say.

It is also just possible that, since it is now known that there must be undecidable problems in any well-developed consistent mathematical system, physical systems may exist that constitute special cases of models of undecidable problems. In such cases, no general scientific theory may be realizable, but only empirically known special cases which can be classified under some general inductive statement that cannot be properly explicated. The four-color problem on a plane, if it should turn out to be unprovable, would provide an instance of the sort of situation involved, though this is a trivial case scientifically, however deep it may be mathematically. At least these two kinds of examples should prepare us to accept uninvestigable aspects of reality.

At the present time there is an enormous technological growth of machines for performing operations that are ordinarily thought of as human. These may be of the nature of goal-seeking devices as in certain kinds of automatic weapons, or they may be computers capable of performing elaborate operations which formerly would have required impossibly large numbers of human arithmeticians. In practice we do not award posthumous decorations for valor to exploded missiles, and membership in learned societies is for the designers of computers rather than for the computers themselves. In practice, thoughtful people appear to be able to distinguish men from machines. A number of machines, however, are capable of quite dramatic learning, such as Shannon's maze-running electronic mouse and the various devices of Ashby and of Grey-Walter. It is, moreover, quite possible in theory to build a self-reproducing machine, though in practice the expense might well prove prohibitive. Machines can obviously be taught to answer nonoperational questions, such as "Are you conscious?" or "Are you aware of the presence of God?" in the affirmative. In spite of this, most people would feel able to distinguish in a practical way between men and machines. Actually it seems probable from the various discussions of the problem, that the criteria of distinction are empirical characters, such as chemical composition, size, shape, rapidity of output, none of which has any obvious fundamental connection with the problem.[4]

In principle, if we can build machines which can calculate, make decisions, embark on new courses of action, communicate with one another, make unverifiable remarks, exhibit neurotic behavior, and reproduce, there is no theoretical reason why a single machine incorporating all these types of behavior should not be built. It is indeed usually conceded that, if we really understand a process, we can in theory design a machine that will imitate the process. This proposition depends on the meaning of "understand," but in the ordinary reductive sense in which the word is commonly used in science, the proposition is certainly true. From a strictly empirical point of view, we should have to admit that the difference between such a machine and a living being would be that it was of an entirely different shape and size, was composed of metal, various dielectrics, and gas under low pressure, rather than of proteins in an aqueous phase, and that it used the sun as an energy source via the waterfall or heat energine and power station instead of the cornfield or the ox, and that initially it had been created by man.

Even though the machine should protest when tampered

with, no one at first would believe that it felt pain, and, if some people came to believe this, we should feel justified in regarding them as neurotic sentimentalists. The ordinary objection to regarding the machine and man as both living is that if the man says he is conscious of his own activities, we believe him, but if the machine were to say so we should not believe it. It is obvious that this criteria is completely nonoperational. It begs the question it asked in S, and can never be applied in making an actual decision.

It is evident to the present writer that, in the greater part of biology as in the sciences of the inanimate world, a reductive theory in which no concepts that are not ultimately based in physical theory are needed, is quite adequate for the present state of our knowledge. Occam's razor warns us that, if we attempt to stray from the reductive path, we shall run into a tangle of hypotheses of every degree of complexity and that, even if one happens to be truer than anything we have, we should have a very small chance of finding it in the tangle. The only way in which we might be able to discover if the reductive procedure can let us down is to start investigating those areas in which it seems least likely from previous experience that it will work. We must then make every effort to find a reductive explanation in such areas; only after such efforts are exhausted have we any right to conclude that something other than physical principles are operating.

Since we have run into an impasse about the consciousness of a machine built to imitate cerebral behavior, while no such impasse exists anywhere else in biology, it would seem worth while to consider whether in the study of purportedly conscious behavior[5] we might find nonreductive processes. Logically perhaps there is no reason why the epistemological difficulties of the conscious machine should suggest that reductive theory might break down. It is, however, reasonable to suppose that situations of this sort, since they involve to each of us experience of noninvestigable subjective elements, are likely to be fertile if faced imaginatively. This view, that conscious behavior involves something special, has been strenuously opposed by most academic psychologists, partly because they rightly feel that reductive theory must come first and partly because they are quite wrongly afraid, like so many primitive people, of sorcery.

The particular phenomena to be considered are what are commonly called parapsychological, a category including primarily the various kinds of extrasensory perception and of psychokinesis. The experimental basis for accepting extrasensory perception is largely that when certain people are asked to write down a series of symbols, there is sometimes fairly clear evidence that the frequency and order of the symbols is determined either by certain material series of marks that are not physically accessible to the subject (clairvoyance) or by sequences of images in other people's minds (telepathy). The experimental evidence for psychokinesis is based on the position of dice thrown at random when someone is wishing for a particular number or other kind of position. The effects can be positive or negative; in the case of dice-throwing significant negative results (i.e., statistically too few sixes when six is wished for) seem to be particularly common. There are sometimes curious displacements in time, so that later events reported in the mind of one person appear to have a statistical effect on earlier events in the mind of another.[6] In every case the experiments have to be described in sentences in some of which reference is made to reports, not in S language, by some of the participants.

Until recently, most investigators have tended to shy away from this field. More recently, it has seemed to many that only two alternatives are offered by the published data. Either the whole thing is a gigantic hoax, or the main results of the best parapsychological experiments are in the main valid, i.e., the propositions describing such results are with a very high degree of probability likely to be true.

The hypothesis that the results are a hoax involves systematic dishonesty on the part of a number of supposedly respectable people. It cannot ideally be proved untrue because, whenever anyone previously skeptical does an experiment giving ostensibly positive results, the remaining skeptics can merely claim that the experimenter has joined the hoaxers. It is claimed by those who adopt the hoax hypothesis that the latter is a priori much more probable than is telepathy, clairvoyance, or psycho-kinesis, that no amount of evidence in favor of these classes of alleged phenomena can counterbalance their negligible probability of existence.

This argument is hardly based on prescientific experience prior to scientific study, because the impression given in daily life due to coincidence, simultaneous reception of identical sensory cues, and the like, is that there is far more telepathy actually occurring than anyone who seriously studied the matter would claim.

From the standpoint of the present work, the important results of such researches are first, that it seems very unlikely that any reductive theory, based on our present understanding of the inanimate part of the universe, is likely to be of help here. Ultimately, some sort of unified theory including para-psychology may become possible, but it is unlikely to resemble the physicochemical theory believed to underlie most of biol-ogy. It must, however, be pointed out that it is not inconceiv-able that further progress along these lines may be virtually impossible owing to the phenomena being too sensitive to uncontrollable parapsychological influences of the experi-menters. It would seem not impossible that a sort of uncer-tainty principle, presumably only faintly analogous to that encountered in physics, is involved. This possibility should not be used as an argument against research in this extremely important though often discouraging field. Even the smallest positive results, such as we now have, challenge the commonly accepted view of the content of scientific theory. The area should obviously be investigated far more intensively, but with the full understanding that the results may be very few, though enormously significant.

There is no guarantee that we can investigate everything that exists. The known existence of undecidable problems in mathematics and the possibility that some unsolved problems which may, like the four-color problem, be general models of physical situations in nature and may reflect some undecidable situation, suggests that uninvestigable areas may exist. It would seem that the criteria for discriminating between living systems of the highest degree of complexity and inanimate artifacts may involve properties such as shape, size, or kinds of atoms involved that a philosopher would hardly consider to be fundamental. The problem of the machine built to say that it is conscious raises the difficulty of how one knows that it is not.

Parapsychological phenomena which are apparently associated with conscious human minds seem to be nonreductive in the present state of knowledge. It is possible that investigation of such phenomena may lead nowhere should they prove to be, as by their nature seems almost inevitable, continually interfered with by the personality of the experimenter.

Wittgenstein's famous dictum "whereof one cannot speak, thereof one must be silent" has seemed hopelessly constricting to most people. Since it is apparent that communication of a nonverbal sort is continually going on even if we try to remain silent, it is not only constricting but completely impractical, even lethal.

Most people now recognize the propositions of religious belief and the sentences of religious ritual as continuous attempts to do what Wittgenstein told us we must not do and what humanity continually declares it must do. The justification of this behavior is obvious. We cannot neglect that part of reality about which we cannot make publicly verifiable statements. Being social and cultural animals, we want to transmit our insight into the uninvestigable parts of the universe no less than our discoveries about the investigable parts. We have a language in which publicly verifiable statements about the latter parts can be made. We borrow its elements, make them into metaphor, add everything we can think of, and fail to make ourselves clear when we try to deal with our insight in the inductively uninvestigable parts. *Introibo ad altare Dei* means one thing at the beginning of the Roman mass; it may mean something quite different at the beginning of Joyce's *Ulysses*.

At the present time all that I would as a scientist ask of the theologians and of the nonrigorous philosophers is that they make quite clear in what language they are talking. It is for instance extremely cruel to torture the minds of the young with problems relating to free will and determinism in which half the propositions employed relate to the scientific S language, and the other half to a metaphorical T language developed for theological purposes. In S, the dichotomy is presumably between determined and not-determined, and in some cases a continuum of partially determined states is permissible. In S, the not-determined is presumably random. The moralist not sure of his language is likely to protest, though in vain, that he wants nonrandom, nondetermined behavior on the part of responsible free human beings. But in the metaphorical language T, we may pray "O God, who art the author of peace and lover of concord, in knowledge of whom standeth our eternal life, *whose service is perfect freedom.* . . ." In such a statement as that italicised, considered as a statement in S, there is an obvious inconsistency, for the service of God at any given time, for any given individual, presumably presupposes a unique mode of behavior. Considered as a statement in T, the verification of which is a matter of individual experience, and in which the meaning of "service of God" and that of "freedom" are implicit in such a nonpublic verification, the statement can at least personally be known to be both true and nonparadoxical.

Margaret Masterman, moreover, has given indications (*Theology* 54 [1951]: 82-87) of a most penetrating and ingenious way in which statements of an apparently paradoxical kind in theological language can be submitted to a quite rigorous kind of logical analysis. The possibility of such an analysis is a matter of very great importance. There are far too many Christians who, catching desperately at St. Paul's remarks about "foolishness to the Greeks" and finding the existentialists easier reading than either the scholastics or modern logic, glory in the absurdity of their faith, until religion is regarded as shallow unless intellectually ridiculous, and intellectual activities immoral. To such ends surely we were not born.

GEORGE N. SHUSTER

Religion and the Professions

CHAPTER XI

Training for the professions has become the principal business of modern higher education in this country as well as in foreign lands. This fact probably more than any other differentiates our practice sharply from that of the past. It is noteworthy, for example, that so far as one is able to determine the Romans knew neither schools of architecture nor colleges of engineering. We are left to surmise that the men who erected such glorious functional structures as the aqueduct at Caserta and the Black Gate, the *porta nigra* of Trier, must have learned their craft as members of a guild fostered by the army. Of equal interest though of more recent vintage is the circumstance that during a century of discoveries as brilliant as those of our own, the Royal Society could bring together, discuss, and promulgate the findings of otherwise isolated thinkers, Newton and Halley among them, who to our way of thinking had been trained for mathematical studies only. Drawing generalized conclusions from such data would be perilous. They serve both critics and commenders of our time. Perhaps one may not injudiciously say that what is most novel and significant in this development is that a procedure has now been established for readily bringing the discoveries made by men of great stature to the attention of the many fledgling scholars so that they in turn can embed the meaning of these discoveries in a growing awareness of that "accumulated knowledge" which, as Dr. Conant has said, is another name for science. This knowledge has now become the principal source of dynamism in a highly complex industrial society.

So far-reaching in pertinence for the social well-being of the race has this change in educational method become and so difficult is it now to master the data made available to the student for a profession that several fateful consequences have ensued. First, professional education has forced its way back into the colleges by means of what has until recently been an ever-increasing demand for prerequisites, and at the same time it has forced its way into doctoral programs. Of course it has not everywhere succeeded in having its way, and there are even some indications of a change of heart. Yet who will deny, in spite of many protestations, that a "broad, general training" is favored by business and some of the professions, that for very many young people, male and female alike (as well as, perhaps, for most of their teachers), the vocation remains the solely significant consideration and that whatever hampers pursuit of it is likely to seem peripheral or even a waste of time? Second, the number of professions with which the college and the university are at present concerned has notably increased. To use just one example, training for "commerce" is now capped with instruction in business administration. Similarly, the "calling" of yore has become the "profession" of today. Thus home economists are no longer women who have learned to cook, sew, and mind the baby but are masters of the chemistry of nutrition and students of the sociology of family living. The third consequence is no doubt materialistic but, even so, important: the financial support required by the major kinds of professional education is tremendous, and in not a few instances the sums needed can be secured by university administrations only by curtailing other scholarly activities.

Although I am here discussing the professions as a single group, it is important to note a few of the contrasts among them. Most of the guidance professions—notably medicine, law, and teaching—are as old as recorded history, though new ones like social work and psychological counseling are seeking to establish themselves in our society and have to some extent succeeded. The technological professions, such an engineering and architecture, are relatively new, whereas those identified with administration, in a variety of forms, are quite modern. True enough, a number of European educational institutions, primarily the German *Handelshochschule,* have in the past manifested some concern with the arts of management, but this was usually casual and never systematic. At any rate, it seems rather significant that the guidance professions have had and still retain a greater interest in the liberal arts and specifically in religion than do the others, exception having been duly made in this country for the War College and certain other establishments for the training of government personnel. This is in part no doubt attributable to the fact that the guidance professions, as counseling agencies, must take into consideration every aspect of human life and behavior. It is not unrealistic to believe that teachers and students of the law may be concerned with Plato, or Kant's *Critique of the Practical Reason,* or the Canon Law. Yet no doubt the impact of modern life has also made itself felt in the trend towards exclusion of all but professional interests. Who would suppose, for example, that an up-to-date school of business administration would normally make a point of discussing Paul's Epistle to the Romans?

If, then, this is the situation—if the subject matter of professional education has become so many-sided, so hard to master, and so completely absorbing, and if there be that in the time which has seemingly dictated a retreat from concern with religious and humanistic subjects—how shall one counsel the university to foster a living interest in the literature of the spirit? Let us note first of all that whenever religion is of primary importance to an individual he will seek it out, even if need be by retiring in high dudgeon to a Trappist monastery. "Every spirit," said Emerson, "builds itself a house; and beyond its house a world; and beyond its world, a heaven." This is probably as true in Russia as it is with us. But our trouble generally, I believe, is hardly that most of us do not want a place for some kind of religion in our mansions, but that we think first of the plumbing, the furnace, and the kitchen. When we get round to planning a room with a shrine in it, all that is usually left is the attic. And of course there is forever with us the fear that becoming too deeply immersed in religion involves the danger of drowning. Or at least of having to wear a special brand of bathing suit. "Philosophy," said Newton, "is such an impertinently litigious lady that a man has as good be engaged in lawsuits as to have to do with her." No doubt many feel, secretly or overtly, that way about religion.

At any rate, religious issues or commitments currently play a very minor role in professional education conducted under public auspices. As a matter of fact, the lines assigned to them are not particularly impressive in private institutions either, even when these are directly associated with a church. Sometimes courses of formal instruction in what is called theology are offered as are classes in philosophy; but conversations with persons teaching these do not convey the impression that students look forward to them with impatient enthusiasm. This does not by any means indicate that the official attitudes of the schools themselves are hostile or perfunctorily tolerant. On the contrary. The prevailing frame of mind in publicly supported institutions certainly appears to be one of benevolent neutrality. While many administrators and professors think they haven't time to bother with such matters, they usually have a feeling that religion is something that quite reputable people cherish, or that it is much better represented in thoughtful literature than used to be the case. Surely *Life* would not offer its readers a series of expensively illustrated articles on the great faiths of the world and then reissue these in a handsome volume costing a tidy sum if there were not "something to them"! In addition the clergy, if not held in high esteem, at least are likely to be tolerated or even befriended. With us, for example, the popular institution of Masonry is not anticlerical though it has been that in a number of European countries. There is a good deal of criticism of the local priest or minister, but so is there of the mayor and the Secretary of State. On the whole, the American attitude seems to be that a clergyman is at least a necessary evil. To paraphrase Voltaire, if he did not exist it would be necessary to invent him.

But what is the educator to do about it? There is no campus outcry for the healing of the spirit. The religious practice of the professional student (even when he is in the strict sense a preprofessional student) naturally varies greatly, but is as a general rule an unperturbed reflection of commitments made during earlier years. Parental allegiances, young people's groups of many kinds, talks with clergymen, Sunday morning instruction—all these leave marks, more or less indelible, on the prospective engineer or chemist. But, exception having duly been made for elites, the average professional student's association with religious life appears to be shallow and perfunctory. In his better moments he considers it a valuable moral prophylactic agent but not a quest which can enlist in any notable way the active powers of his mind. That it might do him good he is likely to surmise, but that he might devote himself to it with gusto is another matter. To these conclusions one is led by a variety of forms of evidence, ranging all the way from public opinion surveys to sociological studies and to what is garnered through personal experience. There are medical students, for example—I have met some of them at Harvard and have been greatly impressed with their earnestness—who are on fire with zeal. But there are very many such students who do not greatly care whether the soul be in the pituitary gland, the cerebrum, or nowhere in particular.

That this constitutes a grave danger, quite apart from all considerations of an individual's well-being in the life to come, is obvious to anyone who believes that the assumptions of religion are correct. For with what moods and goals in view is a man to lead his life? It is fatally easy to fall into the habit of thinking that technical ends are good in themselves if ends established through contemplation of the transcendental are not normally, naturally, the firm props of one's spirit. It would of course be easy to buttress this view with quotations from saints and theologians. If Newman was right in saying that there are only "two luminously self-evident beings—myself and my Creator," a man to whom neither is at all "luminous" must be sitting in spiritual shade. But there are many more mundane commentators. How one could wish that many educators would read and ponder carefully The German Catastrophe by Friedrick Meinecke, the unforgettable teacher of a generation of

American historians! This little book chronicles step by step, as it were, the way in which the moral consciousness of a great nation's elite, engrossed with the power of doing, could descend irrevocably from awareness of ethical ideals to their complete insensitivity. No one can leaf through the great, tragic debate between the spokesmen for Nazism and their noblest antagonists without seeing how the descent to the abyss took place. Consider, for instance, a secret memorandum, recently come to light, which Heinrich Himmler wrote on the subject of the education of youth in conquered territories:

> A basic question to be put when considering these problems [i.e., those of the Occupation] is, what is to be done with schooling, and therewith what is to be attempted in the supervision and sifting out of youth. For the non-German populations of the East, no higher school must be permitted to exist than an elementary school limited to four years.
>
> The objective of such a school can only be to teach simple arithmetic to a peak of the number 500, and to expound the teaching that there is a Divine command to obey the Germans, and to be honest, diligent and considerate. Reading I do not consider necessary.
>
> Apart from the school thus described, there are to be no educational institutions in the East. Parents who seek to secure a better training for their children at the elementary as well as at the higher levels must make application to the principal officers of the SS and the Police. Each such application will be considered in the light of whether the child is above criticism from the racial point of view and conforms with our other requirements. If we accept such a child as being of our blood, it will be explained to the parents that the youngster is to go to school in Germany and is to remain there permanently.

It may seem incredible that such sentiments could once constitute the official educational philosophy of a mighty power. But if one accepts Himmler's premises the conclusions are inescapable. German blood is the highest good; all other blood, particularly that of the Jews, is the property of menials; and accordingly the first is entitled to education while the second is not. This reasoning is no doubt based on lamentably bad genetics, and yet not too many years ago doctrine akin to it was widely credited in the United States, and not only because men responsible for it were antagonistic to the Negro. At all events, it was scarcely a wonder that almost the last and bravest deed of the illustrious physicist Max Planck was to speak eloquently to his students about the necessity for a theistic religion. Where else, in the laboratory or outside it, might one expect to find a convincing answer to the monstrously cruel abracadabra which was then bent on leading the world to destruction? And in a comparable, contemporary fashion, the same protests have been voiced against Communist rule.

Many Americans do not wish to consider this form of argument. They feel that it is lacking in validity insofar as the concrete present is concerned. I cannot refrain from saying by way of reply: what has happened elsewhere does as a matter of fact take place here. During the heyday of the Communist movement in New York, we saw that colleagues who were good, indeed in some instances first-rate, scholars and quite affable persons did not hesitate to undertake the basest acts of character defamation, dishonesty, and utterly indefensible cruelty if the party line demanded it of them. As a friend said of an especially agreeable comrade, after he was caught in an act of flagrant and harmful lying, had he been a commissar he would cheerfully have stood the rest of us with our backs against the wall. I recall that one amiable Communist said to me during the course of an animated conversation that he was devoting all his spare time to the study of Freud. A few weeks later, Moscow announced that thenceforth no party member in good standing would deviate from the teaching of Pavlov. Needless to say, the psychologist in question discarded Freud even as a moth does its cocoon and was soon exclusively engrossed in the works of the author of the conditioned reflex.

What interests our countrymen very much more at this time is the uneasy awareness that membership in the "managerial class," which is the ultimate social reward for having survived the particularly strenuous varieties of professional education, includes a gilt-edged subscription to "conformism." This phenomenon, as presented in dark outline by David Riesman and

William H. Whyte, may or may not be as disturbing as they maintain. It nevertheless is widespread, and as a result raises questions about intellectual and spiritual values that cry out for answers. Not a few of them are directed to our system of education, as Whyte in particular makes evident. If educators accept as the purpose of education the studious preparation of our most gifted men and women for "belongingness," they must inevitably assume responsibility for the results. So also, however, must religion. If the growing church membership in suburbia is just one more approved form of "belongingness," then it is surely incumbent on the churches to study carefully the social ethic of which they have become the staunch if sometimes unwitting supporters.

As Will Herberg, commenting on Whyte's book, has indicated, the problem to be faced is one of "personal authenticity in a world of all-engulfing mass heteronomy." Assuredly this problem is one which drives education and religion into at least an uneasy partnership. Is there something which they must, and therefore can, do together in order to foster the freedom of awareness which is the significant first half of freedom of conscience? Certainly this, whatever it is, will not be achieved by a proclamation, an addendum to the curriculum, or even a Religious Emphasis Week. It can only come into being as a result of a thoughtful, uncompromising study of the general spiritual situation in which we now find ourselves.

The few words of comment on this situation which I shall offer here form only a short and very meager prolegomenon to such a study. If they can evoke dissent and spur on thought they will have served their purpose adequately. We live in a world whose destinies are being determined by science and from which since the middle years of the nineteenth century religion has stood apart. It seems to me that the fundamental difference between the religious and the scientific attitudes is that the second inevitably rests on a principle of agreement, while the core of religious experience is differentiation, which upon occasion can be a very rugged kind of individualism or, indeed, heresy of no indecisive kind. As the lives of Pasteur and Einstein will illustrate, most newly discovered scientific formulae are, to be sure, born to the tune of disputation. But once established they are necessarily assented to, because they are adequate to account for the phenomena they describe. This is true also of certain areas in the social sciences. But every great religion is a corporate union of individual persons, each of whom has his wholly separate, startingly lonely, relationship with the Lord God. "The way to God is the way of God," Abraham Heschel has said profoundly, noting the awesome truth round which mystical theology revolves, namely that the adventure of faith belongs in the first instance to the Divine Huntsman seeking his quarry. The uniqueness of the religious experience will become still more apparent if one uses the word "ad-venture" in its primal Latin sense. "A coming to" God is not something anyone can arrange even for a friend. To realize this we have only to recall Augustine and his mother.

It seems to me that the basic reason why science and religion have been scandals unto one another is therewith laid bare. Men strictly brought up in accordance with what for lack of a better term is called "the scientific method" are first of all repelled by the fact that there are so many religions in the world all claiming to be true and evoking acrimonious discussion which cannot be resolved. They conclude, often regretfully, that since there is no way of bringing about agreement on one formulation, the verity that may be in the theologies can never be known. Or, alas, they may even decide that since Divinity is *Deus absconditus*, the hidden God, he is probably a fabrication. More generally they will feel that since the subject matter of religion is of a character wholly alien from that of science they should be content to leave it to others.

Religious men, on the other hand, are repelled by the absolutism—in their eyes a cold and sterile standardization—of science. They frequently tend, therefore, to fight it off, often hastily and angrily, whenever it seems to affect the core of the human personality. As a result, thought, which in the strict sense is not scientific at all—for example, the psychoanalytic procedures resorted to by Sigmund Freud—is rejected upon occasion as being an unholy concoction of the laboratory. But no doubt evolution is still the classic illustration. Because faith in Christ is historically allied with credence in the Scriptures, spokesmen for Protestant and Catholic churches permitted, during a fatefully long period, a very naïve and literal reading of Genesis to bar acceptance of facts that Darwin's studies of the origin of species had brought to light. This attitude was not merely obscurantist but foolhardy from the point of view of Christianity's own mission. Churchmen were correct, however, in opposing the truth they had learned through lives of prayer to doctrines which for a while seemed to be implicit in what Darwin and his associates were saying, namely, that all existence is at bottom only a fierce struggle for domination and survival. For through prayer, in its corporate historical forms and also in the actuality of personal realization, the truth of the reality of love is established.

The cleavage between science and religion cannot be surmounted by trying to prove that all faiths are, when one gets down to bedrock, the same. Arnold Toynbee has devoted his genius as a historian to this task, coming eventually to the conclusion that love for one's fellow men, as expressed in a purified Christianity and one form of Buddhism, is the fundamental religious commitment. Aldous Huxley's "perennial philosophy" establishes a comparable thesis with different argumentation. But interesting and useful though their speculative essays may be as expositions of religious positions arrived at by modern men of great talent, they do not help to dispose of the problem. It is true that Jesus Christ taught that the noblest commitments were to the love of God and of neighbor, but He also said with the strongest possible emphasis that there was no way to the Father save through Him. This "way" He outlined with dramatic clarity. It leads to the Cross, and there is no other route for Christians. Therefore, however deeply he may revere men who subscribe to other faiths and hold them in unwavering affection, he cannot escape the conviction that the roads down which they travel are the wrong ones. No one can doubt that the "exclusiveness" of Christianity is one highly important reason why science and religion have been in conflict. The Western world has been the cradle of scientific inquiry. It is also, uniquely, the area in which the basic cultural questions have for two thousand years been these: did Jesus have the right to say of Himself what He did say; and, if so, am I walking in His footsteps as he would have me do?

It may also be useful to consider briefly certain aspects of Christian history that appear to reinforce what has been said. The "existentialist" revolt against established Protestantism and the philosophy of Hegel that was set in motion by Sören Kierkegaard resembles in impressive ways the Protestant revolt against the Catholic church and the Scholastic philosophy that had its greatest spokesman in Martin Luther. In both cases the dominant convictions were that the ecclesiastical organization had become bureaucratic and therewith spiritually dull, that prosperity had paved the way of the Cross with asphalt and set up roadside inns on Calvary, and that acceptance of a philosophy (for Luther the target was Aristotelianism) making claims to universal validity crushed the personalism of religious experience. For many reasons it is unfortunate that Luther's uprising could not have assumed the form of a major house-cleaning within the Church, just as it is that the drastic, un-compromising Kierkegaard should have possessed so lim-ited an awareness of the social framework within which life is necessarily lived. But both do make clear that religion, even the Christian religion, is not a tranquilizer but an explosive, not just another prerequisite for club life in suburbia but a going out alone to the rim of the world, not soft music played at funerals merely but also a sudden clash of cymbals in the night and a man answering on his knees, "Depart from me, O Lord, for I am a sinful man!"

Of course, the religious community may also most legiti-mately be identified with warm human experience. Indeed, with us how regrettable that it is frequently not so associated —that the parish church is often like a doctor's office, to which one goes at regular intervals for a checkup; that usually the congregation is preached at and not talked with; and that the expression of love for others that normally accompanies wor-ship is dropping a dollar into the collection basket. From this

point of view certain trends in suburbia are promising and
might be aped on the campus. In their rescue of the individual
Riesman and Whyte outdo Kierkegaard. However greatly one
may disapprove of "belongingness," the fact remains that man
is not only a gregarious animal but a friend seeking friends.
It may be too bad that suburbia is serenely Catholic, Protestant,
and Jewish. But one surmises that even so it is better to live
in White Plains than it was to reside in Magdeburg during
the Thirty Years' War.

The conclusions to be drawn are not at all simple. Men need
in an age of the masses to deepen their awareness of personality
and conscience. They are driven also to find community with
their fellows on a basis that transcends material interests and
recognizes the worth of profound and holy aspirations. From
both points of view the race has never known any substitute
for religion. But the architect of the time is science—a builder
with whose genius we cannot dispense, for if he took his hand
away for an hour the edifice already erected would collapse.
On its ability to supply a steady stream of well-trained scientists
our society depends not merely for its well-being but for its
survival. Unfortunately, there is a gulf between the man of
science and the man of religion. This is not due to any gain-
saying of the one by the other, but to the undeniable fact that
the intuitions of the one are not those of the other. This is a
hard verity. Even harder is its corollary: if the two are not
conjoined, a man will be only half of himself.

So much for the prolegomenon to a study which, let us hope,
someone will sometime undertake. I am led by it to believe
that the task of the educator in any school for professional
men and the task of the teacher of religion is—to use a phrase
not unlike some of Luther's—to stick pins into each other
until they are awake and sufficiently agitated to do something
together to prepare young people for a nobler world than one
in which the best-tasting toothpaste is sold with the help of
the latest group dynamics by the glibbest advertising agency.
After they have got through eying each other askance, they
will have to reckon with the fact that young people will not
acquire religion by stirring a spoonful of it in their tea. A

number of uncomfortable facts will also have to be faced. The most immediate of them has already been alluded to— the plain, simple, sober truth that most of the young people under consideration have their eyes on a ranchhouse within commuting distance and often on precious little else.

The first remedial step is obviously to put religious teachers on the campus and see what they can do. In other words, Mark Hopkins must come and he will need a log to sit on. But when one tries to draw a blueprint of the characteristics of such a teacher working on a campus dedicated in whole or in part to professional education of first-rate quality, a number of queries present themselves. First of all, the man must have been adequately trained in his own theological discipline, which of course means that he will practice and expound a creed and not a common denominator of creeds. Second, if he is to succeed as a teacher his right to membership in the faculty must be based not on courtesy but on unimpeachably evident intellectual stature. He will possess insight into at least some of the philosophic and methodological implications that the habit of quite wholly absorbed living in the world of science has for the men and women about him. It seems to me self-evident, for example, that if he be stationed at a university or college where his principal concern will be with meeting students specializing in education, he will have made himself familiar with behaviorism as professed in many branches of psychological study, and with its achievements and limitations. All this does not mean that he is to bandy phrases about with the profession or to engage in useless controversies. What matters is that he knows intellectually those he meets. And finally, as a thinker in his own right, he will realize, with whatever measure of sadness, that engrossment in science has crowded out of many lives the practice of dialectic in virtually all its forms; and dialectic, whether it be that of Socrates or Aquinas, of Kierkegaard or Martin Buber, is the method by which religious insight has traditionally developed from naïve belief to intellectual realization. Ingrained habits of "positive" thinking are bound to be a theologian's major impediment to success.

When one tries to visualize whence religious teachers of such description are to come, and how they might be induced to undertake their mission with intelligence and enthusiasm, one is squarely face to face with a major conundrum. Such men are to be found, but they are very busy in theological seminaries, religiously affiliated colleges, editorial offices, or research institutions. The fact that in the United States theology is never a discipline in a university under public auspices (as it often is in Europe) is of major importance. If it were, teachers of the kind indicated would develop naturally on the campus. Therefore, if the study of religion is to acquire rank and status in our professional schools, particularly those on the graduate level, church sponsors have no choice save the education of trained and experienced representatives. They must also be ready to take for granted an environment that will not take kindly to old-fashioned interconfessional philippics. Conflict cannot be avoided altogether, but open and venomous warfare is a scandal to the young and a topic of derision for their elders. No doubt Americans do too often believe that sitting round a table will solve all problems of an intellectual character, but these faults cannot be corrected by highhanded and in a real sense scurrilous conduct.

We shall now assume that the requisite religious teachers have been found and that places have been made for them on the campus. What is the situation they will normally encounter? Administrators will be affable and attempt to reveal as little as possible of their traditional stuffed shirts—which are usually no more than the standard appendages of diplomacy and decorum. Inwardly, of course, they will feel a bit constrained or even worried lest something go awry and thunder be heard in distant episcopal sees. A few members of the faculty will lend ardent support, and a comparable number will prove irreconcilably hostile. But the great majority will pay no more attention to the representatives of religion than chemists do to astronomers, or the devotees of pedagogy to instructors in the "content subjects." There will be a student flock, sometimes prodded into membership by anxious parents, and also upon occasion, thank God, spurred on by their own deep convictions and ideals. In almost every instance, the religious culture of young people, as distinguished from religious practice, will have been developed prior to entering the professional school. This means that startling variations will appear. Sometimes, especially if a student has attended a good college, awareness of religious history and values will be quite adequate. But in general the training received will have been rudimentary, however satisfactory young people themselves may consider it; and unless a good deal is done the roots of faith will wither, sending up no shoot other than the instinct for "belongingness," which is unfortunately responsible for very much of what we currently term the religious revival. I think therefore that the initial stage of the academic mission must be the building of a community round the center of worship. This will make it possible for those less well prepared to be stimulated and encouraged by their better-trained companions, even while meeting the teacher in a familiar environment.

It is my profound conviction that once the community has been established, the first-rate religious teacher will find a deeply interested audience, like Newman's at Oxford or—in a quite different mode—Alain's in Paris. Granted such a following, there will be no barrier to the desired goal—namely, that courses in religion be offered for credit to students who wish to take them. For the most part, however, the student will come of his own volition to the religious center, in which we hope vigorous and fruitful discussion of life issues and problems is habitual. We very much need this kind of discussion for graduate students in particular, who are now the abandoned sheep of American university life. Let me add that at least a minimum of discreet and friendly co-operation between the protagonists of varying creeds is desirable (as indeed Pope Pius XII has indicated), though a perfunctory display of sham solidarity may well do more harm than good.

Now what of the campus as a whole? There are, I believe, two principal ways in which concern for religion can be developed on the campus, and these we shall now explore. First, habits of intellectual formation fortunately exist in professional schools that afford opportunities to religion, odd and paradoxical though they may at first sight seem. Let me give an example. American observers of medical practice returning from tours of exploration behind the Iron Curtain were struck by the impersonal, quite mechanistic approach to the patient as compared with our own, which when it is at all contemporary in spirit holds that therapy must begin with a consideration of the patient as a person. This difference some of the observers have attributed to the influence of psychotherapy on American medicine as contrasted with Communist reliance on a strait-laced version of Pavlovian psychology. Now it is well known that the art of psychoanalysis (for despite its use of scientific pigments it is an art) was at the outset definitely antireligious. The reasons why this was so were many and certainly included evidence (of which a great deal was made) that many neuroses could be traced to fears and inhibitions suggested by religious precepts. But as time has passed the fact that sound faith and good psychotherapy both establish the existence and paramount importance of the personality as an indubitable if always inexplicable entity has led many soundly trained and widely experienced medical men to conclude that the healing process of sublimation can be aided by religious practice as by nothing else. This is not because such practices are "tranquilizers," but because they assist the individual in probing to the depths where his decisions are formed. It is quite strikingly true that although some clerics still fulminate against Freud, much of the most penetrating comment on religious writing is currently made by practicing psychotherapists.

Such confluences, and they exist in a number of professional fields, need careful exploration and irenic discussion. An additional illustration from the realm of educational theory may be adduced. Many religious people tremble at the mention of John Dewey's name as they might on the approach of Satan himself; and it is of course true that this philosopher's later discussions of "scientific pragmatism" were as "a-theistic" as can well be imagined. They clearly reflected the crisis of belief which set in after the turn of the century. Yet that which is essential in the pedagogical theory of Dewey and his associate

Kilpatrick stems from the days when both were religious men who employed the old American concept of the community co-operating for good ends in formulating a philosophy of education which in essence wanted children to be given a chance to become part of a functioning community while in school. Wherein does this differ radically from the wisdom of Pestalozzi, Montessori, and others who were as deeply Christian as human beings could well be? The proper critique of Dewey, insofar as his practical pedagogy is concerned, therefore will not be based on antipathy to his cloudy metaphysics but solely on whether the "school community" he envisioned gets its work done and whether the number of policemen and tax collectors in it ought to be increased.

The second way that opens before us is formal instruction in religion. Certainly this is very badly in need of revamping, particularly if it is to be effective within an environment so greatly influenced by scientific inquiry and methodology as ours is. Comment so astringent may at first seem unwarranted. There can be no doubt that the books available today on all the major faiths are vastly superior to the dull, schematic outlines in vogue half a century ago. Major seminaries have likewise given a great deal of thoughtful attention to the problem. The trouble as I see it is that instruction is given as if the young person interested in law, engineering, or some other profession were in fact preparing for the sacred ministry. He is expected to respond in a personal way to material which would be entirely appropriate were he in a theological seminary. On the other hand, the teacher of religion to lay college or university students tends to feel that his discipline will lose its pertinence and value if he proceeds in any other fashion.

Here no doubt European experience can be of value to us, not because of cultural inferiority on our part but because a long period of corrosion of the religious sense, as well as decades of devastating warfare that gave prominence to the problem of evil even while destroying long-established communal solidarities, has compelled teachers in the Old World to revise drastically their concepts of the mission to intellectual men and women. What Romano Guardini and Joseph Pieper have done in Ger-

many, or Yves Cougar and his associates in France, or the inde-
fatigable Jesuits of Liége in Belgium has set an example that
needs only to be followed imaginatively on the American scene.
Professor Guardini's *Glaubenserkenntnis* (Realization of Faith),
for example, presents a course of lectures in dogmatic theology
which, while quite orthodox from the Roman Catholic point
of view, are nevertheless vividly modern in feeling and concern.
The fact that more than a thousand students, of varied church
allegiances and academic disciplines, go to listen to them
clearly indicates that when the sheep have pasture they will
feed. I hasten to add that these lectures are substantial, having
nothing in common with peace of spirit or televised dramatics.
Even so, religious teaching could undoubtedly take a leaf
from the book of modern education and discover the usefulness
of audio-visual materials.

For my part I believe that it is not the religious commitment
of the young man or woman which has been subjected to
fearsome erosion—for as Augustine has said the human heart
remains unquiet always—but the intellectual acre in which
that commitment must be planted if it is to flourish. The problem we face, therefore, is how to enrich the soil. Accordingly,
religion must not shy away from using the treasure made available to it by the centuries during which it has been so
important and creative a force in the shaping of liberal culture
and ethical reflection. These may not seem to an exacting theologian much more than exercises designed to discipline the
mind so that it may be ready for contemplation of Divine
mysteries. But today they assuredly provide far, far more than
the normal ration of spiritual food. The standard program of
the European humanistic secondary school, with its emphasis
on the moral teaching implicit in literature, is likely to seem
to many of us merely a somewhat sublimated version of
McGuffey's readers. But if our generations are fed on the cereals
of utility only, thereby limiting their imaginations to the horizons of science, how can one expect them to hang over the
ledge from which alone one can see eternity in time?

The liberal arts have a way of living up to their origins.
That T. S. Eliot could pack a great hall at the University of

Minnesota with people anxious to hear him lecture is not without its significance for religion also. The more room we provide for the liberal arts in high school, college, and professional school, the less need we shall have for being worried about the specifically religious part of the course of study. But worry we should have to, even then. For however diligent his man Friday, the master theologian is indispensable. Take, for instance, the problem of justice. What is this, for which the whole world cries out, and to what does it obligate a man? What are the major areas of modern life which it affects? How is the individual to shoulder his own responsibility for its attainment? We can and should endeavor to deal with these questions in historical, legal, and philosophic terms. But is not Emil Brunner right when he contends that justice means giving every man his due, and that as a consequence it is the realization in action of that love of neighbor which religious contemplation confronts as a divine demand? Such love is either a movement outward into the world of the religious spirit or it is a delusion with which one must deal logically, mechanistically as do the Communists. Was not the initial appeal of their doctrine rooted in the widespread irritated conviction of the masses that those who professed the Judaeo-Christian faith did not practice what they said they believed? Yet it is now made manifest that the repudiation of justice in its totality by the atheistic on pantheistic totalitarians is not accidental. Justice was discovered, revealed, for us in the Scripture. It is to be found nowhere else. And so, do we not see here the outline of a course that the American professional campus badly needs?

There are certainly any number of worth-while things which might be tried not with a view to stripping religious teaching of all respect for systematic treatment but in the hope of clothing the bones of the "system" with recognizable flesh and blood. If this is done, young people will gladly leave their mathematics texts and their treatises on anatomy for precious hours during which their awareness of themselves, of their obligations and their destinies, can take them beside still waters more profound than any others. I am optimistic enough to believe that in the development of this awareness the gulf between scientific inquiry and religious belief can be crossed by very many. As I have tried to say elsewhere (in a talk given at the University of Michigan during the summer of 1946), there is a point of light at which meet the great men of science and the saints who are the final teachers of religion this side of God Himself. This is the point at which the demonstrated integrity of both is made evident. Yet one must remember that for our time the discovery of it is far from easy. As I then said:

To ask the saint and the scientist to give an account of themselves is not to suggest that either will immediately be believed. For those of us to whom the ancient Christian and Jewish faiths bring not defeat but joy, not doubt but confidence, it may be difficult to understand why the urge to holiness which glows so warm in our tradition should be so invisible to many. The Christian is aware that the Beatitudes, eight in number like a round of dancers, are fruits hung too high on the tree of life for him to pluck. None the less it seems to him that nothing more glorious was ever said of man than that some day his reach might attain even unto them—that he might be rich because he was poor, and mighty because he was humbly selfless. But he must be patient. He cannot help knowing that a curtain has fallen between him and the rest of men. He must give them an example before he can furnish them with a doctrine.

An example shown in patience, not with furor but in quietness! That is the essence of the religious education program for the professional school also. While making it evident that religious thinking can color all human reflection and add a needed dimension to science, the teacher must remember that he too sees through a glass darkly. Perhaps in the end the follower of Newman will meet in friendly company with the disciples of Newton and Blacktsone, Pasteur and Horace Mann. At least of this one can unfortunately be certain: our time will not have a soul until it is shown what having one means.

The Community—Campus Life

ROBERT M. STROZIER

Analysis of the Student Community

CHAPTER XII

In many ways the personalities of the American colleges and universities are reflected in the buildings that house them. The classrooms in which the teaching occurs stand alongside the elaborate hospital systems, the complicated new science institutes and laboratories, the libraries, the efficient administrative headquarters, and the chapel spires. Among these buildings on most campuses are numerous others in which teaching and research occur less frequently, if at all: the oval of the football stadium, the rows of fraternity and sorority houses, the blocks and blocks of dormitories, the sleek and streamlined student union buildings. The campus is a place of learning. In our definition of "campus" we usually do not make exclusions. I have sometimes observed the puzzled look on the face of a visitor from abroad as he has inspected the various rooms of our strange house. Occasionally, a guest from another land will be so bold as to ask what the bowling alley, swimming pools, and ballrooms have to do with scholarship. This is a fair question.

The personality of higher education in the United States is dominated by an important political fact and emotional attitude. In theory and generally in practice the American college campus is open to everyone as a matter of right. In every nation the institutions of learning play an important sociological role. In the United States the colleges and universities selfconsciously play a socializing role. Our campuses are not only congregations of minds dedicated to the pursuit of scholarship. They are also communities of bodies and souls, complete with all the material and physical paraphernalia and shortcomings attending human life.

The right to learning is one of the expressions of the strong American drive toward equality of economic and political condition. The attempt to provide learning opportunities for millions undoubtedly has had an effect upon the quality of the education ultimately provided. In any event, the millions have carefully policed their political right, and the masses have naturally been articulate about the results they expect educational opportunities to achieve. Colleges and universities in the United States are sensitive to the popular will, which largely accounts for the multiplicity of purposes assigned to higher education in this country. There is strength in a multiplicity of purposes. The plethora of our purposes, however, often seems to paralyze our ability to assign an order of values to the various things we do. Student life on the campus puts to a test our value structure.

The United States is still a nation of great economic and social mobility. Mass higher education plays a vital part in keeping things mobile. The public in this country thoroughly appreciates the relation between advanced education and economic and social mobility. Those who support the colleges and universities with taxes and contributions, and the students who come to partake of the education, not only expect the educational experience to equip people for fuller and more prosperous lives, but also to duplicate roughly the lives they already know. The American success story is broadly understood. Most American students need only look at their own parents, relatives, or neighbors down the street to observe some phase of the story in action. How natural it is for these young people, when they leave home for the collegiate experience, to take along with them the prejudices and expectations to which they have been conditioned. The mood of the general American public is directly injected into campus affairs through the conduct of the students.

The student community, therefore, is a ramification of the

adult community. The character of student life is always colored brightly by the events of national history.

The Roaring Twenties produced a generation of students who also roared. The campus life of these students could only have existed in a national climate of bewildering expansion. Prohibition, raccoon coats, jazz, and the gentlemanly "C" did not, of course, characterize or mold the majority of the students of this decade. They simply accented an underlying attitude. The Veterans of World War I thought themselves sophisticated. They had seen gay Paree, and they read and aped F. Scott Fitzgerald. Their younger brothers and sisters, like all those who copy the original, produced a kind of superficiality under the guise of sophistication which today seems ludicrous. This was not a decade of democratic spirit in student life. Still, the campuses drew more students to them than ever before, setting the stage for what was soon to follow.

The contrast between the twenties and the thirties is striking. The unhappy Depression Years brought a new sobriety to the campus. Matters of social importance were natural for young men and women whose parents had lost everything and were unable to finance a higher education for them. Campus jobs, snobbishly avoided in the twenties, became the order of the day. Glittering social functions were few and unpopular. The schools themselves suffered severe financial pangs, and the students in the schools were acutely concerned with their own future economic security. Young and idealistic minds toying with all the popular political panaceas and isms and the faculties existing on substandard incomes were part of the prevailing tone. Our campuses were populated by intense people.

World War II broke suddenly on the United States, and its impact on the campus was immediate. The older male students began to leave. Those who were on call were restless and frustrated, often unable or unwilling to study. Younger men were eager for their time to come, anxious not to miss the Great Adventure. School officials suddenly found their student bodies decimated and upset, and their budgets hopeless.

Many colleges and universities were saved from financial

disaster during the war by the establishment of military train-ing programs on the campuses. The strict discipline of the armed services' program contrasted sharply with the general university atmosphere in the larger schools, whose student bodies consisted mainly of the young, those physically unable to enter the armed forces, and the women. Teaching and research—except for that carried on in the government pro-grams—fell to a low ebb.

As the war drew to an end the leaders of the colleges and universities began to anticipate with mixed emotions the pros-pect of thousands of returning veterans. Preparations for their return assumed that the veterans would be a problem. Wash-ington assured the universities that demobilization would be an orderly process, and that the "problem"—whatever else it might become—would not be one of sheer physical chaos. Things did not work out that way. Men who had served gladly were unwilling to remain in the armed forces when the conflict ended, and their sentiments were effectively articulated by their parents, and thus by their congressmen. When it finally rained, it poured, and for a while it seemed that the campus would be inundated by the returning flood.

A problem existed in the years 1945–49 on most campuses, but the veteran was not the problem. His numbers helped to create the problem, which had been inadequately foreseen. Additional students created immediate needs for faculty, hous-ing, equipment, and services. Men and women who had faced the fire of battle, who confronted futures already foreshortened, returned in a serious frame of mind, naturally impatient with petty rules and red tape, poor instruction, inefficient adminis-tration, and the supine acceptance of anything whatsoever. They were young people in a hurry, definite in their aims, mature in outlook, and quite realistic in judgment. Some of the best students this country has ever known were present in this veteran group, and many of them would never have had the opportunity for higher education had it not been for the War and its unique educational aftermath—the "G.I. Bill."

In their eagerness to recoup financially, many institutions admitted more students than they could effectively instruct or accommodate. Fly-by-night trade schools flourished briefly, taking advantage of the five-hundred-dollar government allotments for tuition. Adequate controls for the approval of study programs were not instituted by the government, and there were many abuses of the opportunities afforded by the G.I. Bill. Despite these abuses, the impact of the bill on the educational scene was profound. The result persists, long after the majority of the veterans have exhausted their benefits under the law.

Local, citizen control of education in the United States is a deep-rooted tradition. Federal interference has long been avoided, and the fear of federal control—of a uniformity imposed by support from the national government—is a live and effective force in American politics and society. The G.I. Bill served as an example of federal economic support free from federal political control of educational policy. Those who most feared federal intervention in education came to realize that this particular federal legislation had democratized education in a way which many thoughtful people had considered impossible. The G.I. Bill brought this whole issue to the campus at a new level. What has since happened makes some administrators schizophrenic. On a grand scale, this unique instrument opened the door to higher education to young Americans from every economic and social stratum.

After this experience, colleges and universities were both ready and eager to absorb the returning veterans of the Korean action. Thus the wars at mid-century thoroughly democratized the opportunities for higher education in the United States. From this adversity blossomed into reality one of the great American ideals, and no one can understand succeeding student communities in this nation without first appreciating this monumental fact.

Religion assumed a more important role on the campus after World War II. The scepticism and agnosticism, prevalent in the twenties, had been succeeded by a marked concern with social issues during the days of the depression. Where independent thinking in the past had seemed to lead the student away from religion, it has, in recent years, seemed to bring him closer to it. State and private institutions have seen a great increase in participation by students in the religious groups. Students are just as much interested in matters of social import but less likely to substitute such interests for religion. The larger religious groups have their own centers on campuses. They co-operate closely with the personnel officers and contribute to the extracurriculum and advisory programs. If the representatives of the various faiths felt in past years that they were only tolerated by the administration, today they feel welcome. It might be added that the quality of the men and women assigned by the religious groups to campus positions is quite superior generally.

The student body constitutes one important link between the institutions of higher learning and the general community. On still another front colleges and universities meet the public directly in an influential context. This is the economic front —the sector in which the educational institutions fight their battles to finance their operations. The ebb and flow of this battle also helps to shape the forces that both expand and restrict student life. For most schools this battle is fought in relation to three major sources of power—government, the great private foundations, and private foundations and private industry.

The relationship between the federal government and the colleges and universities remains ambiguous. Land-grant schools have been recipients of the largess of the government for many years and have worked out a *modus vivendi* which seems to have left their policy-making powers completely intact. Not all state universities have been so happy in their relationships with their own controlling legislatures.

The participation of the federal government in research during and since World War II has been enormously expanded. Almost all the larger universities and many colleges have obtained grants from the government for special research activities. This represents a natural—though often difficult—union of interests and talents. In an atomic era, the government naturally has need of research for which it lacks human talent, technical equipment, and resources. Academicians usually prefer to remain in their professions rather than to join government service. Academic participation in such vast projects as those at Los Alamos and the Argonne National Laboratories are only the most spectacular examples of a trend very much in effect today.

To the extent that the government may give or withhold its resources for specific research objectives—and may always, of course, withdraw its support at the expiration of specific contract periods—the influence of the federal agencies is felt sharply on the campus. An abrupt decline in government support would seriously cripple many excellent educational institutions. On some it would have a disastrous effect.

Moreover, the interests of the national government have predominantly concentrated in the applied sciences. This fact has had a variety of mischievous effects on work going on in the other disciplines. It has created gross inequalities in faculty salaries. It has directed the use of academic resources within the science fields themselves. These concentrations of monetary power and resources within the university naturally influence the quality and the numbers of students who take up those disciplinary pursuits.

Federal influence in higher education at this level presents a very different set of problems and consequences from those implied by the federal scholarship program symbolized by the G.I. Bill. Those who remain adamant in opposition to all federal assistance often fail to honor the distinctions involved.

No college of quality can rely wholly on tuition income for financial security. In most institutions tuition-free income accounts for one-half or less of the total operating costs. No modern business or industry can escape the increasingly acute need for college and university-trained leadership and personnel. On the basis of this mutuality, the educational administrators have turned increasingly to business and industry in recent years for financial support. By and large, industry has responded to this situation generously and wisely. The Ford Motor Company has established its own educational program, as have DuPont and many other corporations. Each year finds new examples of either private programs for the children of employees or direct, general support of the colleges and universities. In their fund-raising efforts the schools have, with increasing frequency, turned to the medium-sized and smaller industries.

Quite aside from the influential role the leaders of industrial corporations play on the governing boards of universities and colleges, reliance on industry for direct grants presents new issues concerning the independence of the educational institutions from the particular interests represented by industry and business. Industry—like government—has its special concern with the applied sciences and with a relatively few other disciplinary areas. Industry has stepped up its campus recruiting activity, and through a variety of doors enters the campus in a manner which influences the choices that both students and faculty members make regarding study and career pursuits. The modern college curriculum reflects the specialized and vocational needs for success in the American industrial and commercial organization. Modern student life reflects the cultural patterns resulting in a society in which business success is the dominant model.

Foundations for educational purposes are not new, but the emergence of the Ford Foundation, with its galaxy of subsidiaries, has been a matter of national importance. Universities turn with more frequency than ever before to the large foundations—Ford, Rockefeller, Carnegie, and Kellogg—for special project support. At the same time, hundreds of smaller foundations have been and are being established with more limited areas of interest. The present tax policies in this country make gifts to foundations favorable to persons of large fortunes who are seriously interested in promoting education. The $500,-000,000 grant by the Ford Foundation in 1955 to private colleges and universities was the largest ever made, and it set a new pattern for foundation giving. Instead of grants of from three to five years' duration for special projects which the school is often committed to continue—assuming they succeeded—the Ford gift was both for endowment and operational purposes. Administrators have long argued that the colleges and universities have greater need for unallocated funds than for special project grants. In any event our schools are now, more than ever, dependent upon foundation support for the continuance of important segments of educational programs.

Curiously, the postwar national prosperity has in some ways adversely affected the economic welfare of educational institutions and their students. Inflation, the explosive growth of national population, and the broadening educational opportunities for our young people have revolutionized the financial situations of the students themselves. Tuition costs in our schools have advanced from an average of around $500 in 1950 to more than $1,000 per year in many of our private institutions. The state universities have also uniformly found it necessary to increase their fees. The student activities fee has become an accepted part of student expense at almost all institutions. It usually includes tickets to athletic contests, support for student publications, and social events. This taxation has led to a strong student voice in the distribution of funds. The associated student organizations in the major schools on the West Coast have almost exclusive representation in financing and controlling the extracurriculum.

Consequently, almost all institutions have been subjected to sharp pressures to increase their funds allocated for scholarships, fellowships, and aids for students. The state schools have expanded their resources for these purposes through special grants from the legislatures and private sources, and the other schools have drawn from unendowed funds as well as from industry, private individuals, and government. Many scholarship programs have been established on a nationally competitive basis—of which the National Merit program is an example.

In 1950 tuition at Harvard College, in the oldest university in the United States, was $600. Today it is $1,000. As President of Harvard University from 1933–53, James Bryant Conant established scholarships on a national basis with competition conducted in regional areas. Alumni who had previously recommended promising young men to Harvard now were asked to assist the Admissions Office to locate talented young men regardless of their financial circumstances. Thus, the scholarship program at Harvard has had a liberalizing effect upon the make-up of the student body of the College. The increased

demand for student financial assistance, and the vigorous efforts
of the colleges throughout the nation to meet this demand,
have been additional factors accelerating the democratization
of higher education in the United States.

At the graduate level the size of the fellowships given has
increased markedly with the national inflation of the 1950's.
The National Science Foundation, the U. S. Public Health
programs, and other grants are larger than most universities
have been accustomed to award. Competition for the qualita-
tive science students, as a result, has been very keen. This is
the day of the multiple applications from students for admission as well as for grants-in-aid. Member institutions of the
American Association of Universities by common consent do
not announce graduate fellowship awards until the first of
April each year. Then they are confronted with a period of
anxious waiting for acceptances by the more promising young
scholars. Obviously, the quality of the educational institutions
is affected by the outcome of such competition. The American
universities not only compete for faculty members and general
public support, but also for superior students.

The economic affairs of national life frame acute problems
for the institutions of higher education in the United States
and add an important dimension to the character of the student
community. Through these problems the campuses are subjected to a variety of pressures. All segments of national life
compete for the attention and talents of the academic world.
Indeed, in obtaining competent teachers in the sciences, the
academic world is itself a competitor with the government and
industry. This intense competition not only affects the kind of
educational opportunity ultimately presented to the students,
but also has an impact upon the decisions students make about
their career futures.

Because the typical American student is young, generally
without dependents, and during his school years not engaged
in full economic productivity, it is sometimes felt that his
immersion in campus life is artificial, detached from the main
currents of the general community. National and international
events, however, reach into campus life and shape what the

students do and think. Occasionally, campus affairs become national events. Though most campuses are separate plots of ground, they are not isolated. They could not be isolated, even if they wished it that way.

Long before the U. S. Supreme Court decided that equal educational opportunities meant something more than the provision of separate but similar facilities, this issue was vigorously faced by the American campus. Since the Court's opinion, this issue has focused on the South, where the great battle against segregation is still in progress. But the plight of minority groups has long concerned American society and the universities.

The segregation of the Negro is central. Discrimination against Jews has been less discussed, but its existence is tacitly recognized. The private quotas of many colleges have been relaxed. In the social life of the campus, integration of the various races has been rapid. The fraternity facet of student life is an example of recent progress.

During World War II the fraternity system in America suffered, and many educators thought it probably would never return to its former strength. This has not been the case. Fraternities provided much-needed postwar housing for many returning veterans. The veteran, tired of the disciplined life of the military, found gaiety and relaxation in the unstructured environment of the fraternity house.

Thanks largely to the influence of these returning veterans, a plan originated among the students at the University of Michigan designed to deny the use of campus facilities to student groups who practiced membership and social discrimination. The plan, which stipulated a given period of time during which the student organizations could alter their practices before censure, gained national importance through its sponsorship by the National Student Association. This proposal stimulated intensive debate within the American student body, and it spurred many colleges to examine more closely the rigidity of their social groups, fraternities, sororities, and clubs.

At the present time many Jewish students are initiated in the traditionally "Aryan" fraternities. Some formerly restrictive

fraternities have pledged and initiated Negro members. Many
national fraternal organizations have officially removed restrictive clauses from their constitutions. This legal action
does not always insure perfect practices, but it does testify to
the growing impatience of students with discriminatory practices. The shape of things to come is demonstrated by the keen
sensitivities of our students, sensitivities often keener than
those of their elders, the alumni, whose student days now rest
in a remote and very different past.

Another important result of the postwar veteran ferment
was the emergence of a genuinely representative, national
student organization. While national student unions are traditional in other parts of the world, the scope and diversity of
the American continent operated against such a federation.
The U. S. National Student Association now has a history of
ten years. It has grown to represent more than two hundred
student bodies of more than a million students. In its formative
years NSA experienced a rare and mature leadership and
reflected accurately many national political tensions. Veterans
were in the majority from 1946–50, and a struggle developed
between extreme leftist and conservative student elements.
With maturity a middle-of-the-road policy evolved, which has
greatly enhanced the influence of the organization. The evolution of NSA has afforded hundreds of student leaders an
extraordinary, practical education in the political dynamics
of American life. But many American educators, trained in a
different age, still look askance at student interest in practical
politics.

Aside from its efforts to stimulate student interest in international student affairs, the most important consequence of the
national organization has been its encouragement of campus
student government. The development of vigorous self-govern-
ment encountered a paternalistic tradition in many colleges
and universities. While the curricula of our schools preached
the democratic doctrine, little opportunity for the practice of
democracy existed in campus life. Today student government
is judiciously and calmly accepted. As the students have
matured through the intelligent acceptance of the responsi-

bility which accompanies increased freedom, so the administrative authorities in most schools have matured by permitting greater freedom to the students. The regulation of student life itself is now frequently placed within the jurisdiction of student government. On some campuses student government is encouraged to share faculty deliberations concerning what is taught and the methods of teaching. But on almost all campuses through committees, through round-table discussion and debate, the lines of communication between the students, the faculty, and the administration are firmly established. The paternalistic approach is no longer tolerated. The paradox of attempting to teach students to think, while directing their every act, is fortunately passé.

Even at a much earlier point in our national history, De Tocqueville observed the American passion for joining organizations and participating in public political and social affairs. He saw these peculiar American propensities as manifestations of the democratic spirit, the conviction among our people that each man was as good as his neighbor and thus entitled to mix fully in all aspects of public life. But one of the prices of equality, said De Tocqueville, was loneliness. The equalization process, he thought, erected impersonal mass models, which motivated the American to join with his fellows in public and social endeavor in an attempt to escape from his feelings of isolation.

Taking modern student life as a whole, perhaps the two dominant qualities are its informality and the way it seeks to encourage broad participation in a variety of activities.

Informality is the keynote to the social life. The student union movement has provided a central meeting place for all students. It has broken down the barriers between formal social activity and the more frequent, unstructured mingling of students of all backgrounds in social intercourse. Clubs and activities on the campus now follow easily the natural, ever-changing interests of the students rather than set and traditional patterns.

The spread of coeducation has accelerated the demolition of social convention and tradition on the campus. The women's colleges in the Eastern region still flourish, but there has been little expansion of these schools in recent years. In fact, some smaller women's colleges have become coeducational, and others have ceased to exist. The finishing school for young ladies has shown a marked decline in the East and the South —the only areas where it ever had importance. The woman's role in American society is reflected in campus life. Women students move with ease into student leadership positions on the newspapers, in the governments, and in the national student movement.

Campus attitudes toward sex have altered considerably. Aberrations which formerly could not even be discussed now are faced for what they usually are—symptoms of deep-seated maladjustments. Sex education and preparation for married life are subjects found either in the formal curriculums or in informal lecture and discussion series on the campus. These subjects are received by the students with frankness, intelligence, and curiosity.

In the athletic programs, attitudes are changing too. Many of the older traditions persist; football remains king of the campus, though some smaller colleges and a few larger institutions have withdrawn from intercollegiate competition. Two major team sports—football and basketball—attained a measure of notoriety in recent years as a result of some abuses: gambling, the excessive subsidization of athletes by the colleges, and promiscuous recruiting practices.

But the most important change is the resurgence of intramural competition. In most schools today participation is at a high level in the intramural programs. This is a manifestation of the desire to shift emphasis from spectating to participation. While the spectator sports are for everyone—particularly for the alumni—modern sports programs are aimed at the individual, not only while he is a student but as a preparation for his active, maturer years. While team sports remain popular, the present trend emphasizes anew the individual sports— handball, tennis, golf, swimming, squash, fencing, gymnastics, and skiing.

Notwithstanding the informality of student life, conformity is still apparent. The crew cut, the white buckskin shoes, and the skirts and sweaters suggest an even greater conformity than actually exists. Conformity in social groups is much less marked. The independence generated by an active student government is the result, not the cause, of this intelligent informality.

With social informality has come a relaxation of outward standards of conduct, which in another day would have seemed to produce immorality. The restrictions on hours for women students have been relaxed in almost all colleges. Smoking, long forbidden, then tolerated in restricted areas, is now casually accepted for women almost everywhere. Drinking is still taboo, but practices vary considerably in the different regions of the country. Most universities leave this indulgence to the discretion of the older students.

Prefabricated houses, trailers, and temporary housing of all kinds emerged after World War II to accommodate the veteran population, many of whom returned to the campus married. Universities have recognized the phenomenon of early marriage and replaced the temporary housing units with permanent apartments for student families. Until the late forties few colleges permitted married students to attend, and many had regulations which automatically dismissed students who were married during the educational term. This has all changed during the fifties. The baby carriage has become familiar on the campus.

The growing concept of residential education in America illustrates best the blending of formal and informal education and the all-permeating nature of the collegiate experience.

The residence halls and dormitories were once considered places where students slept and ate—necessary but distracting services on the periphery of the main educational experience. Today the planning of the residential units is as much of an educational programing task as it is an architectural one. The modern residence hall is seen as a focal point of the student's life in which the arbitrary line between the extracurriculum and the curriculum disappears.

In most American universities, even in the urban areas, the majority of the students in attendance reside in the university community rather than at the residence of their parents and families. Thus, the typical American undergraduate severs the home tie at the age of eighteen and, given the geographic breadth of the United States, this break means that the distance between the youngster and the adults who formerly supervised his conduct is great.

A major shift of this supervisory responsibility has occurred from the home and church to the campus and the dean of students. The college houses the student, feeds him, oversees his moral development, and attends to his emotional and physical health problems as well as to his intellectual maturation. In addition to all of this, as curriculums have expanded and specialized, the college assumes an important role in guiding the student through the academic complexities of the institution. Many students come to college under extraordinary economic pressures which cannot be ignored. Finally, as the student terminates his education in college, his introduction to a productive career is often facilitated by vocational guidance and placement.

To manage these affairs many schools have established deans of students with general responsibilities for this administration. These deans are assisted by staffs of experts: psychiatrists, psychologists, religious counselors, residence hall counselors, veterans' advisers, and vocational guidance and placement consultants. In addition to these there are special counselors for various student activities plus the managers of the student union buildings, the dietitians for the restaurants, and the people who operate the dormitories and the fraternity houses. The titles of dean of men and dean of women are still current, indicating in some places different procedures for handling the two sexes. The dean of students in coeducational schools recognizes certain areas in which women's affairs are different, and his staff includes women in prominent positions.

As a general rule the student's use of these various services is a matter for his own discretion. No one forces him to seek the advice and counsel that the services represent. On the other hand, many schools require students, before they reach their legal majority, to reside in the residence halls rather than off campus. In the event of a serious emotional or physical illness that affects the student's academic status, the use of a particular service may be prescribed. Academic counseling is generally required for all students—at least at the undergraduate level.

It may be argued that these services have very little to do with scholarship itself, that they detract from the central theme of university life and consume unnecessarily both the time and energy of student, teacher, and administrator. To some these accommodations appear to be coddling—crutches which weaken the initiative and independence of the student.

The wise use of the special services on the campus enhance the student's ability to make a wider range of intelligent choices. Students today—in a large, diverse, and free society—are, after all, confronted with a monumental range of decisions. In the totalitarian society many of these decisions are made for the student by his superiors. Others may choose for him his life's work, the field of his university study, his social station. In our country the student must choose for himself his wife, his job, his cultural pursuits, and religious affiliations. But free decision-making should be wise, and a step toward wisdom is the assembly of the relevant facts. Student services principally are mechanisms for the assembly of the facts. Given the best facts available, the decision is still for the student to make.

Educational exchanges of an official character began on a modest scale after the Boxer Rebellion. They were stimulated by World War I, leading to the creation of a national clearing house—the Institute of International Education in New York. But it was only after World War II that exchanges became a large and important affair in which almost all colleges and universities are engaged. At present more than 35,000 foreign students are studying on American campuses, and there are thousands of students from this country abroad. The year abroad for Smith College juniors was established between the wars, and today dozens of schools sponsor special programs of foreign study.

The Fulbright Scholarships established by our government have given a tremendous impetus to the exchange idea. These awards are based on an open national competition and offer study opportunities in nations with which we have concluded reciprocal agreements. Established as a means for the payment for surplus commodities remaining in allied countries after World War II, the program allows students from the United States to study abroad and to receive their scholarships in the currency of the foreign country. From its inception this has been an admirably conducted program. It has made campuses aware of the resources and talents of the universities abroad. It has encouraged faculties to share with their peers abroad the fruits of teaching and research. It has brought to the United States campus a real sense of being a part of the educational process which knows no boundaries and has no restrictions.

The presence of foreign students from almost all countries of the world on campuses has been accepted intelligently and happily. No longer are the people from overseas exploited because they are different. They have become a regular and accepted part of the educational scene.

Barriers remain for the students behind the Iron Curtain. Efforts begun in 1956 to effect exchanges between Russia and the United States have so far been fruitless; the situation in the Middle East may have set this effort back for some time in the future. The Hungarian Rebellion and the consequent admission of thousands of its people to the United States have aided these people, but have not decreased the tensions between the East and the West. Also, no relationships are now established between this country and China.

The World University Service conducts successful annual campaigns for funds on our campuses; fraternities and sororities welcome foreign students into their houses; the Seminars for International Living bring together earnest, dedicated young people; inter-country associations, like the English Speaking Union, the Alliance Française, and the American-Scandinavian Foundation, sponsor educational programs; the Marshall Fellowships, the Rhodes Scholarships, the Lafayette Fellowships, and innumerable other programs all support and extend the spirit of exchange and unselfish dedication to true educational principles.

The international responsibilities assumed by this nation after World War II have awakened American students to their increased responsibilities as citizens.

We have been discussing student life in a prosperous, mass democracy which has quite recently assumed tremendous new responsibilities around the globe, a nation whose power rests on a highly industrialized base, and whose society is mobile, fluid, and free.

Higher education in the United States is a major focus of the cultural and intellectual problems flowing from freedom, materialism, and the necessity to use wisely unprecedented power.

The student community contains all of the tensions that are generated in such a society. In the political life of the United States liberty and the pursuit of happiness have alway been linked to the proposition that learning and education are the keys that open the doors to wealth and success. Material achievements are intimately related to a political way of life—to the ability to think and act freely. Notwithstanding its wealth this is a nation where illiteracy is viewed—even among the uneducated groups—as socially undesirable; where democracy has so thoroughly permeated higher learning that attending college is a standard aspiration among all economic strata.

There are many basic unresolved issues in American higher education; specialization and general or liberal education; the sciences versus the humanities; vocationalism and generalism; conformity and freedom; materialism and spirituality. The exciting thing about students is their eager, fresh, dynamic concern with the important unanswered questions.

SEWARD HILTNER

Religious Counseling

CHAPTER XIII

Jerry is in the office of Pastor Holmes, Director of the Blank Denominational Foundation, which serves the students of a large state university. A brilliant graduate student, Jerry is reflective and articulate but is making no secret of his agitation.

"It was a letter I got yesterday," he is saying, "that made me decide to try to talk with you. Let me try to tell you the story. Especially since I came here to study, I suppose you could say I've been fighting against believing in God. Recently I thought I could end that fight, really believe, and then pray. But I can't. My younger sister is mentally deficient. It isn't that this has hurt me personally, except inside, and my parents have been wonderful about it although it's been hell for them. But ever since I can remember, I've been asking God for an answer to this kind of waste and human tragedy. But I've never had one. I've read, and listened to a lot of preachers, some of them good. I think I know that I ought to be able to see beyond this suffering. But I can't—because it's so senseless. I realize this must be tied up with my personal problems in general, and on those I've been getting some real help over at the Student Personnel Center. But it seems to me now that I need both religious and psychological counseling at the same time."

Jerry made it clear that he did not want discussion merely or mainly of his personal problem but of the religious view of suffering and human tragedy. Pastor Holmes complied with this. Recognizing that Jerry had already heard "the answer" many times without absorbing or accepting it, he attempted to help Jerry think through the deeper situation out of which religious answers have arisen. They discussed, for example, the freedom given men by God in relation to God's sovereignty, the relation of individual and collective sin to human tragedy, and the function of chance in connection with freedom and the creatorship of God. The next week Jerry returned, and reported a counseling session he had had with his counselor at the Student Personnel Center.

"I believe now that I've been asking God to change things so that I would have no occasion for bitterness, and no guilt over my bitterness—rather than facing up to guilt and bitterness as my own emotional problems. I think I must do this before it will be possible for me to accept an answer to the question I put to you last week."

Jerry's was, certainly, a deeply religious problem. But it was so bound up with Jerry's total personal problem as to be insoluble outside that whole personal context. In this instance the primary counseling job was being done by the student personnel service. In another, Pastor Holmes might well have done the counseling, both personal and religious, himself.

Charles, a student in the same university as Jerry, is talking with his faculty adviser, Dr. Hall, about his courses for his next and final year of undergraduate work. He is majoring in Dr. Hall's field of economics. As they have discussed available courses, it has become clear that two crucial decisions depend in large part upon whether Charles will go into business on graduation or will take a master's degree and enter a particular field of public service. Both opportunities are rather clearly open to him. At this point Charles says:

"I see now that I'll have to make some kind of decision, even if I change my mind later, by next fall. I don't know. It seems so mixed up. I do think public service is important, and I'm interested in this form of it. But I think you can do a lot of good in business too. Of course, some people think a businessman can't be concerned with any human values at all, only with his profits. Sometimes I think I'd prefer to get into business if somebody could assure me I'd be able to stand up against pressures of the wrong kind. At those times I feel public service would be safer for my conscience. But then, at other times, I think public service would do more good and be more satisfying. And then I think maybe I'd just be evading the moral issues that I'd have to face as a businessman."

Dr. Hall recognized rightly that this problem of occupational decision now confronting Charles could be aided not only by additional information but also by helping Charles to clarify his personal views about economic life in the larger sense. His helpful counseling with Charles proceeded in that direction. But beneath that specific dilemma, Dr. Hall sensed the deeper religious question of vocation. God might indeed call one man to public service and another to business; but each man should know which. At the conclusion of their discussion, Dr. Hall asked Charles if he had considered discussing this aspect of his decision with the student pastor. It had not occurred to Charles that the problem might be more than technical and personal. But he saw the point, and shortly had three valuable sessions with the pastor.

Here was, on the face of it, an occupational problem containing some technical and some personal elements. The proper decision, even tentatively, could not have been reached if Dr. Hall had not aided Charles with both the technical and personal elements. But either decision Charles would have made at that time, if he had not also had the pastor's counsel, would have left him feeling like a moral coward. If he had decided to enter business, but with a feeling of impending moral defeat, he would have been unnecessarily torn. If he had decided on public service, with the fear that he was more interested in safety than in service, that too would have meant conflict. Above the technical and personal counsel, it was vital that he consider his decision in the larger context of religious vocation.

In the case of Jerry, we saw an obviously religious problem which could, however, be dealt with only by first giving personal and psychological help. In Charles' case, we have seen a technical and personal problem which was, however, handled effectively only by religious counseling accompanying the other. Few student problems are purely and simply religious, and many problems that do not appear to be religious in the conventional sense require consideration at a religious level if they are to find proper solution.

On every large campus hundreds of poignant human problems arise that are religious in the traditional sense, such as that of the boy and girl of different religious faiths who are considering marriage. Here are a few excerpts from a typical situation of this kind described by William E. Hulme.[1] Protestant Ted is talking with the campus pastor about his relationship to the Roman Catholic girl he wants to marry.

"She's all a guy could want, if it weren't for this religious angle. My folks are really up in the air about it—my mother especially. Every time I step into the house it's an argument. . . . They're just downright unreasonable. Oh, I suppose they're right—Protestants and Catholics probably shouldn't marry each other. But they're going at it in the wrong way. . . . It just makes me all the more determined to keep seeing her. . . . I never realized how prejudiced some Protestants can be against Roman Catholics until I'd been going with Esther. . . . [After reviewing the documents he would have to sign if he proceeded to marry Esther according to the Roman Catholic regulations.] That's about what Esther said it was. . . . There's sure nothing fifty-fifty about that. It doesn't seem fair. But Esther just takes it for granted . . . It seems there's only three things—or four, that can happen. Either I turn Catholic, or she turns Protestant, or we have a mixed marriage with our children raised as Roman Catholics—or we break up. . . . I love Esther and she loves me. . . . Yet there doesn't seem to be any good answer."

Rightly enough, every clergyman must adhere to the regulations of his own faith in such matters. And most clergy of all faiths, knowing the probability of future complications beyond the vision of the couple in love, tend to be pleased when, as in the case reported by Hulme, the decision is against proceeding with the marriage. But our society and its universities are heterogeneous. The decision is very often in favor of the interfaith marriage; and every religious counselor, while faithfully executing his responsibility as assigned to him by his church, bears also the responsibility of helping the couple to confront realistically the special hazards to follow from their decision.

A variety of types of problems with an obvious religious significance are initially presented to counselors on the campus today. The following examples of such problems range from the more obvious and external types to the less obvious and internal types.[2] First there is the conflict aroused with old forms of religious faith or unfaith by newly acquired knowledge. The usual form of this is the threat posed to immature faith by findings of the sciences. But increasingly common is the problem of a student with no previous training or commitment in religion who is suddenly confronted by something vital about religion in his study of history, or the humanities, or even the sciences.[3]

Second, there is the situation aroused by negative events; for example, the student's new wrestling with religious faith because of the death of a parent or friend. As described above, Jerry's problem was of this sort.

Third, there are the problems of vocation not only in the economic but also in the moral and religious sense. Charles' problem was of this type.

Fourth, the problem of relationships among members of the several faith groups is illustratively suggested by Ted's story.

Fifth, there are the many sorts of moral problems plainly associated with religion. One aspect of these was seen in the moral dimension of Charles' conflict about what occupation to pursue. Problems of relationship between the sexes fall also into this category. Even the Kinsey findings show that there are very few persons on a campus who regard sexual behavior as devoid of moral significance.[4]

Finally, we shall note the problems of meaning and of meaninglessness. Studies like those of Philip E. Jacob, as well as common observation, suggest that the present student generation, on the surface at least, is more "conformist" than its predecessor, in relation to religion as to other things.[5] This is, after all, only the student reflection of the more general social situation, with the churches having larger memberships than at any previous period. But on the campus as in the local church, we soon learn that beneath the surface there is more anxious or wistful search for meaning than was evident at first glance.[6]

In the previous generation, the troubled skeptics and doubters either evaded all religious counselors except neutrals, or else presented their views with a kind of aggressive challenge. Today the search for meaning is quieter. Questions are more indirect. Indeed, they may be missed altogether if one is not steadily sensitive to what is conveyed beyond literal verbal meaning. But the problems are there, and, however indirectly, are being often posed.

For example, even apparently remote problems such as inability to concentrate may be symptoms of confusion and indecision about lifework, and this may in turn have a dimension involving religious vocation. Just as the clergyman needs to be prepared to deal with many kinds of problems in order to give help in the religious dimension, so the teacher or student personnel worker needs to be prepared for the possible emergence of unsuspected religious dimensions of a problem.

Since the business of a university is education and the advancement of learning, it is especially important that we ask about the relation of religious counseling to that. Granted that such counseling may be important according to the purposes of the several churches, is it nevertheless only peripheral to the university?

Properly understood and effectively executed, religious counseling is vital to the educational process itself.[7] Any counseling may at times have to become therapy in the sense of re-establishing a basic floor that has been seriously threatened. But most religious and other counseling of university students is more than therapy in this sense. It aims at clarification of meaning, at bringing together emotion and intellect, at better symbolization of genuine experience, at deepening or enlarging the perspective from which problem situations are viewed. Where the focus of the counseling is religious, then by our definition there is an attempt to grapple with deeper and more ultimate concerns and meanings. Unless there is some such clarification, the total personal functioning of the student may be impeded to the extent that he cannot pursue the purposes of the university itself. Good religious counseling, when needed, promotes the mind and the intellect no less than the person and the feelings.

On the campus of any state university two groups of people engage in religious counseling. The first are the professional religious workers: co-ordinators of religious affairs, faculty members teaching religion, nondenominational or interdenominational religious workers, denominational religious workers, and pastors of local churches near the campus. Their main concern is religion. While interested in all aspects of the students' welfare and education, their focus is on the religious needs, problems, and searchings.

The second group is the administrators, faculty members, and student personnel workers. Their focal concern with the student is his education. Their counseling of him is as a part of the educational process, to facilitate his learning. Their professional focus is not on his religion. Yet like it or not, since so many personal and educational problems have a religious dimension, they are inevitably engaged at times also in religious counseling.[8]

With reference to those religious needs of students that can best be met by counseling, what relationship do we find between these two groups on the campuses? Occasionally we find open hostility or suspicion. Most often we find a kind of noninteractive parallelism—you help students in your way, and I'll help them in mine. Latterly there seems to be emerging from both sides a desire for active co-operation, though it may be too early to call this a trend.

Each group—the clergyman on one side and the student personnel workers on the other—has been guilty of misreading the other's counseling function. The clergy have accused the personnel workers of being mere technicians, or of being willing to settle for the reduction of tension, or of neglect of spiritual values. The personnel workers have regarded the clergy as inevitably biased in their counseling, of having the answers even before they know the problems, or of focusing on souls divorced from body, personality, and the educative process.

Whatever grains of truth there may be in such projections, there are serious distortions on both sides. And the most important corrective agent to such misunderstandings is being found in counseling experience itself. Among student personnel workers there is increased attention to values, growing conviction that the counselor is unlikely to be helpful unless he likes and respects the person he would aid, and more interest in the person as a whole rather than merely in one's professional slice of him. Among the clergy there is a renunciation of any form of coercion without sacrificing conviction, renewed attention to the wholism inherent in both Judaism and Christianity, and recognition that religious problems and personal problems are intimately interwoven. Wherever there has been opportunity for honest mutual discussion of fundamental questions, both understanding and co-operation have thereafter increased. We anticipate no revolution but a gradual increase in understanding and co-operation.

Understanding is also increased through intelligent referrals. No counselor can handle everything, and an important part of his professional equipment is knowledge of those who can do something better than he. Included in this are such obvious needs as the clergyman's referral of a psychotic student to a psychiatrist, the teacher's referral of a brilliant but failing student to the personnel services, and a dean's referral of an interfaith marriage situation to the proper clergymen. But referrals are needed in many situations less obvious than these. For illustration look again at the situations described at the beginning of this chapter. No counselor should profess to skills he does not possess; but he can have knowledge of his ignorance only as he learns of the skills of others. Referrals are potentialities not escapes. Indeed, the clergyman referring the mentally sick student to the psychiatrist ought still to make a pastoral call upon him; and the teacher rightly expresses a continuing interest in the brilliant but failing student whom he has referred to student personnel. Each group has a focus of function, but each group is also interested in the whole student. If all groups remember this, then the specialized counseling services of the large campus really help without fragmenting the student.[9]

It is our conviction further that better mutual understanding, co-operation, and referral will come about to the extent that both groups see their counseling as a part of the educative process. We sometimes act as if professional religious workers were interested only in a compartmentalized soul, student personnel workers only with extracurricular emotions and technicalities, administrators only with budgets and discipline— and as if only the faculty were concerned with education. But since education is the real business of the university, every service must, in some basic way, be evaluated for its contribution to the educative process.

It is reasoning of this kind that makes us believe the faculty, as the very heart of a university, has a greater contribution to make to religious counseling than has often been assumed. This includes of course the counseling of individual students by individual faculty members, as in our case of Charles and Dr. Hall. Just as important, however, may be the lesson that the faculty member's counseling is, in one basic sense, the norm for all religious counseling in the university. It begins from the concerns of intellect appropriate to the subject matter under consideration. It progresses to personal and perhaps religious issues but with the primary focus still on education. It may indeed need to be supplemented by specialized counseling services. But it shows the proper context for all counseling of university students.

The clergyman who really believes that the best ultimate service to his church lies in the best counseling of the student to maximize his learning cannot possibly possess the counseling vices sometimes attributed to him. The student personnel worker who believes his best service to the student lies in the best fostering of the capacity to learn is similarly protected from the sins of which he is at time accused.

As John and Sue go off to begin study in one of our great state universities, Mother and Father back home may wonder if help and counsel will be available in the event John encounters some apparently godless scientific opinion, or Sue falls in love with someone of another faith, or either of them confronts basic questions of morals or vocation. On the fundamental fact let Father and Mother be assured. If the student will but take the initiative, the right kind of counsel is available on or adjacent to every such campus. Let it be admitted that he may not hit it right the first time. If he establishes contact before a shadow falls, he will be much wiser. But the resources, few though they are in comparison to the quantity of students, are there. And their quality is steadily improving.

We are soon to have, however, a great increase in student enrollment in the state universities. Can the services of religious counseling move ahead in spite of the growing number of students, or can they even keep up with it? The answer to this appears to be less encouraging. In the last analysis, the answer may be "Yes" only if Father and Mother, through their contributions to the church as well as by their taxes, make it so.

Let us look first at the professional religious workers who serve students. The religious co-ordinators, university officials charged with co-ordination of all religious services to students, do much helpful counseling. But the more students, programs, offices, problems, and dimensions there are to be co-ordinated, the less time they are likely to have for counseling. Something similar may be true for the pastors representing the various faiths and denominations. The larger the program, the less time for personal work. Even the pastors of churches near the campus may be swamped by the increased faculties brought to serve the larger student body, and have little time for counseling.

In all such offices on or near large campuses, there is a move toward the creation of more adequate staff so that, with no neglect of necessary program and administration and teaching, there can yet be significant amounts of time left for individual counseling. For most expansion of this sort, financial reliance must be upon private contributions to the church or related agencies such as the YMCA. Although most national church bodies have increased their support to this work in recent years, in none do the professional workers feel that support is sufficient to meet the needs that lie ahead. Because of its quiet and unspectacular nature, it is religious counseling that may suffer most when the staff is insufficient to carry out all activities.

The general prospects in the field of student personnel have been surveyed in another paper. Our question is: in the future are more faculty members, administrators, and student personnel workers likely to be able to help as needed for religious counseling? We doubt very much that the increase in the number of such people will do more than keep pace with increased student enrollment. If, then, there is no more time to be spent, proportionately, will it be expended better? The answer, we believe, is likely to lie in the perceptiveness with which these persons view the student's religious counseling problems within the context of the whole educative process. And that in turn is likely to depend upon whether something significant about this is included in the professional education or in-service training of these persons. There are encouraging signs in the work of several foundations concerned with religion in higher education, in several programs of the American Council on Education, and on many particular campuses.

If we ask whether the professional religious workers are learning more about their counseling task, the general answer is an unqualified "Yes." Among all faith groups there is a marked increase in both the quantity and quality of such training as a part of professional education. The opportunities for later in-service training are also increasing. And research in religious counseling of college students by the clergy is beginning. All these signs are positive.

Against these generally optimistic statements of the prospect for religious counseling must be set three negative factors. Each is formidable but not unconquerable. The first, and perhaps finally the most important, is the tendency for any professional group to become fixed in its ways and contacts and to interact with others only superficially, occasionally, or when compelled. We have suggested strong reasons why such discussion and co-operation are desirable and some bases upon which they can proceed. But without vision and leadership, professional isolationism usually prevails.

The second factor is the sheer problem of size of the schools, especially when the anticipated growth is considered. Bigness often becomes more efficient, and ultimately may even protect individual interest. But there must be a limit. And bigness that is constantly growing bigger is different from settled bigness.

The third problem is financial. Especially in a time of rapid growth, it is the quiet and unspectacular services that tend to be upgraded last. This is human; but unless it is guarded against both in university and ecclesiastical budgetary councils, it is inevitable. Against all these dangers it is not only the professional workers in university and church who can make the difference, but also Father and Mother.

Religious counseling certainly includes the action of the church in following the student from home to university, so that perplexing problems arising in the new context may not isolate him from the church in which he was born and to which, in one place or another, we hope he will return. But it has been our contention that religious counseling, even by the professional religious worker, is more than that. It is counsel given by any responsible professional person concerned in the life of the student and seen within the primary context of the student's education and learning. So viewed, concern for the religious dimension of counseling is shared by the clergy with faculty, administration, and student personnel. It is the private property of none. Attempts at mutual understanding and co-operation are, therefore, not optional but mandatory. Perhaps such a conception in itself may advance the prospect of religious counseling in the state university.

GLENN A. OLDS

Religious Centers

CHAPTER XIV

Few phrases are as multiple in meaning and diverse in description as "religious center." This may be taken to mean (1) a building in which religious work is housed and carried out, (2) a fellowship of students and faculty held together by a central religious concern, or (3) the ultimate loyalty, basic commitment, or framework of faith of a person's life that serves to shape and integrate it. The first is a matter of geography; the second, of function; and the third, of philosophy. No definition would be complete without all three, and each, in turn, is complicated.

How shall one describe the rash of religious centers that has "broken out" on or near the university campus from the turn of the century, and so dramatically since World War II? In round numbers the Catholics list 500, the Jews 200, the Lutherans 400, the Methodists 350, the Baptists 300, the Episcopalians 200, to mention but a few. In value these centers range from modest "homes" to multiutility buildings worth upwards of $2,000,000.[1]

The centers are as varied and versatile in type as the strategy of our pluralistic religious culture over the last fifty years.[2] (1) There is the home, among the earliest, the most economical and persistent forms. Intimate and informal, it houses the priest, rabbi, or pastor, serves as a center for fellowship, small study groups, classes, and activities, and occasionally houses students or small co-operative eating groups. (2) There is the clubhouse, functionally designed for fellowship, recreation, discussion, and study, as at the Lamar Technological Institute. (3) There is the chapel. It may contain offices for counseling, choir, and modest study room facilities; but its form and function are shaped as a "sanctuary." (4) There is the combination, with the intimacy and actuality of the "home," the social utility of the "clubhouse," and the sanctuary of the "chapel." (5) There is the church center, situated in and with the local church on campus. (6) There is the common center, bringing together several or all religious groups in one building with multi-purpose meeting rooms, offices, chapel, and social hall.

How shall one describe the function of these religious fellowships? Up to 1900, in the predominantly Protestant era of higher education, these were primarily "voluntary associations" of, by, and for students. They were bound together not so much by theological agreement as by personal, moral, and religious earnestness. They knew a deeper wisdom of the relation of "wholeness" and "holiness," and sought to translate into the larger life of the campus and the world the implications of their own dedication. Many, if not most, of the services to students later incorporated into official university responsibilities were cradled and carried out by these societies.[3] Walls between students of different races, sexes, classes, and conditions were challenged, scaled, and broken. These fellowships were nonsectarian and nonclerical, having no connection with parent church bodies. They were patterned chiefly as YMCA or YWCA associations which by 1900 numbered "some 700 associations for men and 600 for women, with membership totaling over 100,000—almost half of the students then enrolled in the colleges and universities."[4]

By the turn of the century the communities of faith entered the field through provision of professional and financial help. As early as 1887 the Presbyterians and the Episcopalians had begun work at the University of Michigan.[5] Shortly after 1900, full-time university pastors were provided at Michigan, Wisconsin, and Illinois, both Catholic and Protestant, with a first full-time rabbi at Illinois in 1923.

The phenomenal development in professional leadership, national associations, and co-operative programs and agencies in more recent years has diversified in breadth and depth the nature of these fellowships. The early conferences on "Church Workers in State Universities" at Michigan in 1908 and at Cleveland in 1915 defined the need and scope of trained leadership in the field, collaborated with the new Religious Education Association (1903), and sought to enrich the "content" of these groups. Growing concern with the intellectual content of faith in the life of these groups and the university gave rise to the development of Bible chairs as early as 1893, short-lived interdenominational "schools of religion,"[6] the University of Iowa School of Religion,[7] and the establishment of the National Council on Religion in Higher Education to select and train fellows in all fields of higher education. Miami University prior to 1930, and the University of Michigan in 1934, brought full-time religious directors to their staffs, followed in fresh resurgence since 1945 by Ohio State, Minnesota, Maine, Florida, Georgia, Mississippi State, Louisiana State, and others.[8]

By 1920 and onward, experience of these groups with one another prompted attention to interreligious understanding and co-operation; the founding of the National Conference of Christians and Jews; co-operative religious programs at the University of Pennsylvania, the University of California at Los Angeles, Cornell, and on other campuses; various national student religious bodies—denominational, ecumenical, and international—and the demand for increasingly competent student religious workers. These workers have increased from a handful in 1900 to some 200 by 1938, and to more than 1,000 by 1953, the last official record available.[9] They exhibit a diversity in function and outlook natural to diverse theological backgrounds, personal capacities, and local peculiarities.

The nature of the religious concerns that bind the groups together is equally complex and reflects a comparable development. The early societies stressed personal piety, missionary recruitment, and service; the "middle period," social activity, civic responsibility, recreation, and student services; and contemporary groups are bound together by theological interest. Through all phases these groups have reflected an amazing vitality, versatility, and adaptability.

How shall one describe the meaning of "religious center" in terms of man's ultimate loyalty, basic commitment, or framework of faith by which life is integrated and made whole? Clearly, there is no common core of agreement concerning the particular content or form that such a loyalty or faith takes. There is, however, recognition that religion, from the Latin *relegere*, does mean "to bind together," and that the university, from the Latin *unus* and *versum*, does mean "to turn into one." In intent, both bear witness to man's deep need to unify his life and thought around some ultimate principle, object of loyalty, or subject of faith. In practice, psychological and historical analyses bear witness that most men, institutions, and cultures have their "center" in this sense, which functionally, if not theologically, defines their religion.

The origin and development of the religious center in the two meanings already discussed, as building and fellowship, can only be truly understood in terms of this view of man's nature and need. In the earliest period of the modern university, when theology was queen, religious form and content provided a "center" for the curriculum and life of its students. Even in the state universities of the earlier nineteenth century, the products of a predominantly Protestant culture, concern for the cultivation of man's religious knowledge and commitment was central, through required chapel, courses, and activities.

The steady erosion of this pattern through a growing self-consciousness of religious pluralism, difference, and a consequent emphasis on separation of church and state could not help but alter the role and function of religion in the life of the state university. The growing separation of religious faith and liberal learning, and the qualification, criticism, isolation, and displacement of the common presuppositions and values of Biblical and classical religious faith in the development of the state university required a fresh strategy on the part of the community of faith.

The appearance of the religious center, in its complexity and diversity, bears witness to the experimental response of religious faith to this new and altering university scene. It reflects the confidence that, although the state university cannot enthrone any theology as queen or champion, its students and faculty alike will and must live by some basic loyalty, some kind of religious faith, if not explicitly, then implicitly. The religious center becomes thereby a symbol of this central fact, not as queen but as servant of man's persistent need to "be made whole." It is a place where persons meet, loyalties are found and fixed, faith seeks understanding, and the community of faith ministers to students in search of a "center" for life or fidelity and growth in that already found. It is a fellowship of persons, bound by common concern, steeled and stretched by study and service, and transformed and empowered by worship and love. It is the bearer of a persistent philosophy, meant to complement the mission of the state university.

The philosophy of the religious center, in whatever form, is more than a set of ideas. It is a way of life as well, for religion insists that idea must issue into act and vision into character and community. No simple analysis can do justice to the rich diversity in religious thought and practice that characterizes the religious centers of American college campuses. Still, we need some way to come to terms with a dynamic process. Within the compass of this brief chapter there is room to mention only three features of the basic philosophy of religious centers. They characterize (1) the climate, (2) the functions, and (3) the ideas that constitute a living philosophy informing the religious centers of American campuses.

Religious centers on state university campuses are not so much the product of a finished or fixed philosophy as they are the experimental expression of communities of faith trying to meet new problems in the changing religious atmosphere of the state university. To be sure, the experiment is not without its informing ideas, but its initial intent was nurtured by a general yet persistent sensitivity to growing student needs in the fast-developing state university.

These needs, at once personal and practical as well as theological, called for some strategy fashioned from the message and ministry of the community of faith, with concerns that are intimate, ultimate, and inclusive.

The intimate concern was to meet and minister to human

need at its most personal, decisive, and inward ground: the ground of self-acceptance, self-understanding, self-direction, and self-fulfillment. In the growing state university, numbers had begun to impersonalize and fragment, common worship was often precluded, relationships were increasingly anonymous and academic, and motivation for learning officially void of the religious dedication to God and neighbor in the service of love. How could the religious community minister to the intimate personal and practical need of the student to be a responsible, significant person?

The ultimate concern was to meet the student's growing confusion over what is truly Ultimate[10] and worthy of his complete commitment. How could the religious community keep the ultimate questions alive in a community in which they were precluded or given marginal or minimal attention?

The inclusive concern was to meet the student's hunger for wholeness in thought and life in an inclusive community, a real *uni*-versity. In the state university, frightful fragmentation of both curriculum and community had begun to replace the earlier more homogeneous constituency and objective. How could the religious community, precluded general academic relevance, presume to offer any help? How could it introduce the student to an inclusive community in which all barriers between man and man, and man and God must fall? How could it mediate an inclusive concern to bring all the scattered truths of man's specialized studies into one community of truth?

The ways in which the religious centers sought to implement these persistent concerns in plans, programs, practices, and personnel range over the entire spectrum of human interest and activity.[11] In one of the larger centers, where fourteen religious groups are housed and work together, a recent survey revealed over fifty different kinds of co-operative activity and programs and well over one hundred different activities and programs at the religious group level.[12] The scope of this chapter does not permit even rehearsing the variety and range of these functions. It is possible, however, to discern a few central functions which the centers perform, around which much of their activity can be organized and understood. Oversimplified but illustrative are three central functions performed in every kind of center and type of program, large or small, and irrespective of wide theological variation. They are the creation of continuity in life's values and goals, the maturing of life's loyalties, and the clarification of life vocations. To be sure, other institutions and the university share in these functions; but in a special way they derive from the religious concern of the center.

The center creates continuity. When a student goes to college, he makes one of the most dramatic breaks of his life. Discontinuity is encountered at the "center" of his life, involving the pattern and authority of the character-forming agencies of home and church. The religious center, as a bridge of continuity from one authority to another, from infantile dependence to responsible freedom, from home to a freely chosen community, assists this transition. It seeks to help him build upon the best he brings, without the folly and arrogance of rejection in the name of a fictional freedom. The center provides continuity with the wider spiritual family, the community of faith, without restricting the critical freedom of the student's new status and independence.

The center is especially sensitive to the critical climate of a university, the discipline of doubt in the process of understanding, and the particular period of independence through which its students are passing. It seeks to avoid the peril of religious habit void of meaning, symbol void of sense, and it nurtures in critical understanding the inner meaning of outer form, the religious significance of sacrament, practice, and creed. The continuity it provides is creative and open alike to the past and the future, to the stable values the student brings, and to the creative opportunity for self-determination that the university expects and provides. In the end, its preoccupation is with its students, whose creative passage from youth to maturity symbolizes the flexibility of this function of the center.

The center seeks to help its students mature their life loyalties. The center seeks to clarify the religious conditions that surround life's basic loyalties and to make them sacramental.

The sanctity of sex, the faithfulness of love, the integrity of an ultimate commitment, are not only the subjects of conversation but the climate of life pervading the associations of the center.

Citizenship is also made sacramental in this setting. Not only in its leadership training and nurturing of responsibility, but in its prophetic voice regarding practices and policies of the campus and wider world, the center seeks to translate the moral vision of its faith into the loyalty of its life. One of the dramatic witnesses to this latter function is the way in which the student leadership in these centers across the South has sought to challenge and heal racial segregation in our time.[13]

The center helps to clarify the student's choice of vocation. One of its rationalizations for the wide variety of activity emphases lies here, in providing a climate of student initiative and concern where, free from parental pressures and undue social prestige, God's will, human need, and personal capacity are discovered and related.

Virtually all the activity of the center is designed to provide not only needed help to others, but occasion for self-discovery in a wide variety of vocations through which one can express fully his richest capacities and religious faith. The center's range of activities helps to overcome the persistent notion that only one kind of activity, that of professional religious work, can be a religious vocation. It seeks to show the religious dimension of all useful human activity and serves to recover the dignity of work and the re-creation of play.

Difficult as it is to simplify the concerns and functions of the rich variety of centers at state universities, it is even more difficult to simplify their basic ideas. The different theological traditions, definitions of the "community of faith," conceptions of liturgy and priesthood, authority, and responsibility, make the task in this brief compass virtually impossible. Still, careful study of publications, practices, and judgment of the professionals makes it possible to isolate at least three basic ideas at work in all religious centers. They are these:

1. The self-transcendent reference in the center's life and work derives directly from its religious function, concerned as it is with God. To be sure, man's understanding of the objective

character of God, the Ultimate Religious Object,[14] will vary widely from the religious liberal to the more orthodox. Implicit, however, in all its forms is the "ontological reference" of high religion: the concern to bring man into relationship with what is Ultimately Real and Supremely Significant. To have faith is to be thus oriented.

This serious concern of the religious center—to come to terms with God—serves to judge and instruct man's claim to truth and constitutes a real contribution of the center to the university community. The conviction that all one's seeking and finding is grounded in what is Ultimate, however misunderstood, provides a striking unity to the intellectual enterprise and the mental integrity of the student. All the "truths" found in the university must somehow finally relate to the "Whole Truth." To be sure, this whole truth can be premature, forced, arbitrary, and idolatrous, but not for long. The judgment of expanding experience as well as religious affirmation bears witness that God's mystery outruns man's mastery, and ultimate meaning transcends immediate comprehension. Such judgment, nurtured in natural piety and honest humility, is a permanent warning against idolatry, religious or secular, and narrow compartmentalization of thought.

Free acknowledgment of such self-transcendence judges and instructs motivation for learning as well, saving from subjective self-seeking while at the same time permeating knowing with concern. All religious knowledge is "concerned knowledge." The religious man knows in order to do. His seeking is morally earnest, not neutral, subjectively concerned, not objectively detached. His knowing relates to his being and doing in a radical fashion that gets at the roots of motivation. He who loves God with his whole mind has achieved a condition, through love, whereby the mind is freed of fear of failure, the greed of possessiveness, the pride of performance, and the exploitation of others in the seeking.

Finally, this self-transcendent reference provides a touchstone and offers a corrective to a fragmented university community. In its mature expression it is always unitary and universal. It serves to warn against confusing the idea of God with God, the form of faith with the object of faith, man's broken religious and academic communities with the purpose of God. It symbolizes in ideal a unitary reference toward which the divided communities of faith and learning must move in truth and life.

2. Personal responsibility is the condition for religious discovery. Religious concern cannot be coerced. The self rises to its own self-discovery and personal integrity in the response of its ultimate concern. Religious commitment is the counterpart of freedom disclosing at once something beyond and within. Before God man is most radically and really himself. There is no place for retreat, deception, or duplicity. To respond to God is to leave the crowd for the awe-ful freedom of one's own selfhood. Here is the clearest clue to real responsibility. The religious center understands that this fact is the secret of the substantial student initiative and "finishiative" that characterize the life and work of the center. The voluntary nature of all its activity feeds the freedom essential to mature self-determination. This expectation draws the student from a passive spectator role to that of a real participant. Testimony of students would confirm the view that this is a condition, as well, of all true learning, and offers a suggestive clue to the perplexed educator.[15]

3. Religious maturity requires the interpenetration of worship and work. The center rejects the haunting dualisms that mark the modern world, of sacred and secular, theoretical and practical, and affirms that they belong together in the perfection of whole persons in real community. This rejection is the consequence of the religious acknowledgment that if God is of any importance He is of supreme importance and relevant to the whole of life. It requires that study and service, praying and playing, curricular and cocurricular activity be dynamically related in a total life and whole person. The emphasis is a prophecy not only of religious integrity but of mental health and the possibility of becoming a *uni*-versity community.

These basic ideas are not fixed or final. They are self-creative and self-corrective. They plot out directions and emphases, broad enough to permit the rich particular content of different faiths and diverse programs and functions.

Few religious centers are at the center of the campus. Their location is often a prophecy of their function, linking as they do the community of faith and the community of learning. They are creations of a "boundary situation," with all the torment, frustration, and creativity of borderlines and boundaries.

Their situation is further aggravated by sizable diversities in both the communities of faith and the communities of learning. In the former they are due to theological, historical, and practical differences from extreme left to right; and in the latter to local, political, and institutional differences making easy or difficult this relating. The uniqueness of each is expressed primarily in the way in which the message, ministry, and strategy of each center are bound up in a host of local circumstances, personalities, and attitudes making up its life. Survey of the history of different centers reveals no clear pattern of building type, program function, personnel and staff, or official status on campus by which a tidy classification of significance can be made. The persistent function of counseling bears little correlation with the type of building or activity program and reflects more the competence and accessibility of the student worker and co-operation with allied university services. The various types of interreligious co-operation correlate only vaguely with the kinds of centers involved. As one might expect, the importance of persons in student and professional leadership, in determining the center's role and significance, is substantial.

How, then, shall one arrive at any useful analysis of pattern and function? The "bridging" function of the center, between the community of faith and the community of learning, is suggestive. How these two communities, with their own centers of gravity, interests, and objectives, do relate becomes a means of organizing an analysis of the patterns. This should not be taken to mean that the vitality or value of the relation and work performed is given in the pattern, but only that the pattern furnishes a clue to emphases and possibilities. To be sure, the writer's own "slip of faith" is unpardonably showing. Though the analysis is not meant as "progression in value," there is an underlying conviction that an implicit value and philosophy is contained in the pattern of the relation of the center to the university.

There are seven discernible patterns. They are characterized not only by building location and fellowship emphasis, but by an underlying philosophy regarding the relation of the community of faith to the state university.

1. The center is adjacent, independent, and isolated. It is not only off campus, but is unrelated in sympathy and fact with the so-called secular university.

2. The center is peripheral but penetrating. It may be off campus, but its ministry is to the campus.

3. The center is marginal but co-operative. Although it may be on the edge of the university, it seeks to work in its midst. It recognizes points at which genuine co-operation is not only possible but necessary. These include collaboration in counseling, campus services and charities, supplemental help in moral and morale problems, and minor ministries attending major university events of a quasi-religious nature.

4. The center is informally recognized and complementary. It is informally part of the educational mission of the university, an acknowledged ally in the total enterprise. The center's own autonomy in program, personnel, and support remains unaltered, but it is no longer merely an outsider.

5. The center is formally recognized and officially important. It has official status and administrative recognition. The university frequently provides a building, or space, or helps the religious organization achieve both. At Minnesota and Ohio State, the university has provided a nonsectarian religious officer to facilitate liaison with and co-ordination of the different religious centers enjoying this status.

6. The center is organically important and officially responsible. It figures naturally in the educational process, fulfilling its religious role responsibly. This pattern reflects a long history of co-operation, appreciation, and confidence between the religious centers, and between the centers and the university. Examples of this type are found at Michigan and Florida.

7. The center is integral and central. It symbolizes recognition of the central importance of religion, its integral relation to learning, and its "essential" mission "in the university."

Its best example is found at Cornell University. There the revolving altar in the chapel respects the integrity and difference in the form and freedom of worship yet retains the fellowship of a wider charity and work. The entire center, with its multipurpose public rooms and auditorium and its private offices for chaplains and religious groups, constitutes a bona fide division of the university, guaranteeing religious freedom but insuring an integral religious function in the university.

But if it is difficult to discern a progression in the patterns of center-university relation, how much more difficult it is to spell out functions. This is aggravated because the religious center affirms a "wholeness" to life that makes distinction and separation of function difficult. Beneath the wide diversity of buildings, programs, and activities is a steady protest against the fragmentation and segregation of modern life. The communities of faith knew, in founding their centers, that intellectual brilliance apart from humility and reverence and unrelated to morally responsible action can be bleak, irrelevant, irresponsible, and dangerous.

This cycle in different forms and tempos, in different theological traditions and university settings, can be discerned as a permanent part of the center's life and function. The cycle carries within itself the deeper rhythm of the religious life— worship, wisdom, and work, the movement from aspiration to illumination, to action, the interpenetration of reverence, reason, and responsibility. It is precisely because the religious center has no final option on these dimensions of life and expressions of the human spirit, however central they are to its function, that problems arise in the university.

Problems arise precisely because sometimes, and in different ways, and almost always in isolation one from the other, the university in its own way is involved in all three. This is illustrated in worship. Many of the state universities in earlier predominantly Protestant days had their own chapels and chapel services.[16] Even in states with strong Catholic and Jewish population this was the pattern and practice. Led by the president and professors, the services were nonecclesiastical and frequently nonclerical. Some schools developed nondenominational or nonsectarian chapels led not by university personnel but by visiting preachers. Still others employed a chaplain to care for the public worship.

As university populations became more heterogeneous, reflecting the religious pluralism of our culture, and as, in more recent times, there has been a resurgence of religious orthodoxy in form and practice,[17] the problem has become more acute. The diverse patterns in location and function of the altar in religious centers reflect the uneasy tension in this area. Those centers located in church or synagogue solve the matter simply. Worship is in the sanctuary. Some centers have no chapel for public worship as such but refer the student to the nearest local church or synagogue as his center for worship. Others develop student churches with the total life of a religious parish. Others provide student chapels as part of the equipment and service of the religious center. Still others co-operate with the university in providing several services—Protestant, Catholic, Jewish, or any other distinct type represented in large numbers in the university—as a total university ministry to the campus.

In the last plan there is no longer an inclusive university worship service, but rather several worship services for the university in keeping with its heterogeneous religious population. At this point problems arise. How are these university services to be designed and led and how are they to be related to the local churches and synagogues and the religious centers? Or should they be abandoned and returned to the religious community and centers?[18]

Even more complicated, though not so difficult to solve, is the matter of study. Obviously this is the primary emphasis of the university, but in the area of religion and in the state university this is complicated indeed. Although more than three-fourths of the state universities have some form of official instruction in religion, the pattern varies immensely.[19]

In response to this varied pattern and local contingencies the religious centers have developed their strategies. Religious instruction in matters of faith and morals is a central emphasis not only of the Catholic Newman clubs and the Jewish Hillel foundations but virtually of all the other religious groups as well. This may vary from loosely organized informal Bible study and discussion classes to formal courses offered by the center for credit,[20] co-operative Bible colleges supported by several religious groups and centers,[21] institutes or schools of religion separate but recognized[22] or as an integral part of the university under a director.[23]

Beyond this formal study lies the hinterland of discussion groups, cell groups, social action groups, lectures, panels, and conferences that constitutes much of the life of the center. Varying from the "juicy" and popular "Love, Courtship, and Marriage" series to spot talks on "Fissure and Fusion," the pattern of study seeks to involve and help the student at the level of his interest and need, and in terms that his crowded time will permit.

The problems that lurk here are those of duplication of effort, exploitation of students' time, relative degrees of competence, and the age-old tension between propaganda and persuasion, the intent to convert and the intent to inform. Can you teach about religion without being acquainted with it? Can you be committed yet objective in religious study? How much responsibility shall the university assume in dealing with religious illiteracy, with diverse religious traditions, with religious ethical systems related to pressing social problems, with the framework of meaning and ultimate claim of faith(s)? Shall religious centers give courses? Shall they be for credit? By whom shall they be given? How shall they be administered? Shall religion be taught as part of other disciplines and in other departments? Shall it be taught as a department of its own or as an interdepartmental discipline?

Finally, the most prolific and perhaps perplexing function of the center is in its work, translating faith into action. It has already been noted that many, if not most, of the student services initiated by religious societies have been taken over by the university as part of its student personnel services. These have included employment and housing services, orientation programs, freshman handbook, student directory, campus chest, counseling services, and virtually the entire range of student personnel services. Most state universities have a lively sense of the practical implications of their research and teaching and the service component in all of their work.

The problems here again are those of relation, duplication, and administration. The student union and the social clubs have their recreational side. Shall the religious centers omit this feature from their program, or is recreation essential to the "wholeness" of the center's emphasis? How shall the service projects for relief, community service, and international outreach, and to special students and special needs be administered and related? What should be the relation of the religious center to the student council, the interfraternity council, the foreign student adviser, the deans of students' office, and the president or his representative in student affairs?

Most centers insist that the faith they profess must be embodied in significant human service, that love of God entails love of neighbor and vice versa. But shall the center organize as a religious group to work, or shall it work to have the campus organize to serve? Shall it insist on the religious motive for significant human work, or shall it work to make any human service significant, whatever the motive? These are growing questions requiring radical rethinking.

The acceleration of developments in this field makes prediction about the future as precarious as it may seem foolish. The center's phenomenal recent development in number, staff, buildings, and budget[24] has been matched by growing interest and concern on the part of the university.[25] Nor does this trend seem likely to be changed soon. Within this general development, however, certain local trends with potentially far-reaching significance are discernible. Space permits only their mention, description, and the suggestion of implications. We will consider general trends and particular trends relating to the threefold function of the religious center—worship, study, and work.

Concerning general trends, it may be said that there is:

1. Growing distrust of the segregation of religion and liberal learning.

2. Growing awareness that deepening of the center and widening of the circumference of the religious life must go hand in hand.

3. Growing concern that the large group of students not being reached and awakened by the deepest claims of both communities be found and helped. Certain types of such students stand out in bold relief and persistent challenge. They are: (a) The questioning but suspicious. (b) The indifferent. (c) The apathetic. (d) The unquestioning. (e) The questioning but fearful.

If these students are reached, a radically new vitality and leadership for good will be released within the university. If they are missed, we may expect even further erosion by conformity and mediocrity, with mounting numbers and dwindling moral resources. In any case, both communities have a fundamental stake and complementary role to play in this process.

Concerning particular trends, the following points may be made:

1. Worship. The trend seems away from the late liberal notion of the nineteenth and early twentieth centuries that differences in forms of faith and practice are really not decisive or important.

It is now generally recognized and accepted that for most religious communities worship reflects the highest art and deepest integrity of faith. Here form and content blend into one. For this reason, differences in worship are recognized and respected. This imposes new difficulties and deeper opportunities for the religious center in educating and the university in serving its students. An all-university worship service will likely progressively fragment at least into predominantly Protestant, Catholic, and Jewish student services, and such others as numbers may warrant. There is real gain and real loss in this trend. The gain is in the recovery of religious literacy and integrity respecting the inner form and content of faith and its expression.[26] The loss is in the concession to that deepest of all ironies of religious history—that what represents the highest religious art should be the most deeply divisive.

2. Study. Within the religious centers there is a new and healthy emphasis on theology, the worship of God with the mind. It raises the pertinent religious question regarding the vocation of a student and reinforces with religious significance the intellectual mission of the university. Within the university community are stirrings of special significance for the study of religion. The myth of complete objectivity and value neutrality has been significantly challenged by natural and social sciences alike. The university is coming to recognize that all of its significant undertakings proceed from some value presupposition, some standpoint of faith. The effort to preclude religion from the curriculum on the grounds that it is a faith to be affirmed, not taught, has been weakened by this new mood. Interest in ideology has revived the interest in the psychological and sociological role of religion as well as a concern to understand the motive and meaning of faith itself.

With this trend has gone the awareness that the effort to deal with "religion in general," to avoid sectarianism or any show of partisanship, has frequently led to missing the very nature of religious faith that makes it meaningful in life. A noticeable trend is away from the general treatment of religion and toward a treatment of particular faiths "from without" and often by not only a professional but a "professing" religionist, as at the University of Iowa, Columbia, and more recently at Harvard.

Finally, there is growing awareness that interest in "religion in general'" was evidence of a deeper wisdom concerning a general religious dimension of all life not easy to isolate or segregate. This trend seeks to discover and articulate the religious dimension of man's varied activities and interests, and, as at the University of Michigan, to incorporate within different departments of the university study of the religious phase of history, psychology, sociology, etc.

These trends are equally ambivalent. Theological interests of the center may deepen the life of the mind and the intellectual integrity of faith, or they may tend to substitute in-

tellectual exercise for personal commitment. Recovery of the
"faith standpoints" in all our knowing may alert us to a deeper
dimension to all our knowing, but it may also become the
apology for a new irrationalism with critical consequences for
both communities. Interest in particular faith content may
enrich an earlier religious abstraction, yet it may negate the
important effort to discern fundamental unities where they
exist, and return to a provincial Western religiosity. The imperative to understand the cultures of the East and the Middle
East requires exposure to these traditions often given in the
older "comparative religion" courses.

3. Work. There is a growing convergence between the religious center and the university in the area of student services.
The trend is toward conversation, collaboration, and, where possible, co-operation. This is critically apparent in counseling but
also at the activity and program level. Although there is a trend
toward incorporating university responsibility for co-ordinating
religious activities within the dean of students' office and area,
there is a countertrend that I believe will be eventually more
decisive. This trend recognizes serious jeopardy to the religious
counseling and pastoral functions of the religious staff associated directly with administrative offices, which handle disciplinary and discretionary matters. It resists the temptation
to reduce the work of the religious center to "student activities"
alone, and bids for a wider relevance to the whole student and
the total university.

Only close and continued collaboration at national, professional, and local levels between these groups will provide
clues about how this development will and should proceed.

No appraisal can do full justice to the facts or be even
tolerably acceptable to differing theological perspectives, educational philosophies, and personal standpoints. At best, an
appraisal can lift again to bold relief broad principles that
illuminate the nature and value of the religious center in the
university. These will be gathered around three frames of
reference: educational, theological, and cultural.

Educationally, we are able to see that though we may seek
to separate religious faith and learning in an institution, we

cannot do so in the life of a student. It is unsound to suppose that in all other matters the student should aim for integration but that in this decisive area he must subscribe to segregation. As a psychological impossibility, the effort creates chaos at the center of life. For better or worse, the university cannot fail to deal with the matter of religious faith in its students, and the religious center cannot fail to be in some sense an "educational enterprise."

The task here is twofold: (1) We must train a new kind of chaplain and university religious worker. With few exceptions, theological seminaries are too specialized, isolated, and insulated from the main currents of thought in the disciplines of a university to do this job. Yet the campus religious worker must understand and deal with the impact of these different disciplines on his students and their faith, all in fresh ways and with a marked degree of competence. He must know the university as well as the content and resources of religious faith. In his graduate training he must be exposed systematically to the presuppositions, outlook, method, and implications of the central disciplines of the university. In this task the best minds of the university can be engaged. They must be brought to bear on the issues where religion and the university meet, converse, and challenge each other. (2) We must develop a new kind of university faculty person alert to the twin demands of religious faith and liberal learning. The National Council on Religion in Higher Education and more recently the Danforth Foundation have been breaking ground in this area, but the need far outruns the results to date. What is required is a fresh wedding at the graduate level of theology and the other disciplines, such that the creative interpenetration required of the students at the practical level will have been grasped in some measure theoretically.

Theologically, both the university and the religious center stand in danger of the perpetual sin of idolatry and the peril of segregating God. Any thoughtful person knows, as indicated earlier, that if there is a God, if He is of any importance, He is of supreme importance and relevant to the whole of life. The difficulty is that both religious and university communities tend to force an impossible segregation of the sacred and the secular. The product of such segregation in the religious center is either irrelevance or presumptive pride, and in the university, value-neutrality and emptiness or some form of idolatrous faith.

The saving feature of our religious pluralism and democratic culture is the guarantee against any form of religious despotism capturing the state university. The plurality and particularity of faith that makes impossible uniformity in authority makes equally impossible ready identification of religious faith with any "watered-down" version of "democratic culture" or other forms of religious idolatry.

The task here is twofold: (1) We must translate the theological renaissance of the past quarter century into relevance to the contemporary educator who is perplexed by problems centering around (a) the nature of man, (b) the relation of knowledge to virtue, ignorance to sin, and (c) the religious roots of the institution and practice of democracy. (2) We must translate valid educational methods and liberal humanism into the practice and programs of the religious centers, rendering them more effective without displacing their religious motivation and ministry.

Culturally, both communities realize more than ever that our pressing problems are primarily ideological. They concern the faiths by which men live. Our problem is to discover how to deal with totalitarian "faiths," their power and efficiency, without succumbing to their methods or sacrificing the freedom and plurality of our own. We know no faith is more fanatically powerful than religious faith. Can we learn how to co-operate and federate our religious faiths without watering them down, rendering them instrumental or idolatrous, or robbing them of their free vitality? If there is any hope of learning how to do this, it should be in the state university, mirror in miniature of our complex culture. Can we discover how this can be done? Can we learn how to wed intellectual competence and religious commitment, the critical community of learning and the dedicated community of faith?

Our task here is twofold: (1) We need basic research concerning the relation of faith and culture, religious belief and social behavior, theology and practical ethics. The newly formed institute concerned with these relationships at Wesleyan University is an important experiment in the right direction. It needs expansion in new directions in other settings, including the graduate school of a large university. We have not begun to use the religious center as a laboratory in research-action, to which it would lend itself readily and well. (2) We need pilot faith-action projects aimed at reducing cultural tension, promoting creative intercultural and interreligious understanding. Too little has been made of the role and resources of religion in providing paths and bridges to this understanding. Religious centers collaborating with instructional units in the university are uniquely designed for such projects at home and abroad, more imaginative in character and wider in scope than traditional service and work camp experience.

Finally, whatever else the religious center and the university may do, they must help the student recover and reconstitute a valid center for his life through which life can be seen steadily and whole, and in terms of which both communities may realize their deepest intention as *uni*-versity and religious center.

ARTHUR J. LELYVELD

Interreligious Relations

CHAPTER XV

Several levels of motivation for interreligious co-operation exist on the college campus. They range—or they rise, if you will—from the inescapable practical demands of the campus situation to the distinterested effort to apply brotherhood ideals in the milieu in which they should be most naturally at home.

Whatever the motivation, interreligious activity in some form and in varying degree is omnipresent in the state university and, like all co-operative activity, it seeks structure and machinery and it demands accommodation. Its origin may be the need felt by the administration to present to the community the university's religious "face" despite its heterogeneous religious and ideological features. Or it may be the recognition by campus religious leadership that compelling common objectives are a counterweight to cherished differences, that the menace of shared peril and the tokens of multidenominational failure must neutralize sectarian competitiveness.

There is a growing and healthy unease about the shared peril, a growing recognition that despite swelling membership rolls and the quantitative success of external religion in the community at large, we are not doing too well. If we are transmitting our value traditions to the college generation at all we are doing so largely in terms of vague verbal affirmations; we are not evoking genuine commitment or a will to religious action.

Philip Jacob's excellent compendium of surveys of student attitudes[1] has given wide currency to disturbing conclusions which, though they are admittedly generalizations, probably apply to 75 to 80 per cent of college students today[2] and come as no surprise to those intimately acquainted with student life. Here the religious forces confront together a picture of a composite student who though "nominally religious" is "essentially secular," who is "gloriously contented" and "unabashedly self-centered."

What is more, Dr. Jacob jolts the religious forces by a hint that they are not to be too sanguine about their capacity to change this situation. Indeed he cites evidence purporting to show that the less "religious" the student, the less prejudiced and the more humanitarian he is likely to be.[3] But Dr. Jacob offers no comfort to the social scientists. He adds that there is no proof that a larger dose of liberal education or of social science produces "a more sensitive regard for the humane values."[4]

These facts, along with the prevailing societal attitude that makes material gratification a chief goal and the pursuit of self-interest a common characteristic of our time, are an invitation to humility. They demand that campus religious workers and the university community concerned pool their resources in the effort to introduce students to factors of enrichment and to moral and spiritual values. In this task, they will at the same time be combating a major menace: the multiplication of mass men who take their values from each other and whose goal in life is security within the protecting uniformity of the group.

In this context, religious differences are a good. The cultivation and appreciation of distinctive traditions not only protect society against reduction to universal grayness, but they are also important tools for the preservation of the group sources of societal ideals essential to democracy. Interreligious activity must, therefore, be of such a nature as to make possible the continuity of group distinctiveness and of valuable differences.

What we have been saying makes sense only if we are speaking of dynamic religion, the disturbing kind, not the anodyne kind, the revolutionary kind of thought found in the prophets and the gospels, the kind that makes demands on people. Lack of campus antagonism to religion—and there are no significant, committed antireligious forces today—may well be a danger sign. The university may comfortably make a *pro forma* bow in the direction of the church through the invocation by a religious dignitary on a stated occasion and through other equivalent amenities, when its benign attitude rests on the assumption that religious forces will not be strong enough nor religious convictions deeply enough held to constitute a problem.

The variant religious groups working together may contribute to the revitalization of religion and its acceptance of an effective role in society; they may introduce meaningful commitments into the lives of students, and by the reality of meaningful differences they may slow down the march of conformity.

In the state university, for legal as well as for human and moral reasons, this co-operation must be voluntary. But though it must grow out of the will of the groups themselves and remain free of "interference" by state agencies, the university cannot afford to ignore a development that crisscrosses the campus and lies so close to the heart of its own concern. This creates a dilemma that may belong in the category of those problems that never get solved but only get older. The university must walk the thin line between its constitutional responsibilities and its responsibilities to its students in an area increasingly recognized to be crucially important.

One approach to this dilemma on state campuses today is a technique called "co-ordination" of religious activities. In the proliferating area of student "personnel" services, the university that cares for the physical and mental health of the student, that provides counselors for his emotional and financial problems and guidance officers for his vocational uncertainties, may with equal propriety concern itself with his religious needs.

This approach was fully developed and first applied at the University of Minnesota where, under the leadership of Dean Edmund G. Williamson and Dr. Henry E. Allen, a rationale and a structure within the field of student personnel work was developed. The University of Minnesota Office of Coordinator

of Students' Religious Activities was organized in 1947 and its
"bureau history"[5] gives this description of its origin:

> As the University grew in enrollment, and as the multiplicity of
> diverse faith groups became more apparent on the Campus, it was
> clear that a University-sponsored chapel service or the appointment
> of a University Chaplain could not be satisfactory when there ex-
> isted diametrically different approaches to worship. Logic seemed
> inevitably to spell out a policy whereby the cultivation of spiritual
> growth among students was to be left to private organizations. . . .
> The advising and counselling of these faith groups was plainly the
> responsibility of the national denominational or interdenominational
> organizations with which the student groups were identified. Most
> churches designated a chaplain or counselor with responsibility to
> minister to the needs of these student "congregations."[6]

> Since, however, these diverse student religious organizations were
> an integral part of campus life, there needed to be 1) a pattern of
> liaison which would show the University's appreciation for the con-
> tribution of these religious programs and 2) a method of making
> sure that the contribution of these groups and their advisers would
> be constructive. Student religious groups like all other student or-
> ganizations were under the guidance of the Student Activities
> Bureau, but because of the recognition of religion as a basic motivat-
> ing force, together with a full appreciation of the autonomy of
> religious activity in the American pattern of church-state separation,
> the establishment of a special bureau to coordinate religious activi-
> ties was indicated.

One key to an understanding of this development is the
phrase, "as the university grew in enrollment and as the multiplicity of diverse faith groups became more apparent." Life
on the pre-World War I campus was relatively simple and
nowhere more so than in its religious life. The student body
was so overwhelmingly Protestant that the small Catholic and
Jewish minorities could be overlooked without unfriendliness
or irresponsibility.[7] The academic environment made for a
liberal, ecumenical approach to Protestantism itself, and the
minority religions could be invited in all good will to participate
in "interdenominational" services or in the religiously motivated, secularly expressed activities of the Protestant YMCA

and YWCA's to which the care of the University's religious life was frequently delegated. The fact that this did not meet the religious needs of minority groups was not uncomfortably evident as long as their representatives were few in number and their own communions neglected them.

In 1913, however, the first Newman Club for Catholic students on non-Catholic campuses was founded in Philadelphia, and there are today some 800 units in the Newman Federation of America. Then, after World War II, the Hillel Foundation for Jewish students came into being at the University of Illinois and later, under the aegis of B'nai B'rith, spread to more than 200 campuses, serving a Jewish student population of almost 200,000. Quite unsurprisingly, the major concentrations of these non-Protestant religious groups were on state university campuses.

The value of this change in the religious life of university communities was soon felt. Where formerly an official chapel, intended to include all and offend none, may have been leading to religious stagnation or impotence, the rise of religious differences helped the process of probing and re-examination that has been characteristic of much twentieth-century religious life. There was a dawning understanding of the benefits of religious pluralism.

The greatest contribution to this development was made by the disruptions of university life produced by World War II. The campus was invaded by G.I. students who were more mature in years than the average college generation and who were returning from experiences that had shattered provincialism and opened their eyes to the multiplicity of human types, human beliefs, and human responses. Among them were a host of religious workers whose ministry had been remolded in their service as chaplains to the military forces and who had chosen student religious work as a form of expression analogous to what they had done in the army and in the navy. They, too, brought views broadened by their personal involvement in cataclysmic events.

They had not only heroically served the needs of men of diverse faiths in the midst of razor-keen tensions and soul-smothering violence, but the best among them had also come to recognize, with a clarity sharpened by crisis, how inadequate were their ministrations to men of religions other than their own. In their fellowship with chaplains of other groups they learned that a minister might serve under the emergency circumstances of the battlefield as surrogate for a rabbi or a priest but that he could no more take their places than they could take his—that each faith group possessed depths of tradition, significant shades of difference of associations and meanings, which the outsider could strive to understand, to respect, and to appreciate but could never wholly appropriate while he retained the identity of his own faith. What is more, there was a new conviction among many that each faith deserved to flourish in the wholeness of its own continuity and through the contributions of its own scholarly interpreters.

One such individual, among the many I had the opportunity to observe, came out of military service and by the power of his own understanding revolutionized the chapel structure of a tradition-bound ivy-league school, securing quasi-official chaplaincy status for the professional head of each denominational religious agency. This sort of influence, combined with that of administrators governed by the American tradition of respect for equality of privilege and the rights of groups as well as of individuals, produced comparable changes on many state university campuses. Official chapels that had been taken for granted were now abandoned and several "interdenominational" Student Christian Associations became Student Religious Associations.

These changes have not taken place without understandable pockets of resistance and inevitable awkwardness. Indeed, the vestigial remains of earlier untroubled times frequently produce a measure of benevolent amusement. This is primarily true of the effort to find structural devices in new buildings that will evenhandedly accommodate all. There are three-way revolving altars, occasionally with one-third unsanctified by the church for whose use it was designed, and even four-way altars with one-fourth dedicated to completely innocuous, generalized religiosity.

On one campus where the wishes of the donor made necessary stained-glass windows not wholly acceptable to one faith
group, specially designed window shades carrying symbols
acceptable to that group were installed. The administration
of another state school succumbing to the anachronistic impulse
to build a chapel for all its students whatever their religious
backgrounds was surprised and even a bit offended to learn
that a motif of crosses in the brickwork made it difficult for
conscientious Jewish students to use the building. On another
campus where a new "meditation chapel" was built it was
equipped with offices for each of the "associate chaplains,"
making it necessary for some of the satellite agencies' leaders
to leave the comfort of their own well-equipped buildings to
make a periodic bow to the new structure in the name of unity
and good will.

The students of another tax-supported school have been
provided with an interreligious building—three-layer cake
in design so that there is a floor for each faith—the ground
floor of which is the scene of an annual struggle conducted
with restraint and yet with firmness about display space—for
the convictions of the group which displays madonnas will not
permit the madonnas to associate with the symbols of the Feast
of Lights, and the followers of the Feast of Lights are unwilling
to be relegated to an upstairs corner while Christmas takes
charge below.

Only one school, a privately supported one, has made the
logical response to the demand of the times for evenhandedness
without the watering down of significant differences. Brandeis
University has built three separate and equal chapels around
an interfaith area where a common altar is the focus of official
University events such as the annual baccalaureate service. But
this bold solution is obviously not without its own complications—nor could it be easily imitated by state universities.

In all this the Jewish minority, as the only non-Christian
group in substantial numbers on campus, has a special problem.
It is not one that is the result of ill will or of a fault in the
organization of activities; it is one that grows out of the situation itself. It is the problem of the unconscious dominance of
the majority culture. The Jewish minority is affected by it

even in its popular understanding of distinctive Jewish traditions. More frequently than not, they are identified by untutored Jews in Christian terms: Passover as a kind of Jewish Easter, the "sefirah" period between Passover and Pentecost as a kind of Jewish Lent. The very structure of society is undergirded by Christian assumptions.[8]

Thus even the liberal administration of an official chapel will inevitably reflect the Protestant tradition of worship—the underlying Protestant assumptions, for example, as to what prayer is, what its role should be, what the mood of worship should be, and even as to the character of reverence itself. With the best will in the world, a liberal dean on a campus where there is a large body of students representative of strict Jewish orthodoxy finds it difficult to plan a weekend retreat at a resort or camp away from the campus at the beginning of each school year, although she regards it as indispensable to the kind of thoughtful planning together that will make possible a year of meaningful activities. Her wish to provide conditions that will make possible both strict observance of the dietary laws and strict regard for the Sabbath runs counter to her wish to avoid setting up distinctions that would detract from the unity of the group experience. There is no simple solution for her—it is a situation that requires patience, respect for conviction, and above all a willingness to recognize that differences do exist and are important.

This kind of respect for difference, which frequently demands exercise of the Christian virtue of "going the second mile," is part of the moral responsibility of the dominant majority that is frequently more difficult to bear than the legal responsibility. This is the responsibility to recognize that deviations from the dominant norm may have intrinsic value; that they must not be crushed by the weight of numbers. It is of vital importance if we are concerned about the almost irresistible march of society toward monolithic, deadening uniformity.

Fortunately, this problem has won respectful attention, as may be seen by the wide variety of forms of interreligious organization with which state university communities are now experimenting.

The first such form is the appointment of official university co-ordinators of religious activity, to which we have already alluded. This experiment is in process at Minnesota, where it originated, at Michigan, and at Ohio State. It is noteworthy that these three schools are all large midwestern state universities each with a population of more than 20,000 full-time students of diverse backgrounds. Each has been well served over the past three decades by professionally staffed voluntary religious work agencies, many of which have fine physical facilities on the perimeter of the campus. Indeed a building boom during the last ten years has resulted in the multiplication of new, modern structures for the religious foundations on these and many other campuses.

At Minnesota, there are twenty-three such student religious work units, inclusive of the YMCA and YWCA, on the Minneapolis campus alone—from the large Lutheran Student Association, the Wesley and Westminster foundations, the Newman Foundation, the B'nai B'rith Hillel Foundation, the Pilgrim Foundation, and the Canterbury Club, through all the denominations and faith groups to the small Eastern Orthodox and Buddhist student fellowships. This is the situation into which an academically appointed co-ordinator, now holding full professional rank, was introduced—not to "originate religious programs but . . . to assist groups of all faiths to fit harmoniously and constructively into campus life."

As one of the "student personnel services" under the office of the dean of students, the co-ordinator's office serves as an information center and provides an "interreligious reading room." The co-ordinator is described as a "liaison official." His post is "in no sense . . . a directorship or a chaplaincy." Among the present functions of his office are (1) the processing of voluntary religious census cards, (2) providing a program consultation service for interreligious activities of a co-operative character, such as Religion-in-Life and Brotherhood Week programs, (3) arranging seminars for the professional workers of the voluntary agencies to increase their "student personnel" skills, (4) offering "impartial guidance" to students with personal religious problems, (5) occasional teaching of courses and "arranging institutes concerned with religious values," and (6) speaking on interreligious understanding and interpreting the University's attitude on religious matters.

I have quoted extensively from Minnesota's own statements concerning this office, not only because it is the pioneer bureau providing a pattern for other campuses, but also because even this sketchy outline of its functions suggests the care needed in any effort to nourish religious forces while avoiding favor or the appearance of favor to any religious group. The restraint in the outline hints at the way in which this kind of effort may arouse and indeed has aroused what Thomas Jefferson called the "asperities" of interchurch competitiveness. The new office is being watched most conscientiously, particularly in respect to the area of guidance to the so-called "uncommitted," and it has even been the target of attack by advocates of the "high wall of separation" between church and state. And indeed, when a university bureau presumes to seek to create "a method of making sure that the contributions of these (voluntary religious) groups and their advisors would be constructive," even those groups that co-operate officially in the program will be vigilant to protect their own freedom of action.[9]

This is given point by the fact that such efforts are motivated not only by a need to "co-ordinate" but also by the will to fill a gap and to provide a kind of nondenominational, "nonreligious" counseling service, to serve those who cannot be reached by, or may be dissatisfied with, the existing sectarian campus agencies. It is the product of dissatisfaction with "unofficial" religious work and its presumed ineffectiveness when left totally outside the structure of the university itself.

What co-ordination there is at Minnesota is carried on through the Council of Religous Advisors on the professional level and the Student Council on Religion on the student level. Working with the co-ordinator's office this latter council sponsors the religious emphasis programing in special weeks, freshman orientation, and the like. There is common agreement that the co-ordinator's office has facilitated interreligious co-operation by its administrative contributions, has opened the door to contact with official university life for the student pastors, and has placed the helpful stamp of official university recognition on the work of the religious agencies.

The recently established Office of Religious Affairs at the University of Michigan is like Minnesota's bureau in that it is headed by a co-ordinator and is part of the personnel structure of the University. Along with the Health Service and the offices of the Dean of Men and the Dean of Women, it is under the jurisdiction of the University's Vice-President for Student Affairs. The pattern of operations and of relationship to the separate religious agencies is similar to that at Minnesota, but the Michigan office stresses the fact that it regards University-sponsored program-planning and program-counseling as an important adjunct of its task of co-ordination. Two staff members of Michigan's Office of Religious Affairs give full time to the effort to stimulate and create interreligious programs. They work primarily with student government and major campus organizations. In this effort to influence the campus directly and to build a "climate" favorable to religious activity, the Michigan office may simply be carrying out the implications of its own background, for it grew out of an earlier, University-sponsored Student Religious Association operating under professional direction, which itself was the depression-born successor to a University Student Christian Association.

Here, too, there is co-ordination at the top through professional and student representatives of the voluntary agencies but little actual interreligious activity on the student level. Although the structure at Michigan is still too new to be evaluated, the consensus of those concerned is that the development is constructive and promises to be increasingly helpful as it establishes itself on the campus.

The Co-ordinator for Religious Affairs appointed by the University Board of Trustees at Ohio State in 1948 works with a University Advisory Board for Religious Affairs, which is composed of representatives of the University administration, the faculty, and the student body, along with the professional religious workers and local ministers drawn from the three major faith groups, all appointed by the President of the University. The administrative role of the Co-ordinator's office is similar to that of the office at the University of Minnesota, already described. All twenty voluntary religious work agencies surrounding the campus are represented on two subgroups: the University Religious Council composed of the professional workers and the Student Council for Religious Affairs. It was at the request of the University Religious Council that the University Advisory Board was appointed in 1949.

As on other campuses, this development has elicited some criticism: there are those who regard it as an overorganization of religious interests, which they claim has splintered adult participation and slowed down intergroup religious activities. On the other hand, there is general recognition of the value of the co-ordinator's work in liaison and in executing major interreligious activities such as the annual Religion-in-Life Week, the Convocation for new students, the "Recognition Banquet" for student religious leaders, and campus religious programs on radio and TV. One innovation at Ohio State is a distinguished Festival of Religious Music and a Festival of Religious Art which have served to broaden the area of interest in interreligious activity and to demonstrate the creative relationship between religion and the arts.

One would have expected a similar development of university administrative procedures in religious affairs at the University of Illinois. Illinois was the major laboratory for the birth and growth of off-campus religious foundations in the years immediately preceding and following World War I. Illinois pioneered in this form of response to religious needs, with what has been called "planned maintenance of church and university separation," which at the same time enabled the university to provide hospitality and encouragement to religious groups. However, the development of a University Office of Religious Affairs and the appointment of a University religious co-ordinator have not been contemplated at Illinois, and the organization of a new University Religious Council has encountered difficulties.

This may well be the result of a general university satisfaction with the pattern of leaving religious work to the individual voluntary foundations. Significantly, these foundations at

Illinois have always held a quasi-official relationship to the University through the accreditation by the University of the frequently popular and well-attended courses in religion which the foundations offer. A University Religious Council did exist from 1942 to 1953, but it died of inanition, and recognition was withdrawn from it at its own request. With it, the effort to observe Brotherhood Week with joint activity or to conduct a Religious Emphasis Week also died.

The proposal for a new University Religious Council, which functioned for a time although it had not been officially recognized, grew out of the desire of some of the professional religious workers appointed by the voluntary agencies to foster the development of co-operative activity. It has not been the result of any University-engendered program of co-ordination. The new group sought to be an official body under the supervision of the University and composed of representatives of the campus religious organizations, the residence councils, the faculty, and the administration. Its major function was to have been the planning of campus-wide interreligious activities. But the opposition of the representatives of several religious groups has led the Dean of Students to recommend a postponement of action on the proposal "pending further study." Some of the groups that oppose the plan have requested a final veto power on joint programing, fearing that a University Religious Council may take control of campus religious activities out of the hands of professional advisers and may "disquiet the minds of their students." They are reported to be "a vocal minority, mistrustful of student initiative in the field of religion."

Meanwhile, the Religious Workers Association, composed of the staff members of the eighteen voluntary religious work agencies, which is the major instrument for co-operative religious activity at Illinois, continues to probe the question of what kind of additional interreligious organization, if any, will meet their specific campus needs.

"Definitive and conclusive patterns will not emerge for a year or two and these are initial stages," writes one correspondent. "There is a good deal of groping for the right means."

This kind of "groping" is present even on campuses where

the response to the problem is the antithesis of the Illinois program of "maintenance of separation"—state universities where the pattern of an official university chapel persists. Notable among these are Pennsylvania State University, where a conscientious effort to adapt the old form to the new pluralism is being made, and the University of Maryland, where the chapel idea was introduced after World War II and where a new chapel building was completed some five years ago.[10]

At Penn State, the University Chaplain has been given the additional title of Co-ordinator of Religious Affairs, and the University provides him with an assistant whose function it is to plan interreligious programs. Both the University Chaplain and his assistant are ordained Protestant ministers. But the University tries to mitigate this appearance of favoring one faith group by officially designating several of the full-time religious workers who serve the voluntary religious institutions of the University community as "chaplains to the University." These are ordained clergymen representing the three major religious traditions on the campus. Of course, the chaplains to the University, in contradistinction to the University Chaplain and his assistant, are supported by their own denominations or faith groups. In addition, the University, using private contributions received for that purpose, has built a new "all-faith meditation chapel" whose permanent decor and pattern of use have not yet been fully developed. The pattern at Penn State, as described by the Chaplain, is tri-faith: tri-faith in its official literature, tri-faith in the University's Committee on Interreligious Affairs, tri-faith in the credit course in religion offered by the University, and in every area in which such participation is feasible. But the tri-faith pattern breaks down in the official chapel itself, which by nature and tradition remains Protestant. This is so despite the liberal extension of invitations to non-Protestant preachers and despite the fact that in 1956, of the 92.5 per cent of the entire student body that filled out voluntary religious census cards, 30 per cent noted a non-Protestant religious preference.

There is general agreement at Penn State that the atmosphere of interreligious relationships is "wholesome," but that the student response to interreligious activities is "lukewarm"; the conventional Religion-in-Life Week program has been abandoned in favor of periodic lectures by outstanding Protestant, Catholic, and Jewish leaders under the sponsorship of the Committee on Interreligious Activity and an annual Brotherhood Dinner, which is assured of attendance because of its organization on the basis of official representation of fraternities, sororities, and other student organizations.

On other campuses, the Protestant YM and YWCA's, still playing their traditional role, are important factors in the emergence of a new form of interreligious relationship. At Colorado the regents of the University approved the appointment of a "theologically trained person" to serve as co-ordinator for the Religious Workers' Association, half of the salary of the "co-ordinator" to be paid by the University and half by the YWCA. Then, as the last academic year ended, the post of co-ordinator was abolished and in his place the University appointed a "religious program counselor" who, serving the University half time, employs the other half of his time as a "Y" staff member. The counselor's responsibilities have not yet been fully marked out, but he will advise on Religion-in-Life Week and will work with the student government Subcommission on Spiritual Development. This latter body is currently seeking to establish a small meditation chapel as well as a Department of Religion on campus and is fostering a program of year-round visits to the campus living units by "chaplain-faculty teams."

Some observers have found evidences, at Colorado and on several other campuses, of an incipient rebellion against the "tri-faith" approach, manifested in a refusal of Protestant groups to be "lumped together." "Some of our problems stem from a feeling of a plurality larger, much larger, than three," one correspondent writes.

A period of experimentation marking the transition from a traditional "Y" setup to tri-faith interreligious activity is also in process at the University of Texas where an officially recognized University Religious Council has been formed to work in co-operation with the office of the Dean of Student Life.

The "Y" itself acts as a clearing house and is conscientiously serving the development of genuine pluralism. In the past, student representatives and faculty joined the professional religious counselors in the wholly unofficial University Religious Workers' Association. Now the setup has been reorganized to create a student-run University Religious Council, making its headquarters in the "Y" and on which the members of the Religious Workers' Association serve as "advisory representatives." In addition, there is a Faculty Committee on Religious Life appointed by the President of the University. Texas' major interreligious activity is an annual Religious Emphasis Week but increasingly, it is reported, functioning committees of the University Religious Council are facing up to significant problems of human relations and campus tensions and to the tasks of religious orientation and education on a year-round basis. Through them, the Council is beginning to exercise a direct influence on campus life and values.

The structure at the University of Wisconsin has points of similarity to that at Texas. The "Y" groups, however, do not play a central role at Wisconsin, and the traditional Religious Emphasis Week has been abandoned in favor of quarterly lectures in the Student Union by representatives of the major faith groups. Wisconsin's dissatisfaction with Religious Emphasis Week is reported to have stemmed from the feeling of some that its program tended to be "evangelistic," and of others that its sessions "although well planned and favorably attended . . . presented a false 'united front' of religion to the campus."

The other end of the spectrum from the highly organized University of Minnesota response to the challenge of campus religious pluralism is to be found at the University of North Carolina, where there is neither organization nor the feeling of need for it either among students or denominational workers. An active Campus Christian Council represents the ten Protestant groups and the University administration has customarily looked to the "Y" as the focus of religious affairs. Nevertheless, the influence of Minnesota is felt—at least, verbally—for just last year the University of North Carolina requested the Associate Director of the University YMCA-YWCA "to assume the additional title of Coordinator of Religious Activities."

The problem of interreligious relations has different dimensions at the University of California at Los Angeles and at New York City's Hunter College where off-campus religious centers house all the voluntary religious work agencies.[11]

U.C.L.A.'s University Religious Conference, now housed in a beautiful new building, is a tri-faith venture that has existed for thirty years. It has won remarkable co-operation from lay leaders, clergy, and students of all groups. U.R.C. sponsors not only the usual Religious Emphasis Week at U.C.L.A. but also courses in religion, a School of Religion, and special projects such as its well-known "Panel of Americans" and its adoption of a university in India as its special concern.

Both the University Religious Conference and Hunter's Sara Delano Roosevelt Memorial House are corporate bodies independent of the tax-supported institutions they serve.

A most significant pattern, which has itself been the subject of specific study,[12] is that of the State University of Iowa, where a School of Religion, supported by private funds supplied by the major faith groups but wholly recognized by the University, not only gathers an academically qualified tri-faith faculty for the teaching of credit courses in religion but also serves as the focus of campus religious activity. Supporting its current tendency to place more and more emphasis on its academic function, the School has been encouraging the University's Office of Student Affairs to play an increasingly important role in co-ordinating the activities of the voluntary religious agencies.

At the University of Connecticut, encouragement of the religious agencies has been furthered by the fact that the University has managed to set aside a block of its land on a strategic edge of the campus, parcels of which have been deeded to the individual voluntary groups. As a result, several attractive religious centers have been built.

Through all these variant forms of interreligious organization one finds a surprisingly uniform pattern of programs and problems. The religious forces everywhere confront the crippling indifference of the mass of students, the lack of genuinely deep religious concern in administrative circles, and the secular and sometimes overtly antireligious attitudes in teaching staffs. But something is stirring. As Father Robert F. Drinan said in a recent issue of *America* (December 15, 1956), the "old campus gods of science, progress, secularism and humanism are undergoing an agonizing reappraisal" and educators are asking how the Judaeo-Christian heritage may be presented to college students in a manner more effective than religious organizations or religion courses seem to make possible.

For many years the chief reliance of interreligious programing on state university campuses has been the Religious Emphasis Week program, initiated by the University Christian Mission and recently influenced by the National Conference of Christians and Jews. We have already alluded to instances where this form of program has been abandoned and campus religious forces are actively searching for new techniques that will be freed of the more obvious defects of so-called Religion-in-Life Week approach. Those defects are the once-a-year, formal, and occasionally perfunctory character of this kind of program and its failure to make a meaningful impact on student lives. The new approaches are aimed at creating a year-round, week-to-week program in the campus living units with the stimulation provided by the visits of some of the most forceful personalities on the religious scene.

On one large campus, where Religion-in-Life Week persists, the featured orator last year was the most popular speaking personality of the denomination with the largest representation on that campus. The University's largest auditorium, capable of seating thousands, was set aside for his appearance. But when the great night came, the attendance totaled 150, not all of whom were students.

"Despite fine words, the University says 'no' to religious activity," one observer said in explanation of this disappointment. "After Homecoming Week, Greek Week, and Snow Week, the students are exhausted and barely able to muster up enough energy to study for finals. It is at this point that we come along and cruelly dragoon some student into taking the chairmanship of Religious Emphasis Week, doomed to failure before it begins."

There is, however, one "action project" of national character which is religious in its origins, religiously motivated on the American scene, and struggling to relate its religious values to its program of philanthropy and education. This is the work of World University Service, which annually raises hundreds of thousands of dollars for aid to overseas student communities and for a program of education in international understanding. Sponsored in the United States by the national student work organizations of the three major faiths and by the National Students Association, it has experimented in recent years with a "core" program on several campuses through which it has tried to enlist the energies of local representatives of the national sponsoring groups in activity and discussion related to the meanings that undergird the Service's fund-raising program. This effort has not proved to be easy. American students give, but they give through typically American, organized campus chests that inevitably obscure the causes for which money is contributed. The chests by their very nature substitute "promotion" for education and rely on ballyhoo and time-tested machinery and new "gimmicks" to extract student gifts.

"The Campus Chest contributes quite a large sum of money to World University Service, but though some of the church groups on campus may possibly educate their own students as to the purpose of WUS, they are not vitally connected with the central campus chest committee which is handled by the Student Government," one correspondent writes.

The dilemma is sharpened by an antithetical situation at another school where the campus chest committee dropped WUS and "the University Religious Council has picked it up and has done a much better job of education for it, but has not been highly successful in actually raising funds."

But this is after all the heart of the very dilemma with which campus religious forces must continue to wrestle: to find the means of linking participation with understanding, machinery with meaningful content.

Intergroup and interreligious activity acquire meaning when

they emphasize both service to common objectives and the application of shared social ideals. An interchange that possesses the dimension of depth becomes possible only when it is founded on the integrity and increasing understanding of each individual group, which are then reflected in the program of joint activity.

The organized attention which this problem is receiving is a recognizable new factor in university affairs. The first consultative conference to this end by state university administrators and faculty and religious leaders was held at Minnesota in 1949.[13] This meeting set off a process of continuing exploration and by its example stimulated the holding of several similar conferences. Nourished by the National Conference of Christians and Jews,[14] a conference of university personnel and religious workers at twelve midwestern universities was held at the University of Illinois in 1955.[15]

The fact that these conferences have not failed to recognize the difficulty of the problem and the impossibility of finding a simple solution is encouraging to those who believe that it must be confronted in all its complexity. The difficulty inheres in pluralism itself. The voluntary religious agencies representing as they do the variant individual faith groups must be the foundation for any interreligious structure, and, though there is some justification for dissatisfaction with their present effectiveness, the university must recognize them, encourage them, and thus help strengthen them or it faces the danger of building its new approach in a way which will violate cherished traditions of separation of church and state, infringe upon the freedom of action of individual groups, or offend the sensibilities of the minority denominations.

Sensitive understanding of this danger was expressed at the Allerton Park Conference by Allyn P. Robinson, who said:

A religious group derives its reason for being from its religious faith. This faith is rooted in its heritage . . . To ask a group to disregard or slur over its religious commitments in the interest of "cooperation" or "brotherhood" is to ask a group to do what it cannot do and maintain its integrity . . . Intergroup activities involve more than saying "My door is always open, anyone may come in." Too often this means that the majority groups determine the basis on which cooperative activities are conducted and minority groups are placed in the position of conforming or withdrawing. And if they do the latter, they may be quite unfairly considered "uncooperative." The ethics of a pluralistic society requires new norms, new appreciations, and new skills.[16]

We are today at the very beginning of the task of finding those new norms and new skills. But the hope that a "community of values" can be created is encouraged by Philip Jacob's finding that in certain group situations and in certain colleges where there is "unity and vigor of expectation" there is a "peculiar potency" to counteract the wound-down mediocrities of our times and to lead students toward meaningful and enriching life goals.[17] In carrying forward the effort to build that potency in the state university situation, we bear the overwhelming obligation to grasp both horns of the dilemma. The struggle to provide deep and significant religious educational opportunities must never infringe upon the absolute religious freedom which is the keystone of the American structure and is, at the same time, the expression of a supreme value.

FILMER S. C. NORTHROP

Students from Other Lands

CHAPTER XVI

The presence of students from other lands calls for exceptional religious and educational statesmanship. The task will be misconceived if it is thought of merely as the chance to acquaint them with our religious and social values and to provide them with the facilities here for sustaining their own religious faith. The opportunity is present also to educate American and foreign students alike in interreligious, intercultural, and international understanding and collaboration. President Eisenhower has noted that man now has it within his power to destroy mankind. Either we learn to understand one another and to restrain our culturally and religiously inspired nationalisms and imperialisms or we perish.

The masses of Africa, the Middle East, and Asia are rebelling against Western imperialism. This development includes insistence upon their own indigenous cultural laws. Since the separation of politics from religion is foreign to any people who have not passed through the Protestant Reformation or come under modern Western secular political philosophy, this native cultural renaissance is also a resurgence of their own religion. Note the recent Islamic religious reaction in Turkey against Atatürk's modern secular reforms. Read Prime Minister U Nu of Burma's exposition of Buddhism in An Asian Speaks.[1] Consider the similar synthesis of Buddhist religious values with constitutional democracy in Thailand. Recall Ghandi's statements, "Such power as I possess for working in the political field [has] derived [from] my experiments in the spiritual field" and the Hindu Bhagavadgita is "the book *par excellence*" spiritually. Read Esther Warner's *New Song in a Strange Land*[2] and hear the contemporary Liberian say, "All we got to live under two laws. We got to live under the Liberian government [Western] law. They got plenty soldier. We don't give our heart to that law. The other law is the law of our people where the chief is the big man. That one we give heart to."

Clearly, the era in which religious statesmanship is conceived in terms of converting the world to one's own religion is over. It is by cultivating a respect for one another's differing cultural and religious traditions that religious statesmanship in today's world will find itself. As the Hindu Swami Akhilananda has suggested, "Teachers should not attempt to convert students from one religion to another." The deepening of each student's insight into the richness of his own religion and the expansion of his imagination, intellect, and heart to enter sympathetically and with understanding into the spirit and novel merits of other religions is the wiser course. In any event, it is the only practical one, the mood of non-Western people being what it is.

In fact, their present tendency is to affirm that the Judaic-Christian West, however inspired may have been its founders, is obsessed with material wealth and instrumental gadgets at the expense of the intrinsic religious values necessary to control them. Vice-President Radhakrishnan of India speaking out of his Hindu-Buddhist background, like Iqbal of Lahore speaking for a reconstructed Islam, concludes that the hope of the world centers in the religions of Asia, or of Islam, which, not drawing such a sharp division between the religious and the secular, keeps the details of daily life more continuously and intimately rooted in the spiritual. A recent study of Indian students on an American university campus shows that they leave, even after three years including visits in religious homes, with a conviction that Americans lack a proper appreciation of spiritual values.[3] Even European students often share this opinion. One need not accept these judgments in order to see their practical consequence, which is that the West, and especially the United States, is on the defensive with respect to its religion.

Another fact points in the opposite direction. The people of

Africa, the Middle East, and Asia are demanding both (a) the right to build their social institutions in the light of their own indigenous religious traditions and also (b) the higher standards of living and the democratic political control of their lives which they see the peoples of the modern West enjoy. These two demands generate spiritual conflicts and raise problems which must be understood if the needs of foreign students on American campuses are to be met or if American students are to make correct judgments concerning the introduction of Western beliefs and ways into non-Western lands.

The ways of native non-Western people before the modern Western imperialists and Christian missionaries came were not those of liberal, constitutional democracy. As Sir Henry Maine showed in his *Ancient Law*[4] and as the comparative philosophy of the world's cultures reaffirms, any people not influenced by Western law or religion live under the religion and ethics of "the law of status," and not under the religion and ethics of "the law of contract" from which liberal, constitutional democracy derives. In a perfect law-of-status society, the selection of political leaders is not made in an election guided by a contractually introduced constitution to which all people have in principle given their consent and before which they are all equal, after the manner of the religion and ethic of a perfect law-of-contract community. Instead, all leadership is set by status of sex and priority of birth within the family and by color-of-skin, familial, or caste status vis à vis the tribe, determined by whether one is of the predominant sex from the first family of the tribe.

For example, in a purely patriarchal, law-of-status religious community, the head of the nation or tribe is the eldest son of the first family of the tribe, according to the rule of primogeniture. In a purely matriarchal society, the eldest daughter is both the political ruler and the head of the family by the same principle of biologically bred status. Consequently, family, caste, and tribal loyalty become the primary moral, religious, and political obligations. Furthermore, religious worship is not congregational but focuses around the privacy of the family hearth and the ceremonies of the tribe.

Such was the religious, political, and personal ethic of the ancient cities of Rome before the creation of Western legal science by Roman jurists who were Stoic Roman philosophers or heavily under the influence of this philosophy. The African in Esther Warner's Liberia spoke truly when he said that he gave his heart to "the law of our people where the chief is the big man." In this statement he showed that their morality and religion is that of a law-of-status community. The laws of ancient Hindu India are called the Laws of Manu because Manu was the founder of the Aryan-Hindu tribe. Under the laws of this Hindu religious community, only patrolineal descendants of the first Manu enjoyed political, moral, or religious leadership. The same law-of-status ethic operates in Shintu Japanese society, in the Califate, in many local families in unreformed Islamic society, and to a predominant, though lesser, extent among families in Confucian and Buddhist societies.

This is why the people of Islamic Turkey and Pakistan and of Hindu-Buddhist Thailand, Burma, and India have had to introduce a law-of-contract constitution and a legal system imported from the West in order to bring their domestic affairs under their own democratic control and to introduce the reforms necessary to begin the lifting of their standards of living. But this is to begin the shift, initiated in Western civilization following the Stoic Romans, from the religious ethic of status to that of contract. The effect of this shift is to disassociate moral, political, and religious man from color-of-skin, family-centered, and tribally bred man, and to identify him with universal or cosmopolitan man, that is, any man whatever, standing equally with all other men before contractually constructed and freely accepted universal legal principles.

In the West, with the decline of the Roman Empire, this new religious ethic of the law of contract passed on the one hand to the eastern empire and Justinian and on the other hand into the Roman Catholic Church, thereby creating Western Stoic Roman Judaic-Christian civilization. (In fact, the literal meaning of the adjective "catholic" in the Christianity of the Roman Catholic Church is "universal.") Kant's categorical imperative, to the effect that only that conduct is good which can be expressed as a universal law for everyone, is an example of this ethic. The Declaration of Independence of the American colonists and the Bill of Rights of the Constitution of the United States and the Indian Bill of Rights are other examples.

Because the shift from status to contract cannot be made instantaneously, the Stoic, Roman Catholic, Judaic-Christian ideal historically tended in considerable part to be filled in with the law-of-status content. Consequently, Roman Catholic Christianity became associated with hierarchically ordered aristocratic and regal institutions rather than with democratic and egalitarian ones. The same is true of the Protestant Christianity of Luther's Germany, of Calvinism, and of the Church of England of Hooker, Elizabeth, Sir Robert Filmer, and of the latter's biological descendants, the First Families of Virginia. Hence, if the Stoic Roman Christian ethical ideal was to be achieved, it became necessary to reform not merely the Roman Catholic Christianity of Saint Augustine and Saint Thomas but also the Protestant Christianity of Luther, Calvin, Hooker, and Sir Robert by means of the more democratic values of (a) Nonconformist Protestantism and (b) modern secular natural and moral philosophy, particularly that of Newton, Locke, and Jefferson.

In their zeal, however, to locate the source of religious and political authority in the conscience and freedom of the individual, Nonconformist Protestant Christians tend to lose the Roman Stoic factor in Judaic-Christian civilization. Consequently, for them, unlike Roman Catholic Christians or followers of Islam, legal norms seem to be merely instrumental and to be irrelevant for intrinsic personal moral values or for the religious life; also, political nationalism tends to be fostered at the expense of lawful universalism and of faith in the need for the spiritual foundations of international law. It is no accident, as I have shown elsewhere,[5] that many of the major leaders in the achievement of the transfer of some national sovereignty to the Western European economic, military, and political community have been vital Stoic Roman legal thinkers and Roman Catholic Christians.

These considerations point up the fact that Protestant and

Roman Catholic Christians need one another. Interreligious understanding and collaboration on the university campus is as important, therefore, domestically as it is internationally.

Both Christian groups also need modern secular natural and moral philosophy. Witness the adherence of many Southern Nonconformist Protestants to the color-of-skin law-of-status ethic (derived from Sir Robert Filmer through the First Families of Church of England and Calvinist Virginia) and their resistance to the universal ethic of the law of contract by the Supreme Court of the United States in its recent unanimous decision on segregation in education. Clearly, the reform of Roman Catholic and Conformist Protestant Christianity by Nonconformist Protestantism is not sufficient to achieve the religious and moral shift from biologically bred status to a society in which Judaic-Christian man is universal man. All too often the Nonconformist Protestants, taking the Bible as the literally dictated word of God, go to certain parts of the Old Testament containing the patriarchal and tribal ethic for their criterion of the divine and the good. A third factor has been necessary, consequently, in order to approximate the initial ideal of Stoic Roman Judaic-Christian civilization. This third factor is modern secular, natural, moral, and political philosophy, especially that of Newton, Locke, and Jefferson and the Kant of the categorical imperative.

The foregoing role of the Old Testament in this story shows that Jews as well as Christians need the reforming influence of Stoic Roman legal science and modern secular science and philosophy. Otherwise, more and more Jewish students, persuaded by the latter subjects and convinced of the validity of the universal ethic of Western legal science, while they see many of their fellow religionists pursuing the religion and politics of the law of status, are going to be increasingly alienated from their religion. This, in fact, is the domestic problem of the secularized leaders of contemporary Israel from Western Europe when, in their introduction of a law-of-contract constitution, they are confronted with the religiously orthodox Jews from Morocco and the Arabian Peninsula who outnumber and outbreed them.

It appears, therefore, that if the natives of Africa, the Middle East, and Asia want to retain their indigenous religious and cultural traditions while also achieving the democratic control of their own affairs and the more democratically distributed higher standards of living which they see peoples in the West enjoy, they must amend the law-of-status religious and social ways of the masses in the light of a deep understanding and acceptance of the quite different law-of-contract religion and ethic of the Roman Stoic Judaic-Christian, the Nonconformist Protestant Christian, and the modern secular West. Clearly, the modern West has not merely its efficient instruments, but also its unique intrinsic spiritual values. A wise religious and educational statesmanship on the American university campus will insure that American and foreign students alike have the chance, inside as well as outside the curriculum, to learn what they are.

The Africans, Moslems, and Asians must master these values also if they are to achieve their present insistence upon the more universally spread standards of health and wealth which they see in the Modern West. These medical and economic aims require the introduction of scientific medicine, agriculture, and machinery and the latter's high capital investment. Such finance requires (a) the introduction of law-of-contract control of banking and investment at the federal level and (b) the moral integrity in the handling of finance by public officials who, abhorring nepotism, give greater loyalty to the law-of-contract norms of a dull legislative statute or an abstract constitution than to the concrete blood ties to the members of one's own family and to the first families of one's tribe—a type of financial integrity upon the part of public officials which a family-centered and tribally centered law-of-status morality and religion does not provide, and which only the universalist ethic of the Stoic Roman law-of-contract religion and society insures.

The latter ethic, as the Stoic Roman jurists and philosophers made clear, goes back, as does modern scientific technology, by way of Greek philosophy to Greek mathematical physics with its conception of any truly known individual thing as an instance of a formally universal law. This freed the essential properties of any truly known individual from such sensed properties as color, thereby preparing the way for the Stoic Roman jurists, and the Roman Catholic Judaic-Christians following the jurists, to disassociate moral, religious, and political man from color-of-skin, family, caste, and tribal man, and to identify him with universal man. It follows that if non-Western people want the widely distributed standards of health and wealth, they must introduce not only Western scientific instruments but also Western law-of-contract religious and moral values. Similarly, if Western religious and educational leaders are not to betray their spiritual heritage, they must radically reform their present conception of the relation between the humanities and natural science, breaking down departmental lines by revealing the common philosophical and scientific way of knowing from which both derive and upon which both depend for their validity and effectiveness. This is as important for American as for foreign students.

One final consideration remains. Countless Americans are emotionally disturbed and spiritually empty to the point of sickness. This is the case frequently, notwithstanding a religious upbringing and even attendance at Jewish synagogue or Christian church. Every state government is plagued with the endlessly mounting cost of providing care for the insane and the mentally sick. It is difficult to escape the conclusion that this points to something spiritually lacking in the religion of the Hebrew-Christian world and in the ethic of the modern secular West.

The central place which emotion occupies in these ills suggests that it may be here that for Western man the more intuitive religion of the African Negro, the Islamic Sufi, the meditating Buddha, the nondualistic Vedanta Hindu, and the warmhearted Confucian *jen* come into their own. In any event, Swami Akhilinanda of the Ramakrishna Hindu Society of Boston reports that American students, professors, and businessmen who are eminently successful come to him spiritually unsatisfied and emotionally at odds with both themselves and their mates. May it not be that the religious worship in which they participate in synagogue or church is too much concerned with group sermons, group ceremonials, and pastoral visits and confessionals and not enough given to nonverbal private meditation and direct intuitive communion in silence which religions such as Buddhism and nondualistic Vedantic Hinduism provide? Perhaps, also, the modern West needs those psychological techniques discovered by Asian spiritual investigators which so shift and transform the content and focus of a person's emotive experience that he becomes one with the existentially immediate, undifferentiated, and, hence, timeless and infinite component of himself and of all things. If so, the provision on the university campus of the religious symbols and practices of Africa, Islam, and Asia beside those of the Judaic-Christian West may be as important for Jews, Catholics, and Protestants as it is for enabling foreign students of other faiths to sustain and deepen and discover what is still valid, after the reforms by the ethic of the law of contract, in their own religious traditions.

In this connection, the new modernistic chapel at Massachusetts Institute of Technology is very much to the point. In this building there is but one chapel, completely devoid of symbols from any religion whatever. On the floor below the chapel there are several little rooms each containing the symbols of one of the major religions of the world, Oriental as well as Western. When one religion is scheduled for the main chapel, its symbols are taken there.

In one respect, however, this admirable practice leaves something to be desired. It makes the error of supposing that all religions are congregational, bringing people together to worship as a group. This is true of Judaism, Christianity, and Islam and also of Westernized forms of Buddhism and Hinduism. In her book, *The Hindu Temple*,[6] Stella Kramrisch reminds us, however, that congregationalism is completely foreign to [non-Westernized] Hinduism. The same is true in major part of Buddhism, Janism, Confucianism, and an important part of Roman Catholicism as the presence at any moment of the day of a person worshipping alone before a side altar in a Roman Catholic church demonstrates. Consequently, if the authentic religions of the Orient, in their non-Westernized forms, are to bring their intrinsic, intuitive, emotive values to their own adherents or to others on the American campus, special permanent rooms with their respective symbols, isolated from all outside noise, must also be provided for each of them.

For followers of Islam, the chapel at the Massachusetts Institute of Technology with its blank, modernistic interior is ideal. To a Moslem, the presence of any symbol whatever within the place of religious worship is regarded as idolatry and as religiously shocking. Also, the floor of any chapel should be level throughout and without any slope. Otherwise, the Moslem worshipper runs the risk of being unable to return his body to an erect position when, with his knees on the floor, he swings his trunk forward and touches his forehead to the floor. All pews or seats must be removed if followers of Islam are to worship there. At most, only a huge rug or many rugs should be in the room. Before the single chapel for all congregational religions is built, an astronomer might well be called in to orient it so that its front interior points toward Mecca. In campus meals or invitations to luncheon or dinner, where Hindus are included, the provision of an adequate meal containing no meat and composed largely of vegetables is of equal importance.

Such attention upon detail may seem overdone; yet their neglect may produce unnecessary embarrassment and result in more harm than good. Also, Oriental religions should be presented in their pure, non-Westernized, authentic forms. This does not prevent Westernized versions of Oriental religions from holding congregational forms of service, after the manner of the Ramakrishna Hindu Mission and certain Westernized Buddhist groups. Probably, however, the modern West has enough of such religious worship without going to Westernized Hindus and Buddhists for more. What we, in our hectic, oververbal, overpreached, and overlectured world need is the more private, silent type of intuitive meditation and contemplation that brings the emotive fulfillment and spiritual equanimity which the statute of the meditating Buddha, his eyes half open, half closed, or of the meditating Ramakrishna, conveys. The Oriental philosophical and psychological methods of analyzing and directing attention and modifying its content, described in part by Premier U Nu of Burma in his aforementioned article, need to be introduced by Asian experts and studied by Western analytic, radical, empirical philosophers and psychologists. French philosophers and scientists are already doing this.[7] Such study might revive an interest in and a respect for religion upon the part of faculty and students for whom religious philosophy means merely Hume or Wittgenstein and religious psychology suggests merely Pavlov or Freud.

Cultural anthropologists and philosophers have found that the behavior and ceremonies of one culture seem meaningless and even silly to an observer from a different culture unless the observer learns to understand what he sees in the observed culture's terms. Because very few religious people have learned how to do this, the observations of the missionary of one religion upon the meaning and merits of another religion are, with rare exceptions, of little worth. The same is true of most politicians and laymen in their judgments of a foreign nation's secular behavior. Contemporary social scientists who describe a foreign culture in terms of the concepts of recent Western behavioristic or Freudian psychology commit the same error. If we do not want students on the campus to react similarly to modes of worship or meditation other than their own, the religious and educational leaders must learn from the philosophical anthropologists.

The latter have found that to understand the people of a foreign culture one must think about what one sees or hears them do from the standpoint of their own way of thinking about it, rather than from the standpoint of one's own culture. When anthropologists such as Paul Radin and Clyde Kluckhohn did this, even for people who have no written language, they found themselves confronted in each case with a complete and novel philosophy. Recently the anthropologist Professor Hoebel has made a study of the legal norms of seven different so-called primitive peoples. So different are the norms of any one of these seven people from those of the others that he finds it necessary to set up seven sets of basic conceptions to describe them.[8] Interreligious understanding requires the same approach.

Practically, this means that the authentic presentation of the major religions and their practices on or near the university campus is not enough. The mentality or philosophy behind each must accompany the presentation. To appreciate and understand Roman Catholic worship, one must interpret what one sees in terms of Roman Catholic doctrine and philosophy. To evaluate and gain respect for Islam, one must, in addition to observing Moslems at worship, read the Koran and some of the Sharia (laws), while also having some appreciation of the Greek, Arab, and Persian philosophy of a very high order which has gone into their interpretation. Likewise, to understand the Buddhist's Nirvana, the verbal and nonverbal practices of its Zen sect, the Hindu's Brahman, or the psychological and gymnastic techniques of a Hindu Yogi, something of Buddhist and Hindu philosophy and especially its epistemology must be comprehended. To present the authentic practices without the indigenous theory necessary to understand them is to fail practically.

It follows that ministers, priests, and lay religious leaders must be closely associated with the faculty. The resources in the departments of anthropology, philosophy, area studies, comparative law, and religion must be drawn upon. Perhaps all of these departments will have to be expanded, becoming less culturally provincial in the philosophy, law, and religion which they teach. Also, foreign and American students who are authentic representatives of their respective faiths should be encouraged to expound to one another the inner meaning of each religious tradition.

Since the major point in the coming of any foreign student to the United States is to obtain an authentic understanding of our culture, it is best that they live isolated from one another as far as possible, with American students, so that they see what we do from our specific spiritual standpoint. Otherwise, the differing spiritual mentalities of the different foreign cultures which they represent will tend to reinforce them in the error of judging the United States in spiritual terms other than its own, and instead of achieving an objective understanding of our particular spiritual values, they will leave, after the manner of the Indian students in the aforementioned University of

Pennsylvania study, with their initial, provincial religious and political prejudices concerning the United States reinforced. Hence, the regular university union should be used to bring students together, and a residential international house is probably unwise.

It is, however, wise to have some official person or committee whose responsibility it is to see that foreign and American students alike obtain the experience and training in the inter-religious, intercultural, and international collaboration which our contemporary troubled world so desperately needs. This need is so great that the undertaking is one which merits the attention and aid of every university and public official, every faculty member and student, and every religious and lay leader in the surrounding community.

Campus Myths

CHAPTER XVII

History is a kind of vertical anthropology. The quiet gulf fixed between any two generations is paralleled by the psychological discontinuity between contemporary but widely separated cultures.

When an American from the suburbs of Chicago journeys to the Navajos or the Dobus or even to the dying villages of northern New England or to the sharecroppers of the deep South, he is enough of an anthropologist to recognize another world. But when, after he has turned forty, he observes his own children with their friends, he is less able—or less willing —to concede that here also is another world. Time, even a few decades of time, can make for discontinuity. The failure to recognize this fact is at the heart of the ever-present suspicion and malice existing between the generations. Each generation expects the new one to be a slightly modified version of itself. The breakdown of understanding will be greatest in periods like our own, when a wholesale psychological mutation and shift of values has occurred in the brief span of thirty years.

If anyone of middle age doubts that a real gulf is fixed between the generations, let him chaperon a college dance. He goes with nostalgic memories of exciting evenings. His social tradition had been one of rugged and sometimes jungle-like individualism. His was the era of prearrangements among men to make sure that the girls were "cut in on" an adequate number of times during the evening; it was also a period when social prestige accrued by dating a variety of persons rather than being always seen in the same company. The present reality, except in a few places where old traditions die hard, is utterly different.

The chaperon notes with growing bewilderment that the same couple dances together all evening, or at least until, in apparent ennui, they leave early for the nearest tavern. Very rarely is there any exchange of partners. No stag line loiters against the wall. It seems exceedingly dull to the chaperon and to his wife. For their part, they rekindle ancient embers to a mild glow by trading partners with other faculty couples. The students, observing this polygamous conduct, are gently shocked, as though a breach of decorum had been publicly committed.

The changed customs of the dance floor are merely by-products of a far deeper revolution. The old tradition of dating as many different persons as possible, and postponing the day of commitment, has been replaced by its exact opposite—"going steady." Perhaps the college where I teach represents an extreme development, though a fair amount of experience lecturing on other campuses makes me doubt even this. At any rate, in that college the period of "random dating" hardly extends beyond the third date with the same girl. From then on, there is the tacit or explicit assumption that they are "going steady." This status is somewhat vaguely defined, but it seems to be definite enough so that the young man or woman who casually seeks other dates is likely to encounter social ostracism. "Going steady" leads, sometimes slowly but often with great rapidity, to "pinning," which is usually defined as "being engaged to be engaged." This is an important rite of passage, particularly on those campuses that abound in Greek letters; there may be serenades and special listing in a column reserved for this purpose in the student newspaper. Formal engagement can follow soon or be deferred—this often depends on the two families—but once the "pinning" stage is reached there is a clearly defined status—monogamous dating and the presumption of eventual marriage. Not surprisingly, the percentage of students who marry while in college is steadily increasing.

The older pattern of dating put the emphasis on adventure;

the newer pattern puts it on security. A girl who is "going steady" can be sure of a date whenever a date is called for, and her boy friend has the same assurance. Neither may be the dream ideal to the other, but each has two legs and a pair of eyes and can be depended upon to answer present when summoned.

I have no apology for this somewhat extensive treatment of dating and courtship. Nothing in life tells more about the values by which people live. One should, however, add some mention of the markedly more serious attitude toward marriage now found among college students. If they are less starry-eyed and less inclined toward theories of "finding the only one in the world for me," they seem much more willing to work hard and systematically to create stable and satisfying marriages. When the sociology department, in response to student clamor, offers a course in Marriage and the Family, there are certain to be many pinned or engaged couples taking it together. One sees them afterwards at the student union, decorously discussing what Professor X said about sexual adjustment and the merits of the Okinawa system of child-rearing. The latter topic is not a theoretical one to them: they are counting their children before they are conceived and drawing up lists of suitable names.

The professor also discovers that certain jokes, which were once tried and true for classroom use, are no longer well received. He learns to mention marriage with proper respect and sex with due reserve. A certain neo-Victorianism is evident on the campus. I suppose the job of personal emancipation was done so thoroughly during the 1920's that the students today feel a greater need to put some of the wreckage back together and build a durable habitation for their future lives. This is all the more true because many of them come from broken homes and know from personal experience what it means to be sacrificed upon the private altar of their parents' "self-expression" and "right to happiness." In the new campus mood, even Mrs. Grundy is granted a minor but honorable role. It is perilous to make predictions, but the odds seem good that the oncoming generation, with its new earnestness, will score a better record of marital success than its immediate predecessors.

The more one examines the daily life of the campus, the clearer it becomes that security is the dominant ideal. This is not news to attentive observers, but it is perhaps worth while to spell it out in further detail. Take, for example, the college senior who is looking for a job. During the 1920's, the emphasis was still enough on adventure to lure the senior into taking chances, such as accepting that rather shaky job as a bond salesman in the hope of making the quick million. To learn first-hand how great is the change in mentality, talk with any "company representative" as he makes his rounds from campus to campus in the late winter or spring and interviews promising seniors. One of them, an apoplectic man in his early fifties, once burst forth to me, "I told this boy about the opportunities in our company; I told him there were real risks but if he had the right stuff, he could rise to the top. Then I asked him if he had any questions. Do you know what he asked me? Do you know what this twenty-one-year-old boy, hardly old enough to shave, asked me? He thought a while and then he asked me, 'What's the retirement age and what kind of pension system do you have?' "

To the company representative this seems a failure of character, a downright un-American refusal to embrace the road of high commercial adventure. The college senior views it otherwise. He sees the business world more and more dominated by corporate giants which have lost their swashbuckling splendor and now increasingly resemble civil service. Theoretically, he might aim at heading one of them, but the possibility is so remote that he settles for the comfortable and secure niche, the annual increment, a well-padded retirement.

All that I have said is obviously a generalization and an oversimplification; there are always the nonconformists in any period who go their own lonely way. But in broad terms, it is clear that security is as much the key concept in job-hunting as in dating and courting. It is also one of the prime motives in the somewhat changed attitude of college students toward religion. I do not think it is the only motive. There are deeper currents, and from a long-range viewpoint these are the more important. But in any case, part at least of the changed attitude toward religion clearly stems from the quest for security.

The change in attitude is evident on most campuses. Callow wisecracks about religion are not as good form or as funny as in previous decades. The prevailing attitude is to say that religion is a pretty good thing and the churches are useful institutions. True, the theological content of "religion" is rarely specified. Students are more open to "religion" than to Christianity or Judaism—or Hinduism. When the values of religion are discussed, as they incessantly are in bull sessions organized or unorganized, this is likely to be in purely social or subjective language—"what religion can do for society," "what I can get out of religion." The latter is customarily defined as peace of mind. Religion, thus viewed, becomes an added means to security, this time social and psychological security. Belonging to a religious body gives a social anchorage, and the subjective fruits of religion can be a greatly desired lessening of inner tension. God, in such a religion, is to be sought as one reaches for Miltown; His church is a decorous Sunday morning country club. God is to be used, not served or necessarily loved. I add once more that there are deeper and more abiding currents than this, but part at least of the current friendliness toward religion stems from the desire to use God for social and psychological ends.

At this point, the "other-directed" man described by David Riesman in *The Lonely Crowd* begins to come into focus. He abounds on the campus. He does not abound there only. He has been mass-produced throughout America in recent decades. The public schools, to name only one social institution, have labored mightily to produce him by their emphasis on co-operation, group adjustment, social adjustment, every species of adjustment. The changed emphasis in the schools is probably only a by-product of something more deep-seated in America's psychological and sociological evolution, a really massive shift in values. In any event, the "other-directed man," with his sensitive antennae for receiving the responses of his fellows, is the dominant type on most campuses.

The historical predecessor of "other-directed man" was "inner-directed man," who followed his conscience. That conscience might be a very erroneous one, filled with abominable absolutes, and the net result could equally well be a saint or a robber baron, but in any event he looked to his conscience for guidance. The other-directed man has a different absolute, the peer group. Uncertain whether there is a God who really means business, timid about committing himself to any metaphysical ultimate, half-convinced that the conscience is no more than a superego created by society, he seeks psychological security by craning his neck to see what his fellows are doing and saying. In time, he develops an exquisite skill at this, almost a kind of mind-reading. He can divine other people's thoughts before they think them. By behaving in such a way as to evoke favorable reactions from his peers, he wins acceptance. Being accepted, he has the warm sense of belonging. He is shielded from the leering aloneness of having to consult his conscience or his God too often.

I have no wish to compose a sentimental elegy for inner-directed men. In retrospect, as his era fades into history, it seems that he was more than human size, both for good and evil. Other-directed man is humbler, more the normal size of a man. He is inconspicuous, because he chooses to be so. You do not spot him in a crowd. At first glance, it seems that other-directed man has perhaps the moral and spiritual edge. He is likely to be friendly, helpful, considerate of others, less given to trampling them underfoot at the dictates of his unique conscience. His conduct often appears to grow out of the traditional religious virtues.

The truth is that no simple black-and-white evaluation is possible. Everything depends on what the attitudes of the peer group are. If they are such as to reward high standards of conduct, the individual may be lured and led to a way of life above his natural inclinations. If the attitudes are of another kind, he will be pulled down. The way to be accepted by demons is to become a demon. But whatever the level of the peer group—good, middling, or low—there is nothing to encourage the daring innovator who wishes to introduce new values.

In reality, it is fruitless to compare the outward behavior of the two types and try to draw significant conclusions. More important is the difference in motivation. Generally speaking, the enduring ethical systems of mankind have been built on one or more of three bases. A person behaves in a particular way (a) because that way is traditional, or (b) because reason or intuition demonstrates it to be the right way, or (c) because God has revealed that the way is His will. In all of these systems, there is the conviction that a particular kind of life and conduct are objectively right, without regard to the subjective effect they may have upon the individual who follows them.

Superficially, it may appear that other-directed man is a traditionalist, but actually he is not. Mutations of outlook sometimes occur with great suddenness in the group, and he "adjusts" to the changed outlook rather than clinging to what seemed a traditional pattern of values. No, his absolute is not tradition, not reason or intuition, not the will of God. It is the approval of the group.

Inasmuch as other-directed man constantly seeks approval and acceptance, he is daily tempted to use other people. He does it quietly, subtly, and often without knowing what he is doing. He may seem to subordinating himself to their wishes; he is really manipulating them by his own adaptability—manipulating them into accepting him. He is winning friends and influencing people. The "silent leader," who by acting meek and looking wise is rising to power on some campuses, is a good example of how to succeed politically through apparent lack of ambition.

Perhaps, however, this discussion is going into speculative depths that are not too relevant here. It is sufficient to recall the main point, which is the dominance of security as the goal of college students. Its primacy is revealed almost everywhere you look—dating and courting, job-hunting, much of the religious urge, the dedicated quest for acceptance and "adjusting to the group."

I believe it was *Life* which popularized the epithet, "the silent generation," and I find no reason to quarrel with it. After the flaming twenties and the raucously political thirties, the present generation of students seems curiously subdued.

I do not observe many of them passionately excited about anything. When they flame, it is discreetly and with a subdued
glow. They tend to be apolitical and exceedingly cautious about
taking strong stands on any important issue—the recency of
the McCarthy period is undoubtedly a subduing influence,
but the political and social quietism was already apparent
before the late senator mounted horseback to slay any available dragons.

It is not my purpose to attempt a historical explanation of
the underlying causes for the total change in the campus
mentality and mood. It is worth mentioning, however, that the
nation as a whole has changed in the same direction. Until the
1930's, the tradition of rugged individualism held sway in
America, though the frontier had long since dwindled to insig-
nificance, and year by year the nation was becoming more
urban, more industrialized, more dependent on infinitely complex patterns of co-operation. During the 1930's, the inevitable
and necessary adjustment was made all along the line. With a
splendid if slapdash empiricism, the New Deal remodeled the
political, social, and economic structure of the country, and
did the job so thoroughly that no important faction seriously
proposes that the reconstruction be undone. From the 1930's
on, rugged individualism of the nineteenth-century brand,
though still invoked on solemn occasions, has not been the
living reality of American life. We have moved far toward
group consciousness, toward a more collectivistic way of life,
toward the welfare state. The individual finds increasingly
that his well-being and survival depend on co-operation rather
than on the rules of the jungle. Security and group-mindedness
may be two sides of the same coin. If the nation has moved,
haltingly but surely, in this direction, it should not surprise us
to find college students advancing a few paces farther than
their elders and embracing a less ambiguous faith in security
and social adjustment.

I think there is more to it than this. The peculiarly subdued
quality of college students has something of shell shock about
it or of the hushed waiting in the cyclone shelter. My own
generation, men and women in their forties, can remember

the relatively carefree 1920's, when prohibition seemed the most momentous of human dilemmas. But consider a college senior. He was born during the latter stages of the Depression, about the time that Prime Minister Chamberlain journeyed to Munich and betrayed Czechoslovakia. A year later Hitler invaded Poland and World War II began. The present college senior, at the age of eight or thereabouts, asked his father what was this atom bomb he heard mentioned on the radio. He entered high school as the Korean War began. From that time on, it has been one crisis after another. He is aware that the Fascist threat has been replaced by the steadier menace of world Communism. He knows that in all likelihood the cold war is here for most or all of his life. More immediately, he is faced with the personal disruption of military service.

Born into such a world, it is natural for the student to aim at modest goals. How can he control the atom bomb? What wisdom does he have to solve the problems of the Near East? Can he indulge in collective bargaining with the draft board? The broad decisions, literally of life and death, are not in his hands. A kind of fatalism grips him. If he cannot shape the broad course of human affairs, he can at least build the most comfortable cyclone cellar possible and hope that the cyclone will not pass directly overhead. His cyclone shelter is not to be disparaged. At its center is a wife and children. It also includes friends and a means of livelihood. The mentality of the cyclone shelter may not produce a Socrates, a John Brown, a Thoreau; it can and does produce good husbands, good fathers, good members of the community.

It is tempting to assume at this point that the mood of the campus has been adequately sketched. But all schematic presentations of human realities are false, particularly when great numbers of persons are being forced into conceptual molds. To make the picture slightly more three-dimensional, other factors should be mentioned. One in particular seems to call for special attention. It is nothing new, but rather a frame of mind which has been powerful for some decades. For lack of anything better to call it, I shall use the term popular positivism.

I have chosen the phrase popular positivism to emphasize that this mentality is not usually the result of austere and technical studies in logical positivism or anything else that emanates from the modern centers of philosophy. It is rather a way of looking at life, knowledge, and experience which "is floating in the air." It has little to do with educational level. Popular positivism is simply the belief that something is real if you can bang your shins against it. Every other kind of reality is suspect. Less tangible experiences are usually put in their place by a "nothing but." Love is "nothing but sex," the response to the arts is "nothing but private emotions." God, in slightly more sophisticated forms of popular positivism, is "nothing but a wish fulfillment."

The great success story of the past few centuries has been science, and undoubtedly its triumphal forward march has helped generate the cast of mind I have been describing, though I hasten to add that I do not think the scientists—particularly the really great ones—have been generally guilty of embracing and disseminating popular positivism or positivism of a more rigorous kind. It is simply that science, especially on its simpler levels, seems so very precise and capable of verification, whereas morality, the arts, and religion by contrast appear to occupy a subjective and cloudy realm. There are doubtless other factors than science—one suspects that industrialism and the growth of cities have worked in the same direction—but the priestly role of science in modern life has certainly been a key factor.

Some campus observers would prefer to speak of "the conflict between science and religion," but that is putting it too narrowly. The arts, ethics, and the meaningfulness of personal relationships are in the same boat with religion. The crucial question is whether they have their own logic and rationality (though not that of Euclid), or whether they must be consigned to a domain of pure subjectivity, where anything goes and there are no guideposts except whim and untutored emotion.

Whatever the historical reasons for popular positivism, many students bring it to campus with them, and their classes and laboratories often powerfully reinforce it. This may not be the design of the individual professors. It is the precision and elegance of the scientific method which seem to confirm what has been more vaguely held as true. The counteracting influences are, in most cases, considerably weaker.

The student can react in one of three or four ways. If he has enough imagination and courage, he can take stock of his total knowledge and total experience, which will include everything from Physics 1 to memories of watching a sunset and listening to Vivaldi. He can then try to make sense of everything, without using the escape clause of "nothing but." If he does this, he will be driven to seek a way of thinking that will grant as meaningful a place to love and beauty and wonder and awe as to the pointer readings of the laboratory or the tautologies of pure logic.

Probably few students do this. A more common alternative is to move from popular positivism to a thoroughgoing and intellectually rigorous positivism. The final result can be the conviction that nothing is meaningful except the propositions of pure logic or statements capable of empirical (i.e., scientific) verification. The whole world of love, personal relationships, art, and religion is permanently banished to a sort of limbo where it can be cherished for its emotional satisfactions but denied any real rationality.

The attempt to be a consistent positivist does not, however, necessarily end at this point. Once in a while a student positivist is really consistent, with whatever agony to himself. One by one, he discards everything that fails to meet the standards of positivism. His religion, his moral convictions, his belief that T. S. Eliot is a greater poet than Sara Teasdale—these drop by the way into the wastebasket of mere subjectivism. But being driven by a passion for consistency, he goes yet further. Along the way he is troubled by the surrealistic quality of the newer physics and disturbed by non-Euclidian geometry. Finally, he becomes aware that the vast scientific enterprise rests upon staggering acts of faith—the existence of the material universe, the uniformity of nature, the "law of parsimony," and others, none of which can be proved. He is now staring into a genuine abyss. Nothing is provable. Even his own ability to gaze into the abyss finally falls under question, for if everything else rests on an act of faith, how can he be sure of his own reality as the observer looking down into nothing?

I have not been tracing a merely hypothetical evolution. I have seen it happen with an occasional student, though quite rarely. The intellectual passion and rigor that are required are more than most people, students or otherwise, can summon up. But when it does happen, there are two ways out—frank despair or the sober determination to re-examine all possible acts of faith, making sure that those of science and logic have no inherent edge over those of religion, personal relationships, and the arts.

Most students are content to drift philosophically and avoid the sharp and ultimate questions. If a student has come to the campus a vague popular positivist, he most often remains one, and becomes a little more so. From force of habit he may cherish some lingering belief that there is meaning and rationality in things other than science and logic, but he can't put his finger on it. Insofar as he still takes religion, love, and the arts seriously, he is haunted by the suspicion that he is blindly carrying on an outworn tradition. The practical consequence is that though he may not go all the way toward a consistent positivism, his commitment in realms of experience not vindicated by the positivist canons of genuineness are likely to be wavering and weak.

I have spoken of popular positivism as a legacy from the past. At the same time, it has a curious kinship with the emergence of "other-directed man," who, as we have seen, is engaged in a quiet and infinitely subtle attempt to manipulate his fellows so as to win their approval and acceptance. There is a certain detachment and calculation to his relationships, no matter how much he may appear to be another bee in the hive. As for the person who follows popular positivism, he also is encouraged toward "objectivity," psychological distance, and a refusal to make the complete commitment of the personality to anything or anybody. I should not wish to press the kinship of the two things too far, but they do seem to have this much in common. Both mentalities make it easier to analyze—and use—one's fellows than to know them in a completeness of mutuality.

I do not wish to end without one final impression. There is a pervasive wistfulness on the campus. One finds it is much in the campus leaders and paragons of adjustment as in the occasional nonconformists. It is as though, on a deeper level, a hunger arises for something more than mere security, mere comfort, pleasant social acceptance. There is the suspicion that life is being sold short, for limited and relatively trivial prizes. This restlessness, this yearning without a clearly defined object, may not often find words; it is something which must be sensed by long experience on the campus. But it is there, I am convinced, and growing. It may be the necessary prelude to a further stage in the never static life of the campus—a stage when it will be discovered that security and acceptance and all the standard goals are infinitely desirable as long as you are striving for them, but not enough once you have them.

WILLIAM K. FRANKENA

A Point of View for the Future

CONCLUDING STATEMENT

This final chapter cannot be a conclusion of the sort that may come at the end of a book written by a single author or by a group of closely agreeing authors. It cannot simply summarize what has been said, draw inferences from it, or pull loose strings together. The preceding chapters, while relevant to the subject and helpful to those working at state universities or trying to understand the position of the state university with respect to religion, are too varied in their topics, approaches, and conclusions for any such happy ending to be possible. The best that one can do here, then, is to read them and write another essay, with the future in mind, saying what one thinks needs still to be said or perhaps repeated. But I am a philosopher teaching at a state university; hence what I shall say will be mainly philosophical, and, while it does not represent the official position of my or of any other public university, it will be said from what I take to be the point of view of such universities. Thinking Americans, says Herberg, are dissatisfied with the state of the relations between religion and public education, and they ought to be, not only because an insufficient amount of attention is given to religion by our public universities, but also because the attention is sometimes given in forms that are inappropriate in such universities. This state of affairs, as Bean suggests, is due to a tacit compromise between conflicting tendencies, and, if it is unsatisfactory, our only recourse is to get back to principles, being careful to consider only what is relevant to the problem of the state university.

Such a recourse is all the more imperative because there is, in Herberg's words, a "great upsurge of religiousness . . . sweeping the country today." We may look forward to a period of increasing concern about the treatment of religion in state universities, and we must, therefore, get our philosophical principles straight, as well as our history and our constitutional law. For the question is not merely what our founding fathers and their successors intended, nor what we can get away with in the eyes of the law or the public, as many seem to imply; the question, as Kauper sees, is what "positive considerations . . . are relevant to an appraisal of the university's function" in the area of religion.

I shall take some time, therefore, to state what I regard as the philosophy which must guide a public university in dealing with religion. Much has already been said here about this by Greene, Northrop, and others, but few if any of their discussions are complete or pointed enough in my opinion, and some of them are not restricted to the subject of education in a *state* university. I cannot, however, try to justify the philosophy in question in the space allotted; I can only seek to formulate it, and then go on to make a few more practical observations which seem to follow from it.

The main consideration involved is that of "the separation of church and state." But what, if we take it at a philosophical level and not merely at that of political expediency or even of constitutional provision, does this principle assert? Ostensibly it says that the state is not to establish or otherwise favor any one institutionally organized religion as against others; it must be neutral with respect to the "churches." Now, most influential religions are institutionally organized. Many individuals, however, hold views which are properly speaking religious, without being members of a church, or at least without fully accepting the official creed of any church. Many others, moreover, take positions which are antireligious—agnosticism, atheism, scepticism, etc.—but which incorporate some kind of answer to ultimate questions, as religions do. These positions are not church-related, and it is only confusing to call them "religions" on the ground that they embody answers to ultimate issues or are what a man does with his solitude; they are not views of the kind that are traditionally associated with religion and are better called philosophies, though of course philosophies may also be religious. Indeed, discussions of religion in state universities are often misleading because "religion" is sometimes used to mean any ultimate attitude or belief, and sometimes to mean only the kind of attitude or belief which is associated with the historic religions. In this chapter, unless otherwise indicated, I shall use "religion" only in the narrower sense.

My point, however, is this: philosophically considered, the question of the relation of church and state involves a more basic issue, namely, what is or should be the relation of the state to whatever ultimate attitudes or beliefs its members may have or come to entertain? And the answer entailed in the separation principle is that the state is not to "establish" in any way any such ultimate attitude or belief, religious or nonreligious, rational or revealed, private or institutional, prevalent or esoteric. This is the full meaning of "freedom of conscience" or "freedom of religion," if we add freedom to perform the overt acts which are called worship. It means that here is an area in which the state is to be neutral, an area which is to be left to the control of reason, morality, aesthetic taste, or prophetic or mystical insight, an area in which the individual is to be left alone with his God, his church, or his universe. That this is what is meant was forgotten even by Locke, when he wrote that "those are not at all to be tolerated who deny the being of a God." It is no less forgotten by those who talk as if only three primary faiths need to be taken seriously by a state university, and propose that a privileged position be given by it to representatives of these faiths as against others and as against nonfaiths. But God, if we may believe Jeremy Taylor, does not forget it.

We can now see in general terms what is the resulting position of a state university with regard to the treatment of religion in its academic program. A state university is an organ of the state whose function is to provide, for those who wish it, a liberal or a professional education. We shall assume here that the creation and maintenance of such an institution by the state is justified, but it should be noted that this is an assumption, for the logic of many who discuss our topic seems to point to the conclusion that there should be no state universities. As an organ of the state, however, the university must provide an education under the terms of the above principle, and, as Ingraham points out, this involves a limitation of its freedom as compared with private universities. The problem is not only the relation of the state university to religion but to all ultimate creeds, and the answer entailed by the principle of separation is that it and its staff members cannot in their official capacities serve as the organs of any church, religious faith, or ultimate belief; it and they cannot seek in any official way to inculcate or propagate any religion or other form of ultimate attitude in preference to any other. Private institutions may do so, but not public ones. These cannot in any way establish or prefer any ultimate creed to any other—not by giving financial support, by giving or withholding grades, credits, degrees, tenure, advancement, or salary increase, or by any other official act of their staff members or administration. This means, as religious writers have often pointed out, that they cannot enshrine the "religion of secularism" any more than that of Catholicism, but it also means that they cannot choose any three religions and give them any preferred status, however prevalent or well-organized they may be, as the same writers sometimes propose. It means, further, that the state university cannot prefer religious to nonreligious forms of ultimate belief, or natural religions to revealed ones. It must accord to all of them, to atheism and secularism as well as to Protestantism and Catholicism, an equal status and tolerance. It and its representatives cannot support one by their official acts or obstruct another (except when it violates the law or common morality or contradicts the established findings of science or history). In fact, they must protect each, no matter how weak, against the others, no matter how strong, and maintain a free atmosphere in which new ones may come to life and possibly even triumph over the old.

The state university, then, must be neutral or impartial as

between religions and ultimate views. But, it may be argued, if it cannot in any manner inculcate or propagate any one such creed, then it must inculcate or propagate them all and so maintain a kind of neutrality—indoctrinating the students in Catholicism in one course, in orthodox Judaism in another, in atheism in a third, in Marxism in a fourth, etc., and leaving always one place where some wandering St. Paul may preach an Unknown God. This is rarely, if ever, explicitly advocated, but it is logically implied in one sort of argument that is given for the three-faith approach, and is suggested by those who hold that the university must not stand apart from the present conflict on basic issues. It seems clear, however, that this approach can only be hopelessly confusing in practice, and the three-faith plan is sometimes offered as a compromise which goes part of the way toward this "ideal" but is still feasible. But, if we must compromise, it would seem better to do so in another way, namely, by giving up the effort to inculcate or propagate religions or other ultimate credos at all. This way has rightly appeared, though it is not always consistently or rigorously maintained, in many discussions of the teaching of religion in state universities. The opponents of the three or many-faith approach have naturally emphasized it. But even the proponents of this approach have often disowned any effort to indoctrinate or proselyte, resting their case on the claim that students must be informed about the various religions and that only one who holds a position is really competent to inform them about it.

This second conception of neutrality or impartiality in the treatment of religion has been well-stated by John Stuart Mill in his Inaugural Address as rector of St. Andrews University. Speaking of the teaching of moral philosophy and religion, Mill writes:

. . . it is not the teacher's business to impose his own judgment, but to inform and discipline that of his student. . . . The proper business of an University is . . . not to tell us from authority what we ought to believe, and make us accept the belief as a duty, but to give us information and training, and help us to form our own belief in a manner worthy of intelligent beings, who seek for truth at all hazards, and demand to know all the difficulties, in order that they may be better qualified to find, or recognize, the most satisfactory mode of resolving them.

It would be unfair, however, to regard such a conception as merely a compromise due to the impracticability of an equal propagation by a single university of all the conflicting world-views. For it is doubtful, as a matter of principle, that it is the function of a state university to inculcate or indoctrinate at all, at least in the region of ultimate attitudes and beliefs. All such propagation, one may reasonably contend, belongs to the home, the church, church-related schools, and personal contact between free individuals, and is not the proper province of an organ of the state. This is the burden of the old theme of rendering unto Caesar and God, respectively, the things that are theirs—of delegating temporal power to the state but leaving the spiritual realm to churches and other voluntary associations or to the individual in his solitude. As Father Murray puts it:

. . . the function of the university is not at all messianic. It is entirely minimal. . . . if post-modern man hopes for salvation, he must set his hope elsewhere than on the university.

The state university must remember this, and if necessary remind its students, their parents, and the religious denominations that the primary responsibility for the concerns of the spirit is not its but theirs. To quote Mill again:

The various Churches, established and unestablished, are quite competent to the task which is peculiarly theirs, that of teaching each its own doctrines, as far as necessary, to its own rising generation.

Must the state university, according to this conception, be secular as well as impartial and neutral? The term "secular" is ambiguous. A public university must be secular in the sense that it must not put its official weight behind religious world-views, or in opposition to nonreligious ones. This does not mean, however, that its administrators and professors need to be agnostics or naturalists, though they may be; it does not mean that they must be irreligious in their private views or even neutral with respect to religions in their personal lives. Neither does it mean, of course, that the university must be officially against religion. A private university may, but a public one may not, be secular in the further sense of being opposed to religious faith, to revelation, or to what is not susceptible of scientific verification or objective rational treatment. To the extent to which state universities have espoused the ultimate creed of scientism, or any of the "philosophies of secularism," their neutrality may be rightly criticized as malevolent by those who are religious. But, for all this, they must welcome the antireligious as well as the religious student and tolerate unofficial opposition to religion in members of its staff; they must never allow themselves to be put into the position, because of pressure or because of the plans which they adopt for dealing with religion, of having to appoint or dismiss a man, admit or expel a student, or withhold any degree, grade, or preferment for anyone because of his ultimate beliefs. They may do so only on the basis of his other qualifications, even in the case of the "religious co-ordinator," or on the basis of incompetence, or of overt acts of treason, moral turpitude, and the like.

The task of the state university, then, on its academic side, is to "inform" and "discipline" its students in order to provide them with a liberal or a professional education. Here "to inform" means to pass on to them the generally accepted results of objective inquiry. "To discipline" means to train them to carry on such inquiry for themselves, and in general to develop their critical, imaginative, and intellectual faculties, as well as their moral character and aesthetic sensibility—and, on request, to train them for a vocation. This is why it has the right and the duty to teach history, mathematics, the sciences, the humanities, languages, and professional skills. But if it is fully to carry out its obligation to inform, it must also give an important place to courses about religion and other kinds of ultimate attitudes or beliefs—courses in the history of the

Judeo-Christian faiths, in comparative religion, in the psychology, sociology, and anthropology of religion, as well as in philosophy. This point has been made by Greene, Father Murray, and others, and need not be elaborated here. If the university does not offer an adequate program of such courses, then again it can be accused by the churches of being malevolently neutral, since it will be giving the student the impression that religion and philosophy are of little import in the past or present life of man. Of course, it must see that such courses are objective and scholarly, else they do not inform but mislead or proselyte; but, so long as they are, they are not in the least jeopardized by the principle of separation or of rendering unto Caesar, as Kauper has shown. As Mill has it:

Why should it be impossible, that information of the greatest value, on subjects connected with religion, should be brought before the student's mind; that he should be made acquainted with so important a part of the national thought, and of the intellectual labours of past generations, as those relating to religion, without being taught dogmatically the doctrines of any church or sect?

However, Greene, Father Murray, Miss White, and others are not content with courses *about* religion, courses designed merely to remedy the religious illiteracy so prevalent in the student body. They desire a yet more benevolent neutrality. Is it possible and desirable for a public university in its academic program positively to aid and encourage religion, as well as to inform about it? Not, as we have seen, if this means preferring religious to other forms of metaphysical or ultimate beliefs, and not if it means indoctrination in some religious faith. Yet it is true, as Shuster says, that without any ultimate perspective or center of some kind, "a man will be only half himself." May we assert then that even a state university, if it is to contribute satisfactorily to the development of its students, may and should aid them in the formation or selection of a philosophy or religion? It seems to me that we may, if we are careful in our assertion.

The public university cannot seek to lead its students to one kind of ultimate commitment rather than another, but it may

encourage them to choose or work out some world-view and
to commit themselves to it, although with tolerance for others;
and its professors may even in class, and certainly in private,
make clear their own positions with their reasons, so long as
they do so undogmatically and without propagandizing. This
in itself would be an important contribution, for many in recent
years have accused our liberal universities of preaching agnosticism or scepticism, of propagating a kind of noncommittalism.
But if the university takes this approach it must remember
that atheism, naturalism, and scepticism are permissible ultimate positions as much as any others, so far as it is concerned.
It must not beg any questions about what is "really ultimate."

It must remember also that even by offering its students
information about the various philosophies and religions of the
world, their history, psychology, sociology, their grounds and
methods, the university is helping them to arrive at more enlightened conclusions about ultimate questions. If I may quote
Mill again:

All that social and public education has in its power to do,
further than by a general pervading tone of reverence and duty,
amounts to little more than the information which it can give; but
this is extremely valuable.

There is, however, a "little more." As part of its task of "discipline," the university can and should give its students training
in how to think intelligently, both critically and constructively,
about ultimate issues. In what will be my last quotation from
Mill, he contends:

If teaching, even on matters of scientific certainty, should aim
quite as much at showing how the results are arrived at as at
teaching the results themselves, far more, then, should this be the
case on subjects where there is the widest diversity of opinion
among men of equal ability, and who have taken equal pains to
arrive at the truth.

Here indeed, lies the main point of teaching philosophy in a
state institution, in particular, moral philosophy, the philosophy

of history, and the philosophy of religion. But courses in the history of philosophy, in comparative religion, and in the sciences of religion also have their disciplinary side, and give training in dealing with various kinds of questions about ultimate commitments. It is hard to see how any course with a more "positive religious orientation" can be designed to cultivate intelligent thinking about religious and other basic issues, without being too specifically religious for a state-supported college, but it should be possible to devise courses in the history or comparison of theologies which will do so.

Art and literature also have a contribution to make, which must not be ignored here. The study and appreciation of poetry, fiction, drama, painting, and so forth, have their own function in the aesthetic education of man, which is one of the tasks of a university, but they can also serve to supplement the studies already mentioned as informing and training the student's mind with respect to ultimate questions. For they can give him a feeling for and an imaginative realization of the essence of any given religion or philosophy as this is experienced by one who lives by it, and they can do so without inculcating or propagating it, because, as has often been remarked, the understanding of the meaning of a work of art involves a "willing suspension" of belief and disbelief in any dogmatic sense. Here then is a kind of spiritual enrichment which the state university may provide and which can do much to meet the desire for more than courses *about* religion.

These seem to me important ways in which a public university can and should teach subjects relating to the formation of or commitment to ultimate faiths or views. In these ways it can help to give its students the knowledge and the discipline which they need to make their world-views, whether they are already chosen or not, more enlightened and more intelligent than they would be otherwise. More it cannot do on its academic side, so far as I can see. That is for the individual himself to do or his church if he has one, except for what the university can add through its counseling and extracurricular programs.

In these programs the same goals may and should be pursued subject to the same guiding principles. Here too are many ways in which the university can foster a serious concern for ultimate questions and promote the relevant information and discipline, for example by inviting outstanding representatives of different faiths and philosophies to interpret their positions in occasional lectures or discussion groups. But here also there are many more ways in which the university can helpfully co-operate with parents, religious centers, and other voluntary organizations which may be concerned with "spiritual" matters. These have been outlined in detail in some of the earlier chapters. In extracurricular activities and discussions, furthermore, it is possible and appropriate for a member of the faculty to exert a more positive personal influence on a student's attitude and thought about basic issues than he can in class, as long as he makes it clear that he is not acting in his official capacity and behaves in a manner consistent with his belonging to a community of scholars. Finally, in its provisions for extracurricular affairs the university can do much to initiate or facilitate co-operation between the various student religious groups connected with the campus. It must, of course, leave them free, as Lelyveld insists, but even so it may and should seek to foster democracy, tolerance, reasonableness, and mutual understanding. As Father Murray emphasizes, it must not promote any "bogus irenicisms" or any religions of the common denominator, for then it is espousing a certain ultimate creed. It should, however, draw foreign students and their religions or philosophies into the picture, because Northrop is right when he says that it is both practically necessary and spiritually rewarding for us to understand the spirit and the values of their cultures.

Various plans for dealing with religion, both in and out of the curriculum, have been proposed for or adopted by state universities; and certainly it is wise that such universities should experiment with a variety of arrangements. It is not possible to discuss them at length here in the light of what has been said so far in this chapter; I must simply hope that the application of what has been said will be reasonably clear. Some existing plans, however, do seem to be of doubtful propriety in a public university, and I shall therefore venture a few remarks. As I said before, it seems clear to me that such a university cannot properly adopt any scheme which involves appointing a man because he holds a certain kind of ultimate creed or dismissing him if he changes his mind. It is also inappropriate, in my opinion, for it to adopt a plan which it is not ready to pay for out of state funds. It would likewise seem questionable for it to answer pressure by giving credit for courses taught in religious centers which are not fully accredited colleges, for if they are such that it can properly give credit for them it can also properly offer them itself. As for giving credit for courses on religion transferred from de-nominational colleges, it should do so only if upon scrutiny they are clearly taught in the spirit and with the competence which it would ask of its own teachers if they were to teach them. About the three-primary-faith plan I wish to add two observations. The first is that Catholicism, Protestantism, and Judaism are not the only live options in the western world; there are also existentialism, Marxism, and democratic secular-ism which may well claim to be represented in such a program. The other is that, if Northrop is correct, then Buddhism, Islam, and perhaps still other religions must also be represented. As was indicated earlier, however, I have grave doubts about the validity of any such plan. The argument that only a man who holds a certain position is competent adequately to present it is weighty, but not conclusive, in its favor.

It is sometimes suggested, for example by Greene, that a university should provide opportunity for primary religious experience as a kind of equivalent for the scientific laboratory or the art studio. Now, it is not clear that Greene is thinking of public universities when he makes his suggestion, but to me it is doubtful that such universities can themselves sponsor religious services. Perhaps it may do so if it makes clear that these services are only religious exhibits, but if they are per-formed in this spirit will they be bona fide expressions of religion? It would seem better for all religious services to be sponsored by churches or student groups, perhaps with some encouragement by the university, which might then remind

interested students of the opportunities thus provided for seeing various religious faiths in action.

However, if some existing plans appear to go too far, there
are others that do not go far enough, for example, those which
include little or no university-sponsored academic work or
extracurricular activity relating to religion. Such cautious plans
are hardly required by the present state of public opinion or
by philosophical principles. Where they are or appear to be
dictated by the state constitution, it may be necessary for
interested people to petition for a constitutional amendment.
This would have to be carefully stated in terms of an adequate
philosophy of the role of the state university, and its success
would require its supporters to go about educating the public
in this philosophy. Indeed, since there are those who are
proreligious and those who are con, those who ask too much
of the state university and those who ask too little, such a program of education is imperative anyway even where no constitutional amendment is necessary. In such a program the state
universities must take the lead, and their spokesmen should
be chosen from their faculties and administrations proper;
they should not allow themselves to be represented only by
those who have a vested interest in religion, as they so often
have in the past. But, of course, they should enlist the co-operation of the many able and friendly religious leaders who are
willing to help them.

Whatever the scheme adopted, the crucial problem, as
several previous writers have seen, is to find the right men to
do the teaching, counseling, and co-ordinating that is involved.
The right man can make almost any plan satisfactory which is
consistent with the above principles, the wrong man can cause
even the best-laid scheme to "gang agley." The right man is,
first, one who accepts the state university point of view, which
I have tried to interpret here; second, one who is unusually
able and objective as a scholar, thinker, teacher, counselor,
or administrator in subjects and activities relating to religion
and ultimate issues, whatever his own basic commitment may
be. Such men are hard to find, and it is imperative that careful
thought be given by the universities and by religious leaders

to the discovery and training of people to work in religion at public institutions, and that interested young men be carefully advised about their preparation. The need must be met, but it must be well met. And again a caution must be added: while it is desirable that these people understand religion and philosophy well, and perhaps that some of them be sympathetic with religion or even personally committed to a certain religion, it cannot in a public university be a condition of their appointment or tenure that they subscribe to any particular kind of ultimate belief.

I fear that this chapter will be regarded as hopelessly "liberal" and "modern" by those who believe that we are in "the postmodern age." Perhaps we are in a new age which is to be guided by other ideas than the previous one, if by any ideas at all. If so, the state university must, of course, be realistic and take cognizance of this fact, for it must keep abreast of the times. But it should lead and not merely follow; in Pusey's words, quoted by Bean, it should give "service without servility." The mere fact, if it is a fact, that historical events have pushed us into a new era does nothing to establish the invalidity of earlier ideas. Historical change does not in itself justify the new either in philosophy, in science, or in morality. It may well be then that, in being a leader, the state university must drag its feet somewhat in response to "the current upsurge of religiousness." This upsurge is itself to a considerable extent a product of historical events, of the hot and cold wars, and political uncertainties of recent decades. It must not be presumed to be permanent; theologians themselves have often decried the superficiality of much of this newly acquired religiosity. In any case, the public university cannot take this upsurge as calling it to take on a religious mission itself, even though it may construe it as a call to do something more about religion than it has been doing.

Yet the point of view of this chapter is not really "secularist"; it does not advocate that the state university may or should embody and teach "the religion of the Enlightenment" or "the philosophy of secularism." It holds, rather, that such a university should strive to be neutral in the sense explained above

with respect to such an ultimate creed as well as with respect
to religious ones. So far I am ready to go with those who reject
"modernity" or "secularism." This step of disowning the "secularist" conception of the state university is all that I find
plausible in the arguments of the postmodernists, and it seems
to me merely to involve drawing the logical consequences of
one line of thinking in the democratic liberalism of the past.
If the postmodernists reply that the neutrality described here
is impossible, I can only say, "I am not convinced, but, as we
believe in democracy, let us try in our state universities to
approximate it."

Notes

Chapter III

1. W. H. van de Pol, D.D., *The Christian Dilemma* (New York: Philosophical Library, 1952), p. 21.
2. Nicolas Berdyaev, *Truth and Revelation* (London: Geoffrey Bles, 1953), pp. 47-48.
3. *Ibid.*, p. 40.
4. Edmund W. Sinnott, *Two Roads to Truth* (New York: The Viking Press, 1953), pp. 44-45.
5. *Ibid.*, p. 192.
6. H. Richard Niebuhr, *The Meaning of Revelation* (New York: Macmillan, 1946), pp. 112-13.
7. *Ibid.*, pp. 153-54.
8. *Ibid.*, p. 119.
9. George A. Tavard, *The Catholic Approach to Protestantism* (New York: Harper and Brothers, 1955).
10. Robert J. Welsh, *Religious Education*, Nov.-Dec., 1956, p. 426.

Chapter IV

1. See M. Willard Lampe, *The Story of an Idea: The History of the School of Religion at the State University of Iowa*, State University of Iowa Extension Bulletin No. 704, March 1, 1955; Henry E. Allen, "Practices of Land Grant Colleges and State Universities Affecting Religious Matters," *School and Society*, December 6, 1952; Edward W. Blakeman, "Curricular Religion in Our State Universities," *Religious Education*, July-Aug., 1953; Walton Bean, "Historical Developments Affecting the Place of Religion in the State University Curriculum," *Religious Education*, Sept.-Oct., 1955.

Chapter V

1. For general treatments of the legal aspects of the problem, see A. P. Stokes, *Church and State in the United States* (New York: Harper and Brothers, 1950); L. Pfeffer, *Church, State and Freedom* (Boston: Beacon, 1953); A. W. Johnson and F. H. Yost, *Separation of*

312 RELIGION AND THE STATE UNIVERSITY

Church and State in the United States (Minneapolis: University of Minnesota Press, 1948).

2. For discussions of these questions, see the papers by C. P. Shedd, E. F. Waite, and L. Pfeffer in H. E. Allen (ed.), *Religion in the State University: An Initial Exploration* (Minneapolis: Burgess, 1950); also L. Pfeffer, *Church, State and Freedom*, pp. 421-23; M. Cuminggim, *The College Seeks Religion* (New Haven: Yale University Press, 1947), pp. 123-30.

3. The provisions of the state constitutions are collected in C. H. Moehlman, *The American Constitutions and Religion* (Berne, Indiana, 1938).

4. See, e.g., Maine Const., Art. I, Sec. 3; Conn. Const., Art. I, Secs. 3-4, Art. VII; S. C. Const., Art. I, Secs. 9-10.

5. See, e.g., Ill. Const., Art. II, Sec. 3, Art. VIII, Sec. 3; Mich. Const., Art. II, Sec. 3; Mo. Const., Art. II, Secs. 5-8, Art. XI, Sec. 11. Apart from constitutional limitations, the charters under which a number of state universities and colleges operate forbid sectarian instruction.

6. See, e.g., Col. Const., Art. IX, Sec. 8; Mont. Const., Art. XI, Sec. 9.

7. Wash. Const., Art. I, Sec. 11; Ariz. Const., Art. II, Sec. 12; Utah Const., Art. I, Sec. 4.

8. Thus it may be noted that while in some states the constitutional provisions directed against sectarian education apply only to public schools (e.g., Col. Const., Art. IX, Sec. 8; N.D. Const., Art. VIII, Sec. 152), the constitutional provisions of other states bar sectarian instruction in all of the state's educational institutions. See, e.g., Nebr. Const., Art. VIII, Sec. 11; Mont. Const., Art. XI, Sec. 9. The Wisconsin Constitution (Art. X, Sec. 6) expressly forbids sectarian instruction at the university.

9. For a discussion of the state court decisions pro and con on this question, see A. W. Johnson and F. H. Yost, *op. cit.*, pp. 41-73.

10. *People ex rel. Lewis* v. *Graves*, 245 N. Y. 195 (1927); *Zorach* v. *Clauson*, 303 N. Y. 161 (1951); *People ex rel. Latimer* v. *Board of Education of City of Chicago*, 394 Ill. 228 (1946); *Gordon* v. *Board of Education of Los Angeles*, 78 Cal. App. (2d) 464 (1947).

11. *North* v. *Board of Trustees of the University of Illinois*, 137 Ill. 296 (1891). In a suit brought by a taxpayer against the University of Minnesota to enjoin the University from permitting use of its facilities by student religious groups, the Minnesota Supreme Court, without reaching a decision on the merits of the question, dismissed the suit on the ground that the taxpayer should first have presented the matter to the institution's governing board. *State ex rel. Sholes* v. *University of Minnesota*, 54 N.W. (2d) 122 (1952).

12. See C. P. Shedd, "Religion in the American State Universities: Its History and Present Problems," in H. E. Allen (ed.), *op. cit.*, pp. 20-21, 23; H. P. Van Dusen, *God in Education* (New York: Charles Scribner's Sons, 1951), p. 111.

13. For a summary survey, see C. P. Shedd's paper cited in note 12, pp. 23-26.
14. Substantially the same conclusion is expressed by Leo Pfeffer in *Church, State and Freedom,* p. 453.
15. The U.S. Supreme Court has held that a taxpayer as such has no standing to question Bible-reading exercises in a state's public schools as long as he does not show that this practice involves added out-of-pocket costs at the expense of tax-raised funds. *Doremus* v. *Board of Education,* 342 U.S. 429 (1952).
16. See the opinion of the Michigan Attorney General, July 7, 1950, No. 1256, holding that tax-raised funds could validly be used to build a student center at a state college in conjunction with a chapel built with funds received by gift.

Chapter VIII

1. See Paul Tillich, *Protestant Era, Courage To Be, Systematic Theology,* etc.
2. See my "Art as the Vehicle of Religious Worship" in *Religion in Life,* VII (1938): 93-105.

Chapter IX

1. Adam Smith, *The Wealth of Nations* (Modern Library edition), p. 745.
2. *The Protestant Ethic and the Spirit of Capitalism* (New York, 1930).
3. Emile Durkheim, *The Elementary Forms of the Religious Life* (London, 1915).
4. Gordon W. Allport, *The Individual and His Religion: A Psychological Interpretation* (New York, 1930).

Chapter X

1. The idea of a closed but unbounded system is best grasped by the novice by considering the surface of a sphere, which is of limited area but as a surface has no edges. If we consider not a surface on a three-dimensional figure but a volume on a four-dimensional figure, we should have the required model of a closed unbounded universe.
2. At least according to legend; various estimates of Laplace's own position have been published.
3. The argument of this section, as Chaninah Marienthal reminds me, leans heavily on C. S. Peirce.
4. J. C. Eccles in *Nature,* 168 (1951): 53-57, however, suggests that complexity per unit volume, which is probably greater in the human brain than anywhere else in the known universe, may, in some way not yet understood, be profoundly significant.
5. By conscious behavior, I mean behavior involving report in some explicit language of subjective elements such as images, perceptions,

or any kind of effect. The fact that these elements may succeed one another in an incoherent way is irrelevant to the argument.

6. The best account of telepathy is that of S. G. Soal and F. Bateman, *Modern Experiments in Telepathy* (New Haven, Conn.: Yale University Press, 1954). The best experiment in psychokinesis is perhaps in R. A. McConnell, R. J. Snowdon, and K. F. Powell, "Wishing with Dice," *Journ. Exper. Psychol.* 50 (1955): 269-75.

Chapter XIII

1. *Face Your Life with Confidence* (New York: Prentice-Hall, Inc., 1953), pp. 173 ff.

2. The reader should note that the six categories mentioned here are about "presented problems," or the immediately felt needs. They are useful if this fact is understood. They do not attempt to distinguish, for instance, the student whose underlying problem is gaining independence from his parental home, or the student who has developed compulsive trends that pervade his life and work, or the student who is in danger of alcoholism. As presented problems, felt needs, or symptoms, these have plainly a religious significance; but other people may have religious problems also at a deeper level, even if the religious aspect is not obvious at first inspection.

3. As recently as 1947, a responsible discussion presented the first form but wholly omitted reference to the second. See Kate H. Mueller *et al.*, *Counseling for Mental Health* (American Council on Education, Series VI, Student Personnel Work, No. 8 [1947]), p. 63.

4. See my *Sex Ethics and the Kinsey Reports* (New York: Association Press, 1953).

5. Philip E. Jacob, *Changing Values in College* (New Haven, Conn.: Edward W. Hazen Foundation, 1956), especially pp. 3-4.

6. For a thoughtful psychological analysis of some aspects of the current religious "revival," see the article by Milton J. Rosenberg in *Pastoral Psychology*, Vol. 8, No. 75 (June, 1957).

7. I discussed this question at greater length in the Allerton Park Conference Report, a document issued for limited circulation by its editor, Milton D. McLean, of Ohio State University. This reported on a joint conference of religious workers and student personnel workers from the Big Ten universities of the Midwest, held in 1955.

8. Still notable for its general approach to religious counseling of students, including the responsibility of those who are not professional religious workers, is *Religious Counseling of College Students*, by Thornton W. Merriam, *et al.* (American Council on Education, Series VI, Student Personnel Work, No. 4 [1943]).

9. The fragmentation danger emerging out of increased specialized services is warned against by E. G. Williamson in *The Teacher as Counselor* by Donald J. Shank *et al.* (American Council on Education, Series VI, Student Personnel Work, No. 10 [1948]), p. iii.

Chapter XIV

1. Figures are not available for the total building investment of all groups, though the helpful, unpublished 1953 study of Parker Rossman, "Church Student Work Since 1938," for the Department of Religion in Higher Education, Yale Divinity School, lists some interesting figures. For example, in 1953 the Methodist centers were valued at $8,715,312, the Jewish at $4,500,000, and the Lutheran at $2,000,000. The Catholic centers recently completed were valued at Minnesota at $600,000, at Colorado at $500,000, and at Arkansas at $300,000. The Interfaith Center at Cornell, the gift of Myron Taylor, is valued at more than $2,000,000.

2. See the mimeographed study by John Peter Thomas and Malcolm A. Carpenter, "Religious Centers for Student Work: A Yale Study," (rev. ed.; New Haven: Yale Studies in Religion in Higher Education, 1947).

3. See C. Grey Austin's paper tracing this development at the University of Michigan, "A Century of Religion at the University of Michigan" (Ann Arbor: University of Michigan, 1957), and Richard Henry Edwards' *Cooperative Religion at Cornell University* (Ithaca, N.Y.: Cornell University, 1939).

4. Seymour A. Smith, *Religious Cooperation in State Universities* (Ann Arbor: University of Michigan, 1957), p. 4.

5. Austin, *op. cit.*, gives this whole development.

6. *Ibid.*, p. 24 ff. for this development at Michigan.

7. See M. Willard Lampe, *The Story of an Idea: History of the School of Religion at the State University of Iowa* (Bulletin No. 704, State University of Iowa, March 1, 1955).

8. Smith, *op. cit.*, p. 76.

9. Rossman, *op. cit.*, Table II.

10. The reader will recognize the influence of Paul Tillich in this definition of man's religious concern. See his *Love, Power, and Justice* (New York: Oxford University Press, 1954), pp. 109 ff., and *Dynamics of Faith* (New York: Harper and Brothers, 1957), especially chap. I.

11. For a general survey, see Smith, *op. cit.*, and Austin, *op. cit.*

12. A recent unpublished study made by the staff at Cornell University.

13. Note the way in which local and regional YMCA's and YWCA's in Georgia, Texas, North Carolina, and Florida, as well as other denominational and faith groups, are making slow but steady inroads on the problem. This is frequently in the face of deep and divisive opposition from religious groups and parent bodies, as well as of political and university pressures.

14. The term "object" may be misleading. God is not to be thought of

as an object among other objects in space and time. The term here is used as a referent only, and not as a clue to God's nature.

15. See the suggestive study bearing out this general conviction of the religious center regarding responsibility and learning in Philip E. Jacobs' *Changing Values in College* (New Haven, Conn.: Edward W. Hazen Foundation, 1957). See also the report prepared for the Commission on Student Personnel of the American Council on Education by Harry H. Lunn, Jr., *The Student's Role in College Policy-Making* (Washington, D.C.: American Council on Education, 1957).

17. See Will Herberg's study of the sociology of this development in *Protestant, Catholic, Jew* (Garden City, N.Y.: Doubleday, 1955).

18. Penn State, Kansas State, and the University of Maryland have sought to solve the problem through erecting interfaith chapels with changeable altar and liturgical appointments in order that each faith might worship with integrity in accord with its own tradition.

19. See the unpublished manuscript by Jeanne S. Brown, "Religion in the State University and Colleges" (Yale Divinity School, 1952).

20. University of Illinois.

21. University of Missouri.

22. University of Kansas.

23. University of Iowa.

24. In Rossman's study, *op. cit.*, in 1953 there were 2,971 religious groups on college campuses, 852 full-time and 1,008 part-time professional religious workers, building investments upwards of $20,000,000, and national and local budgets well over $5,000,000.

25. This has been reflected in the amazing increase in number of administrative appointed positions in university religious work, from around 40 in 1945 to well over 225 at the present time.

26. How often has the sensitive Jew been offended by being asked to read a Christological Biblical passage in the university chapel, for instance?

Chapter XV

1. *Changing Values in College* (New Haven, Conn.: Edward Hazen Foundation, 1957), p. 3 ff.

2. *Ibid.*, p. 5.

3. *Ibid.*, p. 22. (This conclusion has been attacked as a statistical finding based on a preconceived and narrow definition of the term "religious," unmodified by any study of attitude changes in the individual.)

4. *Ibid.*, 7 f.

5. University of Minnesota: Office of the Dean of Students. Bureau History: Coordinator of Students' Religious Activities. August, 1954. p. 2.

6. See Cuninggim, *The College Seeks Religion* (New Haven, Conn.: Yale University, 1947).

7. See Edmund G. Williamson, in *Religion in the State University: An Initial Exploration,* Henry E. Allen, ed. (Minneapolis, Minn.: Burgess, 1950), p. 2.

8. An interesting sidelight from the perspective of a Catholic student worker is supplied by Robert J. Welsh, chaplain to Catholic students and Professor of Religion, School of Religion, State University of Iowa (*Religious Education,* Nov.-Dec., 1956, p. 425 f).

"Very often, without thinking about it (and I suppose they might be shocked if they thought they appeared that way) these campus religious councils actually do presume that their organization is a Protestant organization. This is perhaps due to the fact that, numerically, the Protestants are so much greater than Jew or Catholic and because, traditionally and historically, their place in the university antedates our own. . . .

"I have often thought that if I were a Jew sitting in on a meeting of an interreligious group which simply presumed that the statement 'Christian' took care of everybody, I probably would feel that justice was not being done to me."

9. Henry E. Allen quotes a response from one tax-supported campus in which the threat of control is made overt: "The University should insist upon approving the various religious workers assigned to campus groups . . . If college chapters of religious organizations are to function on a campus, it is imperative that the University set up some means of active coordination and integration and, frankly, control." *School and Society,* Dec. 6, 1952, p. 363.

10. The President of the University of Maryland explained that "No appropriations from tax funds have been used in the erection of the chapel. The maintenance of the chapel will be budgeted along with other University buildings. The chapel is to be used for religious purposes exclusively. The University will not assume responsibility for any religious services of a denominational nature, but will conduct, at stated intervals, non-denominational services for all . . ." Quoted by Henry E. Allen in "Practices of Land-Grant Colleges and State Universities Affecting Religious Matters." *School and Society,* Dec. 6, 1952, p. 362. The anachronistic character of this arrangement is made clear in the discussion above.

11. Cornell University has a similar setup in its new Anabel Taylor Hall, but since Cornell is not a state university it has been able to place the hall in the center of the campus as an integral part of the University.

12. See Marcus Bach: *Of Faith and Learning* (State University of Iowa, 1952). The Bible College founded by the Disciples at the University of Missouri has a similar structure.

13. The papers presented at this conference appear in *Religion in the*

State University: An Initial Exploration, Henry E. Allen, ed. (Minneapolis, Minn.: Burgess, 1950).

14. Se Allyn P. Robinson, ed., *And Crown Thy Good: A Manual on Interreligious Cooperation on the College Campus* (New York: NCCJ, 1954).
15. "Religious Pluralism on Campus," The Allerton Conference Report in *Religious Education,* Nov.-Dec., 1956.
16. *Religious Education,* Nov.-Dec., 1956, p. 421.
17. See Philip Jacob, *op. cit.,* chap. VI, p. 99.

Chapter XVI

1. Available on request from the Embassy of Burma, Washington, D.C.
2. Boston: Houghton Mifflin, 1948, p. 36.
3. Marvin Bressler and Richard D. Lambert, *Indian Students on an American Campus* (Minneapolis: University of Minnesota Press, 1956).
4. London: Murray, 1908.
5. *European Union and United States Foreign Policy* (New York: Macmillan, 1954).
6. Calcutta: University of Calcutta Press, 1946.
7. Jacques Masui, ed., *Yoga; sicence de l'homme intégral* (Paris: Les Cahiers du Sud, 1953). See also Pitirim A. Sorokin, ed., *Forms and Techniques of Altruistic and Spiritual Growth* (Boston: Beacon Press, 1954).
8. *The Law of Primitive Man, a Study in Comparative Legal Dynamics* (Cambridge, Mass.: Harvard University Press, 1954).

The Authors

ROLAND HERBERT BAINTON is the Titus Street Professor of Ecclesiastical History at Yale University. Author of *Here I Stand, A Life of Martin Luther, The Reformation of the Sixteenth Century, Hunted Heretic: A Study of Michael Servetus,* he is also a frequent contributor to religious journals.

WALTON ELBERT BEAN is Professor of History at the University of California at Berkeley, an expert on United States history and on the history of the American state university. He is the author of *Boss Ruef's San Francisco.*

KENNETH EWART BOULDING, Professor of Economics at the University of Michigan, was the recipient of the Clark Medal from the American Economic Association in 1949 and is the author of *Economic Analysis, The Organizational Revolution, A Reconstruction of Economics, There Is a Spirit* (The Naylor Sonnets), and *The Image.*

WILLIAM KLAAS FRANKENA, Professor of Philosophy and Chairman of the Department of Philosophy, University of Michigan, has contributed a number of articles to *The Dictionary of Philosophy* and many to current philosophical journals.

THEODORE MEYER GREENE, for several years Professor of Philosophy at Yale University, is now the Henry Burr Alexander Professor in Humanities at Scripps College, Claremont, California. He is the author of *Liberal Education Reconsidered, Arts and the Art of Criticism,* and *Our Cultural Heritage.*

WILL HERBERG is the Professor of Judaic Studies and Social Philosophy at Drew University, where he teaches both in the Graduate School and in the Theological School. His most recent book is a sociological study entitled *Protestant-Catholic-Jew: An Essay in American Religious Sociology.*

SEWARD HILTNER, Professor of Pastoral Theology at The University of Chicago, has served as Executive Secretary both for the Council for Clinical Training of Theological Students and for the Department of Pastoral Services of the Federal Council of Churches of Christ in America. He is the author of *Religion and Health, Pastoral Counseling, Self-Understanding, The Counselor in Counseling,* and is at present a consultant to the *Journal of Pastoral Psychology.*

GEORGE EVELYN HUTCHINSON is the Sterling Professor of Zoology and Director of Graduate Studies in Zoology at Yale University. He has served as consultant in biogeochemistry for the American Museum of Natural History and as a consulting geochemist for the United States Geological Survey. He is the author of *The Clear Mirror, The Itinerant Ivory Tower,* and numerous scientific papers on aquatic insects, limnology, and biogeochemistry.

MARK HOYT INGRAHAM is Professor of Mathematics and Dean of the College of Letters and Science at The University of Wisconsin. He is a former president of the American Association of University Professors and a frequent contributor to mathematical journals.

PAUL GERHARDT KAUPER, Professor of Law at the University of Michigan and a member of the Board of Higher Education of the American Lutheran Church, is the author of *Cases and Materials on Constitutional Law.*

ARTHUR JOSEPH LELYVELD, Executive Secretary of the America-Israel Cultural Foundation, has served as Rabbi for congregations in Ohio and Nebraska, as National Director of B'nai B'rith Hillel Foundations, and in various positions with many other community and religious agencies. He is an outstanding lecturer and a contributor of articles to the *Universal Jewish Encyclopedia* and to numerous periodicals.

JOHN COURTNEY MURRAY, S.J., is Professor of Theology at Woodstock College and editor of *Theological Studies.* He was formerly an associate editor of *America,* and in 1950 was the recipient of the Cardinal Spellman Award from the American Catholic Theological Society.

FILMER STUART CUCKOW NORTHROP is the Sterling Professor of Philosophy and Law at Yale University and Professor Extraordinaire at the National Autonomous University of Mexico. He is the author of *Science and First Principles, The Logic of the Sciences and the Humanities, The Taming of the Nations, The*

Meeting of East and West, and *European Union and United States Foreign Policy.*

GLENN A. OLDS, Director of United Religious Work at Cornell University and former Professor of Philosophy at Garrett Biblical Institute, is a Fellow in the National Council on Religion in Higher Education and the author of *The Christian Corrective* and of articles in the *International Journal of Ethics* and other periodicals.

GEORGE NAUMAN SHUSTER, President of Hunter College, has served as an adviser to the State Department's Division of Cultural Relations, as a delegate to UNESCO conferences, and as Land Commissioner for Bavaria. He is a contributing editor and former managing editor of *Commonweal* and the author of *The Catholic Spirit in America, Religion and Education,* and *Religion Behind the Iron Curtain.*

ROBERT MANNING STROZIER, until recently Professor of Romance Languages and Literature and Dean of Students at The University of Chicago, is now President of Florida State University. He has served as President of the National Association of Student Personnel Administrators and of the International House Association.

CHAD WALSH is Professor of English and Poet in Residence at Beloit College and Associate Rector of St. Paul's Episcopal Church in Beloit, Wisconsin. He is the author of *C. S. Lewis: Apostle to the Skeptics, Early Christians of the Twenty-first Century,* and *Eden, Two-Way.*

ERICH ALBERT WALTER, formerly Dean of Students at the University of Michigan, is now Assistant to the President and Professor of English at that University. For a number of years he was editor of *Essay Annual.* He is also editor of *Toward Today.*

HELEN CONSTANCE WHITE is Professor of English and Chairman of the Department of English at The University of Wisconsin. She is the author of *Tudor Books of Private Devotion, With Wings as Eagles,* and co-author of *Seventeenth Century Verse and Prose.*

Acknowledgments

This book is published to mark 100 years of student religious programs at the University of Michigan. The editor gives his best thanks to the many authors that have contributed to this volume. He gratefully acknowledges the help he has received from the University of Michigan Centennial Commission on Student Religious Work. He thanks particularly the members of the Publications Committee: William P. Alston, C. Grey Austin, DeWitt C. Baldwin, Ronald Freedman, William Haber, George B. Harrison, and Frank L. Huntley—all from the University of Michigan; Allen P. Farrell, S.J., of the University of Detroit; Milton D. McLean, of the Ohio State University; Herman Weil, of Wisconsin State College; and Helen C. White, of the University of Wisconsin. To the resident members he owes a special debt for their willingness to read and reread the manuscripts as they were submitted and revised.

The preparation of this book—as well as of two other publications, *Religious Co-operation in State Universities: A Historical Sketch* by Seymour A. Smith, and *A Century of Religion at the University of Michigan* by C. Grey Austin—has been made possible through the generosity of various donors. Among them, a special acknowledgment is made to the Allen Industries Foundation, Inc., the Holly Foundation, the Kresge Foundation of Detroit, the Lilly Endowment, Inc., the National Conference of Christians and Jews, and the Development Council of the University of Michigan. The Centennial Commission expresses its kind thanks to these donors not only for making the publications possible, but also for the assistance which their gifts have lent to all the other phases of the Centennial program.

E.A.W.